The Rosary in Action

THE ROSARY IN ACTION

by

JOHN S. JOHNSON

With a Foreword by

ROBERT W. BARRON, O.P., S.T.D.

Provincial Promoter of the Rosary
Confraternity, Chicago, Illinois

TAN BOOKS AND PUBLISHERS, INC.
Rockford, Illinois 61105

IMPRIMATUR

✠ Joseph E. Ritter, S.T.D.
Archbishop of St. Louis

July 1, 1954

Library of Congress Catalog Card Number: 54-8388

Copyright © 1954 by B. Herder Book Co.

Copyright © 1977 by TAN Books and Publishers, Inc.

Originally published by B. Herder Book Co., St. Louis, Mo.

PRINTED AND BOUND IN THE UNITED STATES OF AMERICA

TAN BOOKS AND PUBLISHERS, INC.
P. O. Box 424
Rockford, Illinois 61105
1977

Foreword

THE Confraternity of the Most Holy Rosary has been entrusted by the Holy See to the Dominican Order. That is fitting, since well established tradition ascribes the origin of this Confraternity to St. Dominic, who preached the first Rosary crusade in France in 1206. Many popes have called the Rosary Confraternity the highest and noblest of the societies of Christ's Church. Pope Leo XIII exhorted "all priests who are charged with the care of souls—not only the Sons of St. Dominic, to whom by virtue of their Order pertains the leading part in this apostolate—to be zealous in preaching, founding, and enlarging this Confraternity. They will learn that the faithful will be eager to enroll themselves, and to take advantage of the great spiritual benefits in which consist the very meaning and motive of the Rosary." The words of the Holy Father were prophetic in regard to the Church in the United States, where more than four thousand branches of the Confraternity have been established.

The main purpose of this Society is to join the members of the mystical body in a bond of love of God, through the intercession of Our Blessed Mother. There is no doubt that the Rosary is her favorite prayer. The author of *The Rosary in Action* cites many instances of this truth. He points out that American Catholics in ever increasing numbers have come to realize the power and the beauty of the Rosary. Members of the Confraternity have learned for themselves that this devotion provides "a map of human life, a sublime social pattern; that it is a synopsis of Christian doctrine, an antidote for confusion and despair."

In *The Rosary in Action* Mr. Johnson lays emphasis on the essential meaning of the Rosary devotion. When Our Lady commanded St. Dominic to preach the Rosary the new thing which was added was *meditation* on the mysteries. St. Pius V and many other popes have called attention to the necessity of meditation as an accompaniment of the vocal prayers of the Rosary. As the author states, many Catholics who love and pray the Rosary are not aware of this requirement. Moreover, some do not know that meditation is *necessary* to gain the indulgences of the Dominican blessing (although it is not required for the Apostolic, Brigittine, and Crozier indulgences). When they learn of this requirement many clients of Mary are frightened, appalled by the seeming enormity of the task of meditation.

Speaking as a layman from his own experiences, Mr. Johnson first allays such fears by showing that all that is required to gain the indulgences is the sincere effort to meditate, even though that effort fails. He then lays bare the beautiful simplicity and the tremendous benefits of Rosary meditation. He demonstrates to his fellow Catholics how they can meditate, and provides excellent material for each of the fifteen mysteries. Meditation is not necessarily a stupendous work: it is only "the loving thought of the divine plan for man's redemption, as this is revealed in the life and teachings of Jesus Christ."

We recommend this devout guidebook of the Rosary to all members of the Rosary Confraternity. The author has done great service in furthering the work proposed by Pope Leo XIII, to help all to know and to love the Rosary. Mr. Johnson makes application of the words of the Holy Father to our own times: "No remedy is better adapted to turn men away from the evil of these days, and to bring them back to Christ, who is the Way, the Truth, and the Life. . . . This method of prayer—properly carried out as it was instituted by St. Dominic, through meditation on the truths of salvation, and with prayer for the intercession of that Virgin to whom it is given to destroy all heresies—will cause a return of faith, piety, and love, so that the projects and devices of evil ones will fall to pieces."

Robert W. Barron, O.P., S.T.D.
Provincial Promoter of the Rosary Confraternity

Chicago, Illinois

Contents

	PAGE
FOREWORD	v

PART ONE

The Message of the Rosary

CHAPTER		
1	SOME PERSONAL EXPERIENCES	3
2	THE POWER OF THE ROSARY	8
3	HISTORICAL BACKGROUND	21
4	THE PROMISE FULFILLED	29

PART TWO

How to Say the Rosary

5	SOME PRACTICAL HELPS	47
	The Beads	47
	Meditation	50
	Attention: Intention	51
6	PRAYERS OF THE PENDANT BEADS	58
	The Apostles' Creed	62
	The Our Father	64
	Faith—Hope—Charity	71
	The Hail Mary	77
7	THE DEVELOPMENT OF ROSARY MEDITATION	87
	What is Meditation?	87
	A Method of Meditation	93
	Dangers to Avoid	103

CHAPTER	PAGE
8 SUGGESTED OUTLINES FOR ROSARY MEDITATION	107
The Joyful Mysteries	107
The Sorrowful Mysteries	113
The Glorious Mysteries	121
Afterword	130

PART THREE

Meditations for Each Mystery

9 THE JOYFUL MYSTERIES	135
First: The Annunciation	135
Second: The Visitation	146
Third: The Birth of the Lord	151
Fourth: The Presentation	160
Fifth: The Finding	165
10 THE SORROWFUL MYSTERIES	171
First: The Agony	172
Second: The Scourging	182
Third: The Crowning	196
Fourth: Carrying the Cross	203
Fifth: The Crucifixion	207
11 THE GLORIOUS MYSTERIES	228
First: The Resurrection	229
Second: The Ascension	246
Third: Descent of the Holy Ghost	253
Fourth: The Assumption	263
Fifth: The Coronation	268

PART ONE

The Message of the Rosary

CHAPTER 1

Some Personal Experiences

IT IS not so long ago that saying the Rosary was a severe trial to me. We said Rosaries at school, of course, and I have as a boy even led in the saying of the Rosary from the sanctuary, half scared to death at the sound of my own voice speaking out loud. That was in the second decade of the twentieth century just before the outbreak of the First World War; just at the time when the secularized world was lifting its head highest in pride. All the ills we are now suffering from were prepared for us then, but no one seemed to know the world was in great danger except the Holy Father in Rome. Pius IX had called attention to the growing threat of Communism before the middle of the previous century; Leo XIII, the great Pope of the Rosary, had written time after time, begging men to say the Rosary to correct world evils; and the fight was continued by the now St. Pius X, who had recently revived the practice of early and frequent Communion. Meanwhile the world was pretty well satisfied with itself; intoxicated with the thought of Human Progress (spelled with capitals) having outmoded religion (spelled with a small "r"). I believe we said the Rosary in those days mainly because Leo XIII had asked that it be said every day during October, but I am not aware of much active Rosary propaganda.

Nowadays one would not say the Rosary as we did then. I remember not much effort was made even to announce the name of the mysteries. We just went ahead and said the vocal prayers. I notice as I travel around the state that when I drop in here or there for a Mass of a morning that they are now more careful of these things, and often the treble voice of some poor half-scared kid will even add a line or so of meditation as well as give the name of the mystery.

I brought back with me the ruins of the steel beads which I carried through the first World War. One fragment contained almost two decades; the second piece yielded almost a decade; another piece was a decade and a few beads over. In all there were four decades and two beads over I brought back. The triangular bit of metal that held the loop of the beads and connected with the auxiliary beads and the crucifix was broken, and the pendent beads were gone. I say "triangular bit of metal" for in 1917 there were not many rosaries that used scapular medals as dividers on rosaries. The scapular medal was just newly approved then, and most of us were vague about how to substitute the medal. I know that I still used the traditional five scapulars even during the war. I found out later I had rights of self-enrollment in any and all the scapulars while I was in the armed services, simply by taking up the medal, which had to be blessed, of course. I still have the scapulars I wore, and they are in a deplorable state from dirt, sweat, lice, and the subsequent runs through the de-lousing operations. When the scapulars broke beyond repair I simply put them in my breast pocket, not considering getting a new pair, just as I kept on carrying the broken rosary. There is always a danger in spiritual affairs of getting an attachment to the material symbols of the devotion and of cherishing them for their own sake. The thing to do was to have disposed of the scapulars and the beads and to have got new ones, or at least to have had the rosary repaired. Such attachments are inordinate; they bring reproach from unbelievers who say that we cultivate such things as charms, or as lucky pieces. This is sometimes true of misguided individuals, but the Church frowns on making the material carrier of the devotion the important consideration.

I will not believe that the rosary stayed with me as an 1883 nickel I found deep in a corner when I emptied out the contents of my pockets at the hospital after I was hit. I had put this nickel there almost a year before during a card game in New London because I had noted that this nickel was different from others. I had forgotten all about it until I went into every nook and cranny of my pockets before throwing my blouse (if you are civilian—coat) onto a salvage pile. The rosary could not have been so completely forgotten as the nickel, I am sure, as there is a memory of confession before the battle of St. Mihiel in a small church in the Jeanne d' Arc country. I was sergeant of the guard that night and I had a big pistol strapped to my side, and having a duty belt on I was not supposed to take off my overseas cap. I compromised by leaving the pistol on and taking the cap off while I said my Rosary. Surely the beads must have passed through my fingers from time to time—or am I looking back with regrets that I was only *carrying* a rosary during and after the time when Our Lady had appeared at Fatima to tell the children she wanted everyone to *say* the Rosary every day? I remember reading some time ago about an old soldier who, when he learned the joy of the Rosary devotion, had such regrets at the time he had wasted up until then by not saying his Rosary, that the beads hardly left his hands until he had said enough Rosaries to equal the days he had lived upon the earth. While I can say with St. Augustine, "Too late have I loved Thee," I have to an extent caught up on the saying of my Rosaries by this time. Perhaps in my younger days I was just acting upon my lights, which happened to be very dim. What did I really know about the Rosary? Not very much, I fear. Did I even know the names of the mysteries, not to mention being familiar with their content, or digging into their depths? Children get to know more about the Rosary at an early age than we did, and its public recitation by school children is usually much more edifying than our efforts were at that age. However, if this observation should come to the attention of pastors and teachers they may do well to ignore it when teaching their charges to say the Rosary. In fact, simple instructions on the Rosary could be given with profit to adult congregations, as I have met many earnest adults whose knowledge of what is expected of them in the Rosary was of the sketchiest sort. The Rosary is such a familiar object in Catholic piety that we take too much for granted.

But back again to my broken rosary. This was laid aside in a box with other war souvenirs, but I was not, for that reason, without a rosary. There has never been a time when I did not have one, or even an accumulation of them picked up from missions, retreats, and from time-to-time good resolutions. They gravitated to boxes or drawer corners when the zeal that had prompted their procurement had disappeared. Saying the Rosary had always been hard work for me. The repetitions always irritated me, and often I found myself skimming through the task. Many is the time I have had a Rosary to say for a stated purpose and have fallen asleep before it was finished.

About the middle of the nineteen thirties I joined the Legion of Mary, where a Rosary is a part of the daily prayer stint. Often I wanted to jump out of my skin in meeting this requirement. It was not too bad during public recitations, but in private I had trouble. I was saying the Rosary every day but it was still not the way I wanted to say it. I knew the difference had to do with meditation, but since I had too complicated an idea of what meditation is, I never made much headway in mastering it. The great St. Teresa of Avila (Teresa of Jesus) said that it took her twenty years to learn how to meditate. I can well agree with her. If you are having trouble getting through your beads it may be that the trouble is the same as mine was. The truth of the matter is that I was not saying the Rosary the way it was intended to be said at all. For there is a great difference between counting out Our Fathers and Hail Marys and saying Rosaries. It was meditation that made the difference and as far as I was concerned, meditation equaled "distraction."

I wonder if I am alone in this, or shall I find others who have bravely started out to say the Rosary by beginning, as they should, with the first mystery, and then have "come to" somewhere in the third mystery without a clear idea as to how they got across the intervening decades. That is what makes the Rosary so hard to those of us who are unskilled in mental prayer or meditation, and who find that paying any attention to the vocal prayers kills any thought of the mystery that is supposed to be dwelt on; and that conversely by turning the mind to the subject related to the decade at hand, blots out the sequence of the Our Fathers and the Hail Marys. Something like this will always happen as you begin to penetrate the Rosary, but there is a way for it to happen that will not be a distraction. For a very good psychological reason the two processes cannot be carried forward simultaneously, but they have to go on together.

This points up my purpose in writing this book, viz., to give those who would like to say Rosaries, but who have no especial training in methods of prayer, some sort of formula which will take away most of their difficulties. In searching for this formula I bought—or borrowed—all the books I could find on prayer and on the Rosary, and I still do. There are an amazing number of such works, ranging all the way from short pamphlets to deliberate studies of, in one case, four volumes. All of them provided lessons of profit for me. Many of them were written by masters of the spiritual life and contained information much superior to that which I have to offer, but it always appeared to me that it was taken for granted that the reader would know how to coordinate this information with the sequence of vocal prayers, and that precisely is where the trouble comes in. It became clear to me that I should have to devise a method of my own.

CHAPTER 2

The Power of the Rosary

I WAS saying the Rosary every day by this time, as it was a part of the discipline of the Legion of Mary. For the most part I could get through the entire Rosary of fifteen decades because I rode around a lot in my work, and by intense concentration on the task was able to finish it. This did not satisfy me; however I was *saying* the Rosary and yet it did not seem to make much difference in my daily life. Perhaps, I thought, it might help me a great deal if only I could learn the essential nature of the Rosary devotion and see what impact it had made on the world up until the present. Then, if I could say Rosaries *that way* I could perhaps devise a practical method of saying Rosaries to help not only myself but others who may have had difficulties with it. This project of mine was not yet a part of the Fatima crusade for Rosaries. I did not so much as hear of Fatima before 1940. The earliest book I have been able to find in English on Fatima is dated 1939. I just wanted to say Rosaries.

As far as I could see the Rosary was merely a form of Catholic devotion to the Blessed Virgin, just as her litany and scapular devotions are. I have changed my opinion, but it may be well to note in passing that we must watch out that a wide swing of popularity towards the Rosary may make the other devotions to the Blessed Mother fall into disuse. I remember that a few years ago at a Franciscan gathering the question came up about what should be done in regard to the Franciscan Crown of the Seven Joys of Mary, while the Blessed Mother herself seemed to be giving preference to the more commonly known Rosary. It was decided, and with common sense I think, that the Franciscan Crown was very ancient also; had the favor of the Blessed Virgin, and she could not have meant that this form of devotion no longer pleased her. The same line of reasoning is in order as regards the Servite devotion to the Seven Sorrows of Mary. In fact, this devotion with beads and with plaques such as are found in the Stations of the Cross, is increasing mightily in the past ten years. The Scapular of Our Lady of Mount Carmel is also undergoing a revival and extension such as we should not have thought possible twenty years ago. The injunction of the gospel is always in order in dealing with the choice between good works: "This should be done, but not so as to leave the other undone." But still it had to be admitted that the Rosary was taking on such a pre-eminence that it was almost the symbol of being a Catholic. We rarely see a Catholic laid out for burial without a pair of beads in his motionless hands.

When I analyzed my own position I found I had to accept on pure faith the contention of writers, preachers, and even of the popes themselves (although I must admit that I knew very little of the persistent writings of the popes on the Rosary devotion) that there is something in the Rosary which sets it off by itself, and gives to it a peculiar and essential power. Naturally I knew that the Passion and death of Christ figure therein, but so do they also in the Stations of the Cross. Of course I could not say too much from my own experiences as I was doing little besides counting Our Fathers and Hail Marys. Often I listened to an impassioned speaker who begged his hearers to say the Rosary daily for the sake of its spiritual treasures, or I have read a book on the power of the Rosary. At this I would once again dig into my cache of beads and start all over again, only to bog down in the end. I realized that all this was due to some spiritual blindness on my part, since I knew well enough it was the Rosary that kept the faith alive in Ireland during the long centuries of the Penal Times when one could not find a way to hear Mass—even the type of Mass that was then permitted by the Church to outwit the persecutors, in which the priest would lie prostrate in the fields with the Sacred Offerings held on his breast for an altar, while the small group of worshippers hovered around him, apparently at work in the fields. During times like these a person could and did find a way to knot strings to keep tabs on the prayers of the Rosary. In any case, a man generally does have ten fingers.

Recently I came upon a photograph of a rosary made by a German priest in a concentration camp by pressing bits of bread around a string until he had fashioned a pair of beads for himself. I also knew that when Japan was opened again to the outside world after three hundred years of no priests, no Mass, and no sacraments except baptism and matrimony, missioners were asked questions designed to determine whether they had brought back with them the true faith. The first question was: "Where are your wives?" Their forefathers had taught them to know that priests do not marry, and that the expected answer was, "We have no wives." The second question was: "Are you at peace with the Pope?" The answer should be: "Yes." The third question was: "Where are your rosaries?" When the visitors showed the beads they carried they found doors opened to them, and they heard a tale of the preservation of the faith such as is not recorded in the whole history of Christianity. These stories I knew, as well as others I had picked up along the way. Some of these are certainly historical and others are legendary, no doubt. I found them of value in bolstering up my will to go forward, and it may do as much for others.

Perhaps I was then too close to the fringes of the liturgical movement to give credit to anything so simple. I was impressed by insistence on the power of the Rosary, but still I remained puzzled as to the real source of that power. The answer that naturally came to me was that just as the Blessed Virgin gave the Rosary to St. Dominic before the Battle of Muret in 1213 to aid in the overthrow of the Albigenses, so she has added a promise of success to all those who make use of her gift.

Delving further into the history of the Rosary I uncovered the work of the Bollandists on the life of St. Dominic, written in the seventeenth century. This learned group concluded that the tradition of the direct gift of the Rosary to St. Dominic was not based upon enough evidence to support it. They held that the work of Blessed Alan de Rupe detailing the Dominican tradition was unfounded; and that the further writings of the same Alan about visions he had been granted of the Blessed Virgin, and revelations she is said to have made to him about the Rosary were not well authenticated. This was upsetting, as the Bollandists were and are men of undeniable scholarship who set out to re-write the lives of the saints so as to preserve all the truth in their lives, and to weed out legends which had grown up in an age of faith. The legends surrounding the lives of some of the saints are very ancient and stem from an age less critical than ours. Often the legend is an illustration of a deep underlying truth that an age of faith knew how to read. For example, the legend of St. George and the dragon was scoffed at by an unbelieving age which knew there were no such things as dragons that breathe fire. But we know that Satan is called "the Dragon" and we know he can destroy souls by fire. Thus, there is nothing wrong even today in showing St. George in combat with a dragon, since there is in his life and martyrdom a deep victory over a "dragon" who is far more dangerous than the most vicious lizard.

I was disturbed that the story of the Rosary was going to turn out to be a pious legend that grew out of St. Dominic's struggles with the Albigenses. St. Dominic did have a great love for Our Lady as well as for her divine Son. The heresy of the Albigenses centered around the denial of the Incarnation—because to them the mere idea of a "body" was indecent. There could be no reason why Our Lady should not intervene to put into St. Dominic's hands a simple remedy which would go to the heart of the difficulty by setting forth in a complete but easy form correct teachings about the life, death, and Resurrection of Jesus Christ. Many is the time she has helped us by leaving a token of her love; the scapular of Mount Carmel; the Miraculous Medal, or a picture of herself as Our Lady of Good Counsel, or Our Lady of Perpetual Help, or in the apparitions at La Salette, Lourdes, Pontmain, Fatima, or in any of her shrines all over the world where she has left evidence of her love and willingness to help us. But of course the fact that Our Lady could have done this for St. Dominic did not of itself prove that she had come to him in person. I was left supposing that the critics may have been correct after all; that the story is legendary, as far as being an actual historical event is concerned. I did not like to find myself forced to conclude that the Rosary devotion had no better a beginning than the self-deception of Blessed Alan. It just did not seem fitting that Our Lady was to be involved in taking up something that began as a deception, even a well-intentioned one.

Strictly speaking, it should not have made a great difference. For one thing the Blessed Mother has never in any approved Rosary apparition made a connection between the Rosary as it now exists and any theory of its origin. For another thing the origin of the Rosary is not a doctrine of the Church; but still it was upsetting to see the Rosary story set forth according to the tradition in one of the lessons of the Divine Office for the feast of St. Dominic. Moreover, many papal utterances use words that leave little room for any other conclusion than that many of the popes have accepted the traditional story of the Rosary's origin. On the other hand, the popes who came after the apparent overthrow of the traditional story spoke just as clearly about the story of St. Dominic as the popes who came before. The popes were not being moved away from their constant position on the Rosary's origin; so it came either to the fact that the popes had access to a clearer living tradition than their critics, or that the popes did not consider the Rosary devotion as a mere problem of history.

The Church is never upset over matters of historical research. The doctrines and practices of the Church come down to us as a living stream from Christ Himself, and there is never any doubt here. In any historical matter conclusions must follow the evidence. For example, in the list of the popes the first five names were Peter, Linus, Cletus, Clement, and Anacletus. It had long been thought that Cletus and Anacletus might have been the same person. There was an opinion that Cletus had gone into exile and that he had returned after the martyrdom of St. Clement. Thus we should have "ana" Cletus, or "again" Cletus. When it became clear enough that these were two names for the same man, the official papal manual simply dropped the name of Anacletus. The rule for any historical event is that it is to be judged by the physical or moral evidence that appears for or against it. The value of a devotion or pious practice is in the way it leads men to God. The Rosary devotion would be just what it is if it had started in the thirteenth or fifteenth century.

It is strange, but after laying out all the evidence I could to prove that I should not be disturbed, I was still upset at the attempts to set the tradition aside. I could not find it in my heart to blame any of the earnest men who were merely trying to separate legend from truth for the sake of furthering Catholic truth, but for the time my Rosary enthusiasm was dampened. I could scarcely prevent myself from coming to the conclusion that if the Rosary was just another "pious practice" of much later origin than it had been credited with, perhaps one ought not to become too exercised about it, but would do well to stay with the liturgical prayers of the

Church and let old ladies count out beads in sibilant whispers. But that was not the end of it.

If Our Lady had not brought the Rosary with her to St. Dominic, as I had supposed, it was still true that she had brought it with her to Lourdes. Why could we not say, then, that the power of the Rosary was pretty much the same as the power of the waters in the spring at Lourdes; waters that have no curative powers in themselves but which have many times worked even startling cures? There is no evidence of any sort that Our Lady promised to cure anyone at Lourdes, but scarcely had the waters started to well up out of the ground when an unfortunate man in the town of Lourdes asked his daughter to bring some of the water to him. This man, Buriette by name, had had his right eye destroyed in a quarry explosion some years before and it still caused him pain from time to time. He bathed his eye in the water, explaining that if this was from the Blessed Virgin she could cure his eye. The eye was cured. A day or so after this a child in its death-throes was dipped into the cold waters and was restored to its mother alive. At Fatima Our Blessed Mother promised she would work cures, and at Fatima the work of mercy goes forward, intertwined as at Lourdes with the Rosary.

For almost a hundred years the list of cures has continued to grow at Lourdes—of tubercular lungs made whole, and even of missing bone tissue restored, as in the case of Pierre de Rudder who was never near Lourdes in France, but who went to a replica shrine of Lourdes at Oostracker in Belgium. There was also a very famous case which the novelist Zola wrote up in his novel, *Lourdes*. His story followed the case closely enough to the very end. There the novelist had the young lady, who was back on the train to take her home, suffer a relapse and die quite miserably. The truth of the matter is that the young lady continued in her cure until she died a natural death many, many years afterwards, and from another cause. Then there was the case within the past twenty years of the complete cure of a British war veteran from the loss of nerve tissue in his arm. Since His Majesty's medical services could take no notice of a miracle, and since the case was utterly incurable by all medical standards, the man's disability pension was paid to him to the day of his death some time later, from an injury suffered while he was unloading coal.

At Lourdes, very simply stated, Our Lady came and prayed the Rosary with Bernadette. It was a message of penance to the world to help ward off the disasters which were even then impending. She bade Bernadette dig into the bare soil high on the rocky hill above any possible flow-line for water, to uncover a spring which did not until then exist. "The Lady" asked that there a chapel be built, and on her last visit she identified herself. "I am the Immaculate Conception," she said in the patois of the district—but it was an expression that had no meaning at the time for Bernadette, who was sickly and badly schooled for her years. The name given to herself by the Blessed Virgin showed her pleasure in the definition of the doctrine of her Immaculate Conception by Pius IX. The reality of her visitations is proved by the cures effected. A person of good-will can never doubt but that the Blessed Virgin was really at Massabielle with a Rosary.

Whoever objects that but few persons of the crowds who go there ever receive miraculous cures, has missed the point of Lourdes and of the Rosary. Not all twisted legs are straightened; not all eyes that were blind are opened; but the real secret of Lourdes is that whoever goes there prayerfully, does receive a wider miracle. He does have his heart opened to accept the will of God. That is one fact which has struck visitors to Lourdes with tremendous force. The cure of a withered limb is one thing, but the acceptance of the grace to carry it through life without murmuring against God is greater. Too many of us think that all prayers should be directed to having the burdens of life taken away, rather than addressed to the will of God to take them away or to leave them with us as He in His wisdom thinks best. It is hard for us at times to see that sickness and its attendant failures are better for us than the work we feel we should be able to do for God if we had full health and strength; but many a person who was careening straight to the loss of his immortal soul, has been brought to other and better ends through poor health. Incidentally many a person in bad health has taken his illness as a challenge, and has left his mark upon the world; whereas more muscular brothers have spent hours and years learning to hit a little ball into a hole in four strokes, while it takes their less fortunate brethren five strokes to achieve a similar great deed. Not that recreation is wrong; any one who cannot unbend into a little useless puttering, and even nonsense once in a while, should have a talk with his confessor rather than with his doctor. But at the same time it is true that most of the work in this world is done by persons who would be somewhere else if they followed their feelings. The chances are that all of us are going to have to do our work as we are, and that most of our burdens are not going to be lifted from us. God has not willed to restore the terrestrial Paradise. This is one of the besetting sins of our age: to want the answer to prayer to be the taking away of some cross we do not like. If we want to defeat Communism we can do it by being patient in the face of adversities we cannot remove, while doing all we can to better our own and others' conditions. We cannot be apathetic and passive in the face of wrongs and difficulties. Civilization has to be extended and the message of Christ has to be given to every man upon this earth. But work and patience must go together.

This is still a world of sin and sorrow, and God often suffers evil to make headway against us according to our shortsighted view of the matter; but the only evil that can touch us from outside ourselves is that evil which touches the nervous system. Evil can touch the soul only when we act against ourselves. Many a person has learned this at Lourdes, and many have learned it through the Rosary. This is very close to the answer as to what force gives the Rosary a power alongside of which the atomic bomb or the H-bomb is a fizzling fire cracker. Shall we not say that the waters at the Shrine of Lourdes can cure and give resignation because it was intended that Lourdes was to be a memorial and a confirmation of the power of the Rosary? Shall we not say that the Rosary, like the scapular, enters into the great drama of salvation just because the Blessed Virgin said so? The scapular is a simple act of faith; indeed, so is the wearing of the small rectangular piece of woolen material or of the modern substitute—the medal. However, the power of the scapular is not in the external act of wearing it as a charm, but in the fact that Our Lady can get graces from her Son attached to some simple act or practice, just as she obtained the miracle at Cana, even out of due time. Faith is in the Rosary, and the Rosary is likewise simple; but it is more than that. As well as being based, according to the ancient tradition, on a promise of the Blessed Virgin—a promise more than once given—it is in itself an effective means of grace.

There would be great benefit to ourselves in cultivating the vocal prayers of the Our Father, composed by Christ Himself and given to us with a command to pray that way; and of the Hail Mary taken from the words of the Archangel Gabriel at the beginning of our salvation; added to by St. Elizabeth under inspiration of the Holy Ghost, when she first recognized the Blessed Virgin as the Mother of God; and completed by the Church as a recognition of Mary's power to intercede for us. These would be of great benefit to us, and as we shall see there was a "pre-rosary" of this sort.

What is most important is that this is *prayer,* and prayer must always carry with it as an infallible effect the granting of the grace of God to the soul. "Ask and you shall receive," has no sort of qualification attached to it except that it must be sincere and humble. As various saints have said: "You

MUST pray to be saved and if you pray you MUST be saved." It is that elemental. Now when we add to effective prayer the consideration of the life, death, and Resurrection of Jesus Christ we must be made conscious of the great gift of salvation, and if we have any gratitude at all it must have an effect on our daily lives and make us more responsive to grace. This would be the value of the Rosary apart from any consideration of the tradition. We can see from this that there would be nothing amiss for the Blessed Mother to come to Lourdes with such a method, even if she had not brought it to St. Dominic.

But Our Lady did bring the Rosary to Lourdes, and she did bring it to Fatima with a promise attached to it. See then, how great must be the power of the Rosary which takes the best means of salvation and attaches thereto the promise of her who is the established channel of grace. The essence of the scapular is that it is a simple compliance with the Blessed Virgin's wishes; the scapular takes its roots in an age of faith; it is part of an age which is close to the scenes of the gospel; an age which knows and values the reality of the spiritual. It is one of the great encouraging signs of our times that the scapular has had such a tremendous revival. The Rosary in its turn has a different mission.

The Rosary is aimed at the pride of life; its greatest victories have been over the proud and the haughty. Do not take this to mean that the scapular is outmoded in our age of pride. Our Lady still has work for it to do, and this work is being done today right alongside the Rosary. The thing that amazes me is the way the scapular has taken hold especially on young men. The memories of my youth are more filled with examples of defections from the faith. Surely, these youngsters nowadays represent a turn back the other way.

My conclusions at length were ready to take a definite shape about the Rosary. It was not only that it was a chain of the most perfect of vocal prayers as the Our Father, the Hail Mary, and the Gloria; it was not just the meditations on our Lord and His Mother; there had been such a method in another pre-rosary amongst the Carthusians and the Cistercians. The Rosary in the true sense had its beginnings in the combination of vocal prayer and meditation. But it has been given a further efficacy because of promises attached to it by the Blessed Mother herself, who is the portal through which God came to us, and who has been made by her Son the portal through which we go back to Christ. However, grace works through nature, and the secret of the key to the treasure of the Rosary lies in the word "meditation." Without meditation we are not saying the Rosary. Our Lady has made other promises; she has attached her blessings to other devotions, but of late years it would appear that she has turned her favor more and more to the Rosary (but this must not go so far as to exclude other devotions). Our Blessed Mother has attached her blessings to other devotions which turn about the saying of beads. As we mentioned above, the Crown of the Seven Joys of the Franciscans and the Servite devotion to Our Lady of Sorrows are both attached more or less to beads, but not inevitably so. Other promises of the Blessed Mother are almost too numerous to mention. They began with the apparition to St. James the Apostle in Spain as that of Our Lady of the Pillar, and reach through almost countless medals, scapulars, pictures, and places, to our very own day in an attempt to bring us to her Son. How very much like a mother she has been. We find it so very easy to forget our Father, and the labors of our elder brother Christ grow dim in our hearts until our Mother devises some little dainty to attract our childish hearts. In effect she tells us: "If you will just come to this spot and say a few prayers, or if you will wear this simple badge, or if you will just honor this picture of me, I'll get something nice for you." So we come trooping to get the temporal favors she holds out to us, and find that all the while she has had it in mind to get us to go further and to return to God.

Of all the devotions to Our Blessed Mother, and of all

the promises that Our Blessed Mother has made to man to aid him in his difficult lot in this vale of tears, the Rosary alone has attached to it as a part of its inherent meaning the note of meditation. It is more difficult to cultivate the art of meditation than it is to wear a scapular, but the one who will make an honest attempt to learn to say his Rosary well may expect all the intercessory power of the Blessed Mother to help him on his way. That is the power of the Rosary.

CHAPTER 3

Historical Background

IT IS the meditation combined with the beads—not the beads nor the meditation separately—which constitutes the Rosary. Both meditation and prayer on beads as separate devotions or methods of prayer existed long before the time of St. Dominic. In fact the word "bead" comes from "bede" which in early English meant a "prayer." We still "bid" people to do things. The prayers were first, and then a device for keeping track of them came into being, and as sometimes happens in language the device kept the name and the original meaning was lost.

The use of beads or some sort of counters to keep track of prayers is very old. In fact it was somewhat of a shock to me when I first learned that beads are by no means confined to the Catholic Church. Beads are in use, even today among the Mohammedans, Buddhists, Brahmins, and generally in India, China, and Japan. Among Christians, the Copts and other eastern schismatics use beads in prayer. It has likewise been shown that beads were in use in ancient Peru. Even from Ninevah of about the ninth century B. C. there is a sculptured figure which bears a device which may be a string of beads. Due to the stiffness of the sculpturing the interpretation may be mistaken; it may be a wreath. This does not mean that the Catholic use is dependent on the pagans.

It is a very natural impulse to repeat prayers over and over again. A person who relies upon his memory or his fingers will soon lose his count.

In Catholic graves as far back as the third century there have been found devices which look somewhat like an abacus. This is a calculating machine consisting of a series of beads on parallel wires. It was used by the old Romans, and I have seen many a Chinese laundryman run up his beads with great speed to work out multiplications. It seems clear that these abacus-like devices were used in prayer. Prayer beads were found in the tomb of St. Gertrude of Nivelles of the sixth century. In the eleventh century St. Norbert, one of the great defenders of the Blessed Sacrament, used beads in prayer which were found when his relics were translated many centuries later and his coffin was opened.

The early Fathers of the desert were said to have used a bowl in which they placed the number of pebbles to correspond with the prayers they had to say each day. It is this age-old use of beads which had something to do with the denial by critics, even Catholics, that there is any historic value to the tradition that Our Lady gave to St. Dominic the rosary as we know it today, before the battle of Muret against the Albigenses. The fact remains that the Albigenses, who were like the Communists of today in very many respects, suffered a terrible defeat in the battle of Muret. Arms and prayers had no effect upon them for a long time, until a small Christian task force of about 800 men under Simon de Montfort drove into utter confusion a well-armed and disciplined horde of about 40,000. Tradition says this was the beginning of the Rosary. It is certain that the older use of beads in prayer and the older use of exercises of meditation on the joys and sorrows of the Blessed Virgin were not the Rosary. It is the enveloping sequence of meditation set into a pattern of vocal prayers told out on beads that makes the difference. This combination did not occur before St. Dominic, and it can now be placed very close to his day, since

Historical Background

documents not known to the first critics have been found that put the Rosary tradition in a much better light. It helps to explain the success which St. Dominic had with the conversion of the Albigenses after so many years of utter failure.

The Rosary is a combination of many streams of development. This is as it should have been, since devotions grow out of the needs of the faithful. There are always present the liturgy and its principal outlet in the Mass; there are the sacraments with the Blessed Sacrament leading the way; all together giving to the soul the life of grace; all leading the soul in sanctifying grace back to God. Devotions cannot, of course, grow up opposed to the official prayers and practices of the Church; they must not in any case replace the sacraments, but that soul would be shallow, indeed, that did not overflow with some sort of gratitude or joy for what has been done for us by God, or His Christ, or the Blessed Mother, or the angels, or the saints. If no sympathy came from us for the sufferings that have been expended to bring the faith to us each day for almost two thousand years; or if we had no sorrow for the little response we have made to all that outpouring of generosity, we shall be very poor candidates for salvation. Even the reading of the two short lists of martyrs and saints in the Canon of the Mass should leave us aghast at the pain and agony undergone by others for Christ that we might have the faith. Not only did they suffer but they prayed for their tormentors, and that was what won the victory for them and for us. Supposing that St. Stephen had not prayed for Saul, would Saul have been converted, and should we have had a St. Paul?

The earlier ages of the Catholic Church did center most of their devotions about the cultus of the martyrs, with the living—and dying—examples of this Christian fortitude all around them. Then, as paganism receded, the Blessed Virgin came more and more into her own. With the finding of the Holy Cross by St. Helena the yearning of the Western world was to trod the paths made sacred by the Savior during His life on earth. Pilgrims increased their visits to the Holy Land both as acts of devotion and as penances. For those who could not go replicas of the holy places were set up, out of which grew the devotion of the Stations of the Cross.

The liturgical prayer of the Church developed around the 150 Psalms, and at the time of the Reformation almost everyone who could read had a Psalter. Despite all the burnings of Catholic books and the defections from the faith, this is still a fairly common book. Monks sang the psalms in choir, but for the laybrothers, who generally could not read, a substitution was made of Our Fathers, divided for convenience into fiftys. Beads were used to keep track of these prayers.

During the Middle Ages the Hail Mary came into vogue as a prayer; at first only the salutation of the Archangel and the greeting of Elizabeth. The Dominicans, combatting the terrible practice of cursing and swearing that was then all too prevalent, started the first Holy Name Society, and had the name of Jesus added to the prayer. Only this much of the Hail Mary was said in the pre-Rosary as it began to replace the Our Father in the repeated prayers as the devotion became more Marian in character. The ending petition of the Hail Mary was long used in the Eastern Church, but it came to us in common usage only after the formation of the Rosary proper as we now have it. The newer use of the Hail Mary combined with another sort of devotion to the Blessed Mother and became known as "Our Lady's Psalter." Larger beads added to the circlet for spacers became used for saying Our Fathers and helped give form to the Rosary when it arose.

During the Middle Ages much of the devotion to the Blessed Virgin centered about the symbolism of the rose. Roses were woven into crowns with which to bedeck shrines and images of Our Lady, and as they were woven together litanies of praise were said: "Hail Mary, whose feet did bear Jesus to the Temple. . . ." "Hail Mary, whose arms did enfold the Savior of the world." It is not hard to see in the circlet of beads a representation of the crown of roses. This becomes clearer when we recall that the word for a rose-garden in middle Latin is "rosarium." We note in passing that at Lourdes the flower which burst into bloom out of season that cold February was the eglantine, or wild climbing rose. The rose is par excellence Our Lady's flower.

Amongst the Cistercians there grew up about the turn of the thirteenth century in England genuine meditations on the fifteen joys of the Blessed Virgin, each joined with a Hail Mary; a method of prayer close to the Rosary method. In the fifteenth century a Cistercian, Dominic the Prussian, applied such a method of saying a Hail Mary with each mystery of the Rosary. This has survived in two forms. In Germany and in German speaking parishes of the United States there is still the custom of putting the mystery right into the middle of each Hail Mary; e.g., in the vocal prayers of the mystery of the Visitation they say: ". . . and Blessed is the fruit of thy womb, Jesus, whom thou didst take to Elizabeth, thy cousin to sanctify St. John. Holy Mary, Mother of God. . . ." And so through all the remaining mysteries. There is also in Germany, Austria, and Switzerland a "read" Rosary which has 150 mysteries, one for each Hail Mary.

The Cistercian meditations of the thirteenth century were very close to the content of the Rosary mysteries. They were: Birth of the Virgin Mary, Life of the Virgin, The Annunciation, Conception of the Savior, Visitation, Birth of Our Lord, Visit of the Magi, Presentation in the Temple, the Finding of the Child Jesus in the Temple, the Miracles and Preaching of Jesus, the Cross in Joy Purchases the World, the Resurrection, the Ascension, Pentecost, the Assumption and Glorification of the Blessed Virgin in Heaven.

We add the Stations of the Cross which became popular at this time, because crusades and pilgrimages to the Holy Land were almost impossible; the Christians had been forced back by the Saracens and it was difficult and dangerous to visit the actual scenes of Christ's Passion and death. Representations were necessary to call to mind the drama of our salvation. Of course, in nearly all churches in the land there were pictures and statues depicting the scenes of our redemption, but there was need to unfold the whole drama as in a mystery play.

Here all the elements of the Rosary are in place, and at the time of St. Dominic they converged to form the true Rosary. The critics relied mainly on the argument from silence to question the ancient tradition that the Blessed Virgin gave the Rosary to St. Dominic. They should have known that many documents referred to by Blessed Alan may have existed but did not survive the burning scourge of the Huguenots, who destroyed convents, monasteries, libraries, among the thousands of institutions they committed to the flames. The critics went so far as to suggest that Blessed Alan had invented the Rosary devotion out of the whole cloth, and had attributed it to St. Dominic to tie it in with a famous name. But the two persons Alan relies on for his story of the origin of the Rosary had their "Mariales" preserved at the convent at Gand; which library was burnt during the wars of religion. There are other Rosary documents which have been discovered in later years which were from before Blessed Alan's time. The long poem, *Rosarius,* antedates him by a hundred years or so and clearly refers the Rosary to St. Dominic and the battle of Muret. This removes Blessed Alan from all suspicion of inventing his sources. The elements were all in place at the time of St. Dominic; how did they get together into the Rosary? Was the Blessed Mother the first one *ever* to combine all the elements into one devotion, and did she then give this new devotion to St. Dominic as something he never heard of before? Or, as at Lourdes and more pointedly at Fatima, did Our Lady offer the Rosary as a means of saving the world to St. Dominic at Muret? As far as I can determine the words of Our Lady were merely: "Go, take my psalter and preach it constantly; you will experience the greatest marvels of divine Power." There is nothing here to suggest that the Rosary was offered

Historical Background

as something of which the elements were never heard of before. We know that other devotions were leading up to the founding of a true Rosary devotion. Here, I think, the motherly promise of the Rosary's power was added, which alone makes the Rosary to be the great aid it is. If we feel that we can have confidence in the reality of Our Lady's message at Lourdes and again at Fatima, we may have confidence in the reality of Muret; and in each case from the effects that flowed from the incident.

The elements met in St. Dominic at the overthrow of the Albigenses, but it was some time before the physical beads themselves became of such importance as they are now, and it was not until the sixteenth century that the rosary took on the exact form it has today. The pendent beads were carried over from the Brigittine crown of sixty-three beads—six decades, plus the three beads in the pendant to mark the years the Blessed Virgin spent on earth according to an old but dim tradition. There is another tradition of seventy-two years preserved in the Franciscan Crown of the Seven Joys of Our Lady. (No one ever really pretended to know the exact age of Our Blessed Mother when she left this earth to be with her Son). It was in the sixteenth century that Pope Leo X first attached indulgences to the physical grains, or beads of the rosary. In late years so many people are saying the Rosary that the Holy Father permitted all who were engaged in work that occupies the hands to say the Rosary simply by having the beads near by, so again the prayer aspect apart from the beads is coming back into being.

It was the fifteenth century before the Rosary took on the number and sequence of the mysteries as they are today. The external form, the number of mysteries, and all such are mere accidental variants: the essentials of beads, vocal prayers, meditation, and the promise of the Blessed Mother in 1213, came when she offered the Rosary to us through St. Dominic to bring to us the greatest marvels of divine Power.

When we see the effects of the evils that surround us in

the troubled world we live in, we may take heart that Our Lady has promised that she will help us to remove them if we pray the Rosary every day. We may well believe that the Rosary can do this for us today, just as it destroyed the Albigenses in the thirteenth century. The Albigensian movement was not just another heresy; it was one of those periodic assaults of essential evil on the very basis of morality and civilization. It is hard to see how men can be carried away in such large numbers by sheer diabolism, but there it is— an historical fact. When we see what the Albigensian movement had done to men in its day we can better realize what Communism can do today. The Albigenses taught that suicide is praiseworthy; that there is a principle of good that created the soul, and a principle of evil which created the body, and that the body had imprisoned the soul as in a foul dungeon. Hence they concluded that anyone who starved himself to death (the *endura*) had liberated his soul and had done well.

CHAPTER 4

The Promise Fulfilled

AS IS usual with such movements as that of the Albigenses they set up for themselves a code of perfectionism which they freely violated with most revolting excesses. Marriage they considered an evil. They encouraged the desertion of wife by husband and husband by wife; yet concubinage was permitted. Like wildfire this sort of doctrine swept across southern France, killing, burning, and destroying as it went; winning thousands to its side. Such a force was utterly destructive of anything like our conception of civilization. Reason was dethroned and the most primitive emotions were in full control.

What can stop such movements except the grace of God? Surely not all the strenuous efforts sometimes directed against an abuse, only to spread it far and wide. How can one man make another stop to consider the truths of religion when he has fallen in love with what he considers the freedom of his own mind? Only God can convert the human heart and only prayer can cause God—so to speak—to give His graces to those who just do not seem to want them. After years of failure, St. Dominic finally succeeded in stopping the spread of the Albigenses. He did "experience the greatest marvels of divine power." But he found them in prayer; the prayer of the Rosary. Hence we should take heart. Our task is hard and the forces arrayed against us are powerful with the power of hell, but Satan and all his cohorts have no power against prayer, and in particular against the prayer of the Rosary. The Rosary destroyed the Albigenses. The age that followed was that of the Rosary, the scapular, and of the third orders secular. As faith blossomed the human mind was set free. Magnificent cathedrals sprang up throughout all of Europe; universities were filled with eager students. There was a true renaissance of learning which has been mistakenly applied to the recrudesence of paganism of two centuries later. It was a happy world in which civilization made great strides beyond the point where it had been stopped by the Fall of Rome and the barbarian inroads.

But a far greater disaster awaited the world than even the Fall of the Roman Empire and the incursions of the Mohammedans. This time the affliction which befell the world was the Black Death, which took the lives of almost half the people of Europe after starting in the Far East and working its way across Asia. The toll of life was so great that the continuity of history was almost broken. It is estimated that about 25,000,000 people died in three years. Religious communities were wiped out in their entirety; thousands of churches were left without pastors. Untried youths of not over nineteen years were at times consecrated as archbishops of important sees to keep up a semblance of order, while in many cases one bishop had to administer to the needs of several sees. This opened the way to the abuse of "pluralism," as scheming monarchs saw in the Church's need a device for forcing their candidates into office for the sake of the income rather than to promote the care of souls. Often a king would keep a bishopric open and not permit anyone to take over its care. During the vacancy the royal coffers would receive the income from Church property while churches fell into disrepair: worthy candidates were not received for ordination into the priesthood: the people were not instructed in religion: and the forces of evil were gathering strength to tear the

Church wide-open. It was at this time that the groundwork was laid for the Reformation. Rich acres of land which had been used to support monasteries so the monks could devote themselves to the fundamental work of advancing civilization, attracted the attention of the greedy. The civil powers soon had taken over these incomes by appointing as heads of the communities laymen, usually as abbots *in commendum*—generally their own illegitimate offspring. They rendered no religious services to the monastery and used the moneys they collected for their own private secular uses. When the Church later regained some strength and attempted to get back these incomes for their original religious purposes, the holders of the incomes revolted against the Church and went into the "reform." They were careful to bring the properties along with them, either as their own or as grants from the Crown.

The whole world was ready for the next scourge. Powerful families in Italy decided that they would make even the papacy their private institution. There are cases where, when a pope was elected, he would then fill up the College of Cardinals with his family and faction so as to perpetuate the fortunes of his family to the great harm of the Church. A French king broke into this succession and persuaded the pope to move his see to Avignon in France where the papacy remained for seventy years, until persuaded by St. Catherine of Siena to return to Rome. But still greater shocks were in store for the faithful. In 1378 the great Schism began, wherein there were set up rival claimants for the papacy. Each claimed to be the true successor of St. Peter and each excommunicated the other. Often it was impossible for a local observer to say at a given moment where the Church was. Nations divided; even saints later canonized were deceived and were to be found in rival camps. The unity of Christianity was cracking, to be split wide-open in just one hundred years, for the Schism lasted from 1378 to 1417. Large sections of the Eastern Church fell away from unity with Rome, and Constantinople was ripe for its fall into the hands of the Mohammedans.

But God had not deserted His people. Saints were raised up to prepare for the troubles still to come. About this time St. Jeanne d'Arc began her work, with the result that when the blow fell in 1517 there were large sections of Europe strengthened to withstand the "new" doctrines. Whereas conditions were bad enough in France, it was better to have France freed from the domination of England, which was to be torn away from Catholic unity under Henry VIII and Elizabeth. The combined effect was such that the Church must have disappeared from history, if it had not been sustained by the promise of Christ that the gates of hell can never prevail against her. The Church can get into serious trouble both from enemies within and without, and whole countries can be swept away from her when piety wanes and men close their minds to the simple gospel story. But when the end is in sight, the Church has a way of renewing herself from within and of overthrowing or converting her enemies. If our apostolic efforts reach a proper level we need not fear that Russia will destroy the Church. The Church will convert Russia if we pray enough. The serpent is always lying in wait for THE WOMAN, but THE WOMAN and her seed, Jesus Christ, must always crush the serpent's head.

While all the Church's difficulties were causing exultation to her enemies, the Rosary, forgotten during the space of more than one hundred years, was revived during the last quarter of the fifteenth century by Blessed Alan, and also by Dominic the Prussian. The Rosary spread throughout all Europe and thousands upon thousands in every walk of life enrolled in the Rosary Confraternities. Blessed Alan claimed that the revival of the Rosary was due to the appearing of the Blessed Virgin to him bidding him take up the work begun by the founder of Alan's own order, St. Dominic. The Blessed Mother had given him a list of fifteen promises of rewards from her for the faithful recitation of the Rosary.

The Promise Fulfilled

These promises are: 1) Whoever will faithfully serve me by the recitation of the Rosary will receive signal graces. 2) I promise my special protection and greatest graces to all those who will recite the Rosary. 3) The Rosary shall be a powerful armor against Hell: it shall destroy vice, decrease sin, and defeat heresies. 4) I will cause virtue and good works to flourish; it shall obtain for souls the abundant mercy of God; it shall withdraw the hearts of men from the love of the world and its vanities and shall lift them to the desire of eternal things. Oh, that souls would sanctify themselves by this means! 5) The soul that recommends itself to me by the meditation of the Rosary shall not perish. 6) Whoever will recite the Rosary devoutly, applying himself to the consideration of its sacred mysteries, shall never be conquered by misfortune. God will not chastise him in His justice; he shall not perish by an unprovided death; if he shall be just he shall remain in the grace of God and become worthy of eternal life. 7) Whoever will have a true devotion for the Rosary shall not die without the sacraments of the Church. 8) Those who faithfully recite the Rosary shall have during their life and at their death the light of God and the plentitude of His graces; at the moment of death they shall participate in the merits of the saints in paradise. 9) I will deliver from purgatory those who have been devoted to the Rosary. 10) The faithful children of the Rosary shall merit a high degree of glory in heaven. 11) You shall obtain all that you ask of me by the recitation of the Rosary. 12) All those who propagate the holy Rosary shall be aided by me in their necessities. 13) I have obtained from my divine Son that all the advocates of the Rosary shall have for intercessors the entire celestial court during their life and at the hour of their death. 14) All who recite the Rosary are my sons and brothers of my only Son, Jesus Christ. 15) Devotion to the Rosary is a great sign of predestination.

These promises are alike in spirit with the scapular promise made two centuries before, and with the promises of the

Sacred Heart to St. Margaret Mary made about two centuries later. Some of these promises clearly foreshadow Fatima. In a way the uplift given to the Church by the revival of the Rosary was temporary, as man was not ready for a true reform of morals, but much of the ground gained was permanent since the Reformation when stopped at a given point never again moved forward. However, the Church did gain enough strength from the Rosary to meet the onslaughts of those who would destroy her if possible. This example of the role of the Rosary in saving the Church from the impact of destruction should encourage us, for if we look we shall see that the offer of strength always comes before the disaster. When the religious revolt struck in the sixteenth century whole nations were swept away, but at the same time a current ran in a counter direction. A renewed missionary spirit spread the gospel over new parts of the globe so that there were more than enough converts in Asia and in America to offset the losses suffered in Europe, and through the efforts of the Jesuits and other missionaries whole nations were won back. Part of this was the power of the Rosary.

Yet, destructive forces still wreaked untold damage throughout all Europe and a tepidity settled down over Catholic Europe which was as bad as anything that came from Luther or Calvin. It will bear saying that, especially in France, where Gallicanism and Jansenism struck at the Church, disruptive movements within the Church caused more damage than open revolt. The coldness that settled down over Catholic countries drew from our Lord sad complaints to St. Margaret Mary. The Rosary was losing its attraction again, and the cycle was running down from Reformation to Jansenism to deism, to the French Revolution, rationalism, liberalism, and now to communism, the logical outcome of it all.

The Church has been under constant and heavy attack since the Black Death struck in 1348. Perhaps peace should have come sooner, but remember that there will be peace on earth only to men of good will. When we ask God for peace from without we are asking Him to impose His will on man by force; a thing He has never done except when the stench of sin has become too great even for God to endure any longer, or when the preservation of the Church is at stake. In the ordinary course of events God works from within by grace. If we do not keep our hearts open to the promptings of grace something goes amiss with the world. When, then, will the world grow better? The very day when enough men set themselves to straightening out their lives from within. Communists will probably not be struck down by fire from heaven; they will be converted when we have converted ourselves. That is the one great consolation of Fatima. When enough Rosaries have been said there will be peace. The Rosaries we say will bring us peace within ourselves. This peace will spread out to others, and so to the whole world. The only hard thing about converting the world is the difficulty we have in converting ourselves to the love of God and of our neighbor. Let us set to convert; not to kill. The Communists do not care if we kill their people. Their friends are no closer to them than their enemies are. The inner circle seeks only to rule. They know they will get closer to victory as destruction spreads. Victors can be perverted as easily as the vanquished can. In fact, when the victor gets the conqueror's mentality, the spirit of Communism dominates even though that person wears an "anti" label. But the spirit of Communism will not run rampant throughout the world. The Church will triumph, of course, but as Our Lady told us, if we do not turn back to Christ there will be a time when error will be scattered throughout all the world, and the good will have much to suffer. We may have conversion through prayer or through pain. But all this suffering need not be. Our Lady has set her seal of approval on the devotion which will curb the spirit of Antichrist. "Pray the Rosary every day," she tells us, "and these troubles will never come to pass."

The Rosary record is long and brilliant. First, Our Blessed Mother overcame the Albigenses who taught that Christ is not God and that the Incarnation is an illusion. Hardly was this danger out of the way when the Mohammendan peril spread its iron curtain over a great part of Christian Europe, after the quarrels of Christians had opened the way for the fall of Constantinople. Soon the Turks of that day were as close to the Holy City as the Reds are today. In fact, Pope Leo X in the sixteenth century was almost kidnapped by raiders who surprised him fishing just offshore in the Adriatic. Then came Lepanto. Don John of Austria was dedicated to the Rosary by the Pope, St. Pius V, a Dominican. The Rosary went into action, displayed from the topmost masthead. In a day the Turkish fleet was dispersed, burnt, or sunken. In his chapel at prayer St. Pius knew of the victory through the kindness of Our Lady, who showed him the victory in a vision.

The Turkish fleet was now gone, but not the army. Shortly it was on the move against the West. In 1563 Hungary was invaded by the Turks in great numbers, only to be driven back by the Christian forces under Rupert, Prince of Egemberg, who could number only four thousand men. The odds were about twenty to one, since it was difficult to get large armies together in those days because the Empire was committed on many fronts, and had been torn asunder by the Protestant revolt. In France the Huguenots were carrying on a full scale war, aided by Elizabeth of England who saw advantages to herself in the weakening of France. France was helping, in turn, to break up the Empire and was hindering the action of the Empire in the East, while having its own serious troubles with the Huguenots at home. Somehow these Huguenots have had better press agents than the legitimate government of France, so that where thousands of persons have heard of the massacre of St. Bartholomew's eve and fully believe it was a Catholic plot against freedom of conscience, not many know that in the south of France there was a massacre of Catholics on the eve of St. Michael, which was a Huguenot religious uprising. The Huguenots are generally known to history as quiet, peace-loving folk who wanted nothing more or less than to worship God in quiet but were supposed to have been prevented by sheer bigotry. It seems not to be generally known that beginning with the Tumult of Amboise, where an attempt was made to capture the King, Francis II, and Mary Stuart, the hapless Queen of Scots, and for practically the next one hundred years, the Huguenots attempted treasonable alliances with England, mainly, and spread war, death, and ruin through southern France. They were as savage as ever the Albigenses were. Cathedrals, churches, libraries, monasteries, and convents went up in flames. Even the celebrated Winding Sheet of Turin (now widely held to be the actual cloth Jesus was buried in), which was then kept at Chambery, shows burns from the melting of the silver casket in which it was kept, when the church that housed it was burned down. The main citadel of Rochelle had been fortified through English aid under Elizabeth, and English influence still held them in power as a religio-political move against France. Large scale military operations were needed to reduce this fortress and so remove the threat to France. The Rosary played so prominent a part in the success of this campaign that the University of Paris pronounced it a Rosary miracle.

It is true that the government and Crown of France were not too Catholic at the time themselves. Gallicanism and Jansenism were eating into the heart of France, and the counterpart of the doctrine of James of England on the divine right of kings was gaining strength in France. The Jesuits were the principal antagonists of religious separatism and of royal absolutism, and in time were to be suppressed for their efforts. France was at the pinnacle of its power and prestige at this time. It is reported that our Lord asked through St. Margaret Mary that Louis XIV consecrate his kingdom to the Sacred Heart, but Louis preferred to bear on his throne the symbol of the sun. The sun also sets, as he was to learn. It may be a coincidence but shortly after Louis refused the consecration he made bad tactical mistakes in Flanders, which began the long decline of France to her present plight—but France will rise when its Catholic faith rises again. It may be asked why God picked France in her struggle with the Huguenots as recipients of a miracle. It did keep France essentially in the Church and formed a bulwark against militant armed Protestantism which was determined to overcome Europe by force of arms, as is seen in the 1527 sack of Rome. France under Richelieu brought an end to the religious wars. When the south of Europe was undermined by disbelief there was no pillaging army left in the north to sweep down upon it. France in the days of her strength planted the faith in the New World where it has flourished with incredible vigor. Up until the time of the first World War France, in spite of all her own religious troubles still maintained practically singlehanded the burden of the foreign missions. About one hundred years ago French sacrifices were pouring money and men into the American missions of the United States. It may appear that the glory of France is now gone, but she is still the eldest daughter of the Church and can have all her glory back in the fold of the faith. Apart from her Catholic destiny, it appears that only extinction awaits her.

France seemed to be saved with the fall of the Huguenots but in the eastern parts of the Empire there was still serious trouble. The Turks struck time and again at the heart of Europe through the Balkans. They laid siege to Vienna several times; swept into Rumania and Croatia in what is now Yugoslavia. There are still heavy Mohammedan overlays in this part of the world, especially in Montenegro and Bulgaria. In 1683 came the crisis. Egged on by Louis XIV who wore the title of Most Christian King, but who still embarrassed Christianity by endangering the Holy Roman Empire, the Turks swept through Europe and laid siege to Vienna with 200,000 men. After months of valiant resistance by a small garrison, the city was relieved by an army under John

Sobieski, King of Poland. The victory goes to the Rosary, and the date which marks the decline of Turkish power was September 12, a day consecrated to the Holy Name of Mary by the Pope as a result of this victory. Then at Tamisvar, near Belgrade in Rumania, in 1717 the Turk was once more hurled back. In recognition of the help given by Our Lady, the Pope, Clement XI, established the feast of the Most Holy Rosary for the universal Church.

Christendom had been saved from foes without and now fell to the mercies of the French Revolution and all the subsequent waves of unbelief that grew from it. Protestantism in Germany and the north had fallen into rationalism of a sweetish sentimentality of emotion. The Protestants had no more armies to burn and pillage. Spain and Italy went into anti-clericalism. Due to some twist in historical writing there seems to be a belief that Mexico and South America revolted from Spain to gain a freedom of conscience, but the reverse is true. Spain was falling into disbelief, and the American colonies felt that their ancient religious freedom was being upset by the new order. However, irreligion spread to America in the end since Spain still dominated this country intellectually, and through confiscations in Europe the religious orders suffered in America. Religion suffered more through a general coldness and bogging down of religious feeling which permitted rationalistic minorities to work their wills. Church property was confiscated; the religious orders were suppressed and their members sent into exile. Many of the third orders secular, which had had great religious influence in their days, quietly expired and the parent orders were approaching the same unhappy outcome. During the eighteenth century religion reached its low ebb. The one bright spot of the century was the Declaration of Independence and the Constitution of the United States, which rested on principles reaching back into the ages of faith.

The world was now confident that Christianity was breathing its last. The Pope, Pius VI, was in the hands of the revolutionists and died in exile as a result of the mistreatment received at the hands of his captors. Later Pius VII was taken prisoner and carried away to France by Napoleon. After Pius VII the elections of Leo XII and Pius VIII were regarded as death bells of the outmoded idea of the Church. Gregory XVI was supposed to be the "last pope." It was said that at length progress had overtaken Christianity. Or, "enlightenment had overtaken superstition." Then Pius IX was chosen in 1846 by a conclave that was somehow beyond explanation by the rationalists, but they consoled themselves by saying that the experts may have missed the end of the Church by one or more popes. All agreed, however, that it was just a matter of time. They appeared to be correct for in two short years Pius IX was fleeing for his life from Rome to Gaeta in disguise. The Papal States, the last vestige of papal rule, were in the hands of a republican committee.

This was a time of stress and difficulty. Revolution flared across Europe; famine stalked the land. The wheat rotted in France; in Ireland the blight was on the potato. Hundreds of thousands starved in Europe on the Continent, and in Ireland millions starved or emigrated. The industrial revolution in all its savagery crushed workers in England. In truth, religion appeared dead, and who was there to stave off final disaster?

But Our Lady had not forgotten us. At Paris in 1830 she appeared to St. Catherine Labouré with the Miraculous Medal, and predictions of disaster soon to fall on Europe. In 1845 she came again to La Salette with a somber message that her Son's arm was too heavy to hold back from a world run amuck. In 1848 the Green Scapular was revealed to a nun in Paris in honor of the Immaculate Heart of Mary, but it was long in spreading.

Then in 1858 a sickly little girl who could not wade the Gave River in France was forced to stay behind when her companions went across the shallow stream looking for firewood. The little girl, Bernadette Soubirous, wandered along her side of the river to an upjutting rock called Massabielle, at that time the city dump, and all was changed. Ninety years, more or less, have gone by since the little girl, now a canonized saint, and the beautiful Lady who called herself the "Immaculate Conception" passed their fingers in unison over the beads of a rosary. It is hard to realize the changes that have come over the world since that day. The world that sneered at the Papacy now cries out in fear that it has designs upon the control of the world. In numbers, zeal, and fervor the Church has a strength greater in some ways than at the height of the thirteenth century. The enemies the Church had on that cold February day in 1858 are mostly dead now, and the Church is very much alive. The great powers of the world now look to the Catholic Church for leadership against the present enemy, atheistic Communism. The fight is to the death again. Already Communism has enslaved Catholic nations but the outcome so far is that many of those Catholics who were lukewarm have become fervent. Communism has murdered bishops, priests, nuns, and laity on a scale which would put into severe eclipse the worst fury of Nero or Diocletian. In China alone there are hundreds of millions of persons who have become acutely aware of the Catholic Church as their champion against the enemy, Communism, whereas most of these people never heard of the Church's work in better times. However, these victories are all for the future. Today the struggle is grim and the sufferings of innocent people are heartbreaking.

The life and zeal of the Church are new-found. It was not nearly so alive twenty years ago. A cold indifference had settled down on religious life after the first World War, and so were provided all the elements of the second World War. It is now our work to hold back a third World War which will retard civilization for hundreds of years, as the fall of Rome did in centuries past. Our Lady always arrives with the remedy before we become aware of the plight in which we have placed ourselves. There was a visitation of Our Lady at Pontmain, which had a Rosary tinge, and there was, at the turn of the century, a Rosary shrine set up at Pompeii, near the buried city. This helped strengthen the Church locally in a time of great stress. It helped reduce the enemies of the Church who were close enough to harm the pope.

There can be no difficulty about the universal character of the apparitions of Our Lady at Fatima in Portugal. There, as at Lourdes, the Rosary was the great note, but at Fatima the Rosary was offered to men with much greater insistence than at Lourdes. At Lourdes, Mary was the Immaculate Conception bearing a rosary; at Fatima she was simply "the Lady of the Rosary." It is scarcely believable that this apparition took place as far back as 1917 and that it was so long before many persons heard anything about it. The Church, ever cautious about supernatural visitations, spent years investigating; now it appears that we may safely accept it as a genuine apparition of Our Blessed Mother. Again Our Lady was in advance of the danger, since it was only much later that the implications of what she had said about Russia took on a serious meaning. The message was the same in substance as that given to St. Dominic 700 years before. If we say the Rosary every day the enemies of religion will be overthrown and there will be peace. But, be it noted that the message at Fatima was much more somber in tone than that given at the beginning of the Rosary. There is a penalty held out to us, that if we do not heed the message there will be a widespread invasion of error throughout the entire world. Let us, then, say Rosaries every day. Let us spread the work of encouraging others to say Rosaries. Let us keep at the fulfillment of the desires of Our Lady until the conversion of Russia becomes an actuality.

Already there are signs that the solidarity of the Red front is cracking, but surely the time of their dissolution is not immediately at hand. The Reds still have strength enough to hurt the world and their traitors are among us to help them. Yet, no matter how strong they may be now they will all go into the same oblivion that awaited the Albigenses. The danger that lies in our path is that we will not get our hearts into the task and put an early end to the evil. "My Immaculate Heart will triumph in the end," Our Lady promised. She has left it to our zeal to decide whether the triumph will come now or after much more damage has been done.

Some time ago the late Red Joe Stalin sneered at the Pope. "How many divisions does he command?" Let us hope that he will find, from wherever he now finds himself, that the Pope's divisions are scattered all over the world, armed with rosaries. The more who take up the Rosary, the sooner will come the ultimate victory. If the victory comes soon there will be much less damage done to the mystical body of Christ. Between the present and the ultimate victory may lie much danger to the faith of millions. Our Lady told us that if her words were not heeded grave errors will spread all over the world, carrying with them the grievous persecution of the innocent. Part of the fate of the world lies in our hands; a safe place for it to be, if those same hands also hold a rosary.

PART TWO

How to Say the Rosary

CHAPTER 5

Some Practical Helps

THE BEADS

THE Rosary with which we of today are familiar has the following parts: a crucifix or medal on which it is usual to say the Apostles' Creed; a single Our Father bead followed by three smaller beads in a group on which the Hail Mary is said. A Glory be to the Father is then said. This starts the Rosary proper with the announcing of the mystery together with some sort of meditation based on its meaning. The Our Father is said on the final bead of the pendent group. On the ten succeeding small beads we say the Hail Mary, ending each decade with a Glory be to the Father. Then we make a short meditation on the next mystery and follow this with the Our Father on the next large bead, and ten Hail Marys on the following group of ten smaller beads. Then we proceed in the same fashion for all the succeeding decades until the circle of the Rosary is completed. As a variant of the above, the pendent beads are sometimes absent, and the fifth Our Father bead is within the circlet.

The Dominicans who have an especial care for the Rosary have a somewhat different way of beginning. The Rosary was Mary's Psalter and was recited in the beginning as an office. The Dominicans still recite it as an office. They begin, of course, with the sign of the Cross. Then in versicle and response the following: V. Hail Mary, full of grace, the Lord is with thee. R. Blessed art thou amongst women and blessed is the fruit of thy womb, Jesus. V. Thou, O Lord will open my lips. R. And my tongue will announce Thy praise. V. Incline unto my aid, O Lord. R. O Lord, make haste to help me. V. Glory be to the Father, and to the Son, and to the Holy Ghost. R. As it was in the beginning, is now, and ever shall be, world without end. Amen. Alleluia. (From Septuagesima until Easter Saturday in place of Alleluia, say, "Praise be to Thee, O Lord. King of Eternal Glory"). Then continue as with the more general method. There is, of course, no choice or priority between methods. Begin as you please or as the local custom goes. We noted above that the pendent beads came into the present form of the rosary through the Crown of St. Brigit of Sweden. Before the time of Lourdes the six decade rosary was widely used. There exist some of the older statues of Our Lady of Lourdes that show her with a six decade rosary. One such statue is found in the Lourdes shrine in the Church of St. Louis of France in St. Louis (the old Cathedral). Even those who said the Rosary proper often used a six decade rosary, saying the five decades according to the accepted method and then adding the sixth "at choice." There is a Sodality Manual published as late as 1823 under Jesuit auspices that gives such a method.

The Rosary proper starts with the Our Father bead of the first decade. Meditation must begin here if we are to say the Rosary according to the mind of the Church. Without some mental prayer we cannot obtain the indulgences offered to those who say the Rosary "meditating on the mysteries." It is now the custom to say the Joyful Mysteries on Mondays and Thursdays, and on Sundays from the first Sunday of Advent to Quinquagesima Sunday, inclusive. Sorrowful Mysteries are said on Tuesdays and Fridays, and on all Sundays during Lent. The Glorious Mysteries are said on Wednesdays and Saturdays, and on all other Sundays during the year not listed above. For public recitations the above rotation of mys-

Some Practical Helps

teries is closely followed, but we are under no such regulation in private recitation.

If we say more than five mysteries during any one day we do not have to observe any priority of groups of mysteries. For example; we may say the Glorious Mysteries before the Sorrowful, if we wish to; but within any group of mysteries it is necessary to keep to the established order. All who say the Rosary may interrupt it after any decade and resume later without breaking the moral unity of the Rosary. The five decades need only be completed during the course of a natural day.

In order to pray the Rosary it is not necessary to use blessed beads; one would still be saying the Rosary, and a few of the Rosary indulgences would come to him, but it is not fitting that a Catholic should have an object of devotion or of religious veneration which has not been especially set apart as given to God, which is what we mean by a "blessing." A blessed article is in a sense given away, for after it receives a blessing it may not enter into commerce, nor may it be exchanged for anything of value. Neither may it be sold privately, even for the purpose of recovering one's cost out of it. An article which has been blessed and then is exchanged for anything of value becomes secularized. It would not be sinful in itself to sell a rosary if one has to, but if the intention is to transfer the spiritual good by means of a sale, it could be the sin of simony. It is pure carelessness which could prompt a Catholic to use an article of devotion without the blessing of the Church being placed upon it. The principal blessings for rosaries are the Apostolic, Brigittine, Crozier, and Dominican. Almost every priest has faculties for imparting the first three, and many have faculties for the Dominican blessing.

The physical beads themselves now carry the indulgences. Accordingly, the chains may be removed and exchanged at will. One may rewire the beads at will and they need not go back in the same order they had before. One may have such work done by others and pay for the same, as it does not affect the blessings. When beads are lost or broken through no fault of the holder, they may be replaced without loss of indulgences even if such replacements come to include all the beads in the course of time. Some of the beads may be removed even if they are not broken, as long as care is taken not to exchange in this fashion as many as half of the beads. We should not, for example, attempt to divide the beads in such a way as to replace enough beads so as to make one rosary come out as two, so that we have two rosaries that are blessed.

MEDITATION

Besides their physical aspects beads have a mental counterpart in meditated prayer which makes it easier and more reasonable to accept the tradition that the Blessed Mother had a hand in combining the elements of this unique method of prayer, because there is great wisdom in making the manual elements reinforce the meditation. Meditation as an entry into mental prayer has always been practiced by those seeking spiritual perfection, or even advancement, and those who have followed it have profited thereby. But it takes time and practice—more than most persons living in the world can devote to it. It has always appeared to me that meditation and mental prayer constitute a difficult art, but in the Rosary with the hands engaged in a light activity and with the vocal prayers hovering in the background, the mind can be set free for its task of dwelling on the great truths of religion. This type of meditation must be well within the reach of most persons in the world, or Our Lady would not have asked that EVERYONE say the Rosary EVERY DAY.

We have tried to bring out that Our Blessed Mother has a personal abiding interest in her Rosary, and in the welfare of those who say it. This will give us an impulse to make an honest effort to improve our method of saying Rosaries. Our

Some Practical Helps

Lord has said that anyone who asks Him anything *believing* will have his prayer answered. He put no other conditions upon it. However, a lively faith can be well-instructed, and it is better that it should be so. Our Lord will not be outdone in generosity, and he who seeks to improve his method of praying is going to enhance his certitude of having his prayer answered. We read of saints who were illiterate but who were still deeply gifted by the Holy Ghost. That is true—but today there are too many schools. Nowadays, some literate and illiterate people are lazy, and God does not sanctify laziness.

ATTENTION: INTENTION

The main trouble that I noted with myself was that I was not being deliberate enough in my saying of the Rosary. We talk about distraction in prayer, but much that passes for prayer is too automatic for distraction to have much to do with it. Distraction, after all, is at least a sign of some mental activity. When we think, there are side associations that come up into consciousness with the train of thought we are trying to develop. Unless we make some attempt to guide thoughts and repeat our attempts at control, our minds will "wander"; that is, associated ideas will tend to creep back into the line of thought. It takes practice to choose from among the thoughts that well up in the mind and never to pick one that will lead us from the subject. It is not too serious when this happens. There are times in a person's development when it gets almost impossible for him to read a book because at the outset a flood of other ideas springs up in the mind under the stimulus of the opening sentences of the book. This can be cured by trying to read without reference to anything else we may know. Simply read without any attempt to relate what is read to other subjects. When we pray, we should go about it the same way—turn the mind full force to the idea to be meditated. In the present case it will be one of the mysteries of the Rosary. In each mystery as it comes up in turn—be deliberate and be brief. But let us not be vague and half-hearted about our part. Keep alive the two great elements of prayer, deliberation and a lively faith. Sliding the beads through our fingers with no set consciousness of the task before us, and with no apparent expectation of being heard and answered will never develop into the practice of saying the Rosary daily. No wonder people tire of it so soon and give it up, except when surprised into it at a wake, or other public devotion.

No wonder our critics say that the Rosary is a "vain repetition" and quote the Scriptures against us for our "long prayers" like those of the heathen. I have heard the Rosary compared to the prayer wheel of the Buddhists. This is a large wheel which is turned by the "holy one" of India with a crank. On the rim of the wheel are pasted papers, all containing prayers. As the wheel turns the pagan god is supposed to read the prayers and give the one who turns the crank credit for having said these prayers. This is a pitiful caricature of the consolation of the repeated prayers of the Rosary, since in the Rosary the meditation is the important consideration; the repeated prayers form only the background.

If we do as well as we can with the meditations, saying Rosaries will bring home to us the simple import of the Gospel story. It is this which will reform our lives after the pattern of Christ, and also help to reform the world. It is thus we separate the true reformer from the false. The true reformer starts to reform himself first. Then his example spreads out to others; the false reformer wants to impose his own ideas on all who are near him, or under his control, although his own life may be far from what it ought to be. The Rosary will also help to develop a devotion to the Blessed Mother. Our enemies say there is too much of the Virgin Mary in the Catholic Church; the saints say that we can never say too much about her. Don't be afraid that we shall tend to elevate her to a sort of goddess who will encroach on the devotion due to God alone. When we say, "Mary," Mary says, "Jesus." True devotion to the Blessed Virgin will always lead to Christ. Even those who will not concede that the Rosary is the direct gift of the Blessed Virgin must concede that she is the Mediatrix with Christ; and as Christ came to us through Mary, we must go back to Christ through Mary. It is true that great saints arose before the Rosary came into being; it is also true that no saint ever arose without great devotion to the Blessed Virgin.

When we say Rosaries, then, let us not merely pull the beads from pocket or purse and begin to recite vocal prayers, without a deliberate turning toward the meaning of the matter to be meditated as best we can. Let us keep in mind that the troubled old world we live in is deeply scarred across its face by original sin, and that our patience will help supply the painful plastic surgery to heal it. There are lessons in the Rosary which we need, and which the world needs. Let us be deliberate, attentive, and what is more, let us take the trouble to go to some depth in getting at these lessons and the way to bring them home to ourselves.

We are usually full of the world when we start to pray. If we live in the world its cares will always be close to us. Only by a special vocation can we leave the world and retire to the cloister, and that, of course, will not be open to most of us. The world has a way of penetrating us from within, just as many of the children of Israel longed for the flesh-pots of Egypt. Often when we pray to be removed from some evil in this world we know in our own hearts that we merely wish to be set free from the evil consequences, but do not wish to abandon this luxury, that person, or whatever else may have turned the evil loose upon us. Let us do the best we can to throw off the allurement of the world, and kneel or sit with beads in hand to learn what God desires to teach us. This takes a deliberate act of attention.

There are three ways we can pay attention, according to St. Thomas. We can pay attention to the words as they occur and try to analyze their meanings, or we can pay the sort of attention useful for taking notes, or memorizing what we hear or read. This sort of attention can well be used in preliminary studies to learn from the Bible or from spiritual writers the content of each of the mysteries. But the sort of attention to bring to the recital of the Rosary is the "general" attention such as a child uses in listening to an interesting story. With such attention directed at what we are doing we can make a few short statements about the mystery. No attempt should be made to hold this in mind as though continuing to look at a picture. If we do this, the mind will get active about the time that the vocal prayers start, and there we have another distraction in the conflict of vocal and mental prayers. The way I have found best is to name the mystery; make a few short pointed statements about it; and then draw some practical resolution from it. It is not too hard to hold this before the mind for a few seconds, and a few seconds are enough. Don't drag it out at length, unless you are skilled at mental prayer. I am not, and meditation soon becomes sheer mind-wandering with me. Do not try to hold the thought in mind. Let it sink down into the hidden reaches of the soul. It will not get lost there. The mind is a power of the living soul; it knows what to do with thoughts that come into it.

Be brief. Take out the rosary and hold it tightly in your hand. Say: *"I am going to pray this Rosary for . . ."* (for example: for a better job, for a raise in salary, for the conversion of Russia, or for the graces due me from the sacrament of matrimony, or for world peace), *subject always to the will of God*. This will not mean that there is a question of whether God wishes you to have graces, or the world to have peace, or you to have a better job. God always wills the good to happen to us, and He is more willing to give than we are to ask. When we pray it must always be as though there were not a chance that we could fail to be heard—we are to pray "believing," but at the same time we must be careful to avoid the pagan counterfeit of prayer which holds that when we pray we work a psychological trick on ourselves which attracts the good things to us. We should always keep the "will of God" present in prayer and do the very best we know how in helping bring what we ask to a successful conclusion by our own efforts. God will generally answer prayer, so that the unthinking cannot see where the natural effort left off and God's help began. A person who wants to make a success of his marriage must treat his wife with the ordinary politeness he would show to any decent woman; plus the extra consideration she is due as his wife; plus prayers that the graces of matrimony be given him. These graces should come to us from the sacrament, to be sure, but we must ask for them. Grace is not just sent out weekly, or monthly, as a sort of a subscription. Do something about it. Pray for these graces and for all other graces. Pray for everything through the Rosary. As we get back to a sense of dependence on God we draw closer to each other. There can be no such thing as a brotherhood of man without the fatherhood of God. Unless we are of the same Father, we are not brothers; and that is what is wrong with the world. As each of us begins to live habitually in this frame of mind the fact of world peace will get closer. It will not take many to turn the tide. We do not have to wait until the last man is converted. Society takes its color from determined minorities. But there are, unfortunately, millions of humans who will always live subhuman lives. They have minds but do not use them. They have wills but never attempt to will anything. They drift. They will be affected by example, good or bad. It does not take many good people or many bad people to color an entire age, and the good are more effective than the bad.

State the purpose of the Rosary before you start to say it, as we mentioned above, and then add: *I want the answer to this prayer to come through the intercession of the Blessed Mother, who is so powerful with her Son that He worked His first miracle for her, although His time had not yet come.*

On Calvary His hour did come, and there He gave her to us as our mother. He will refuse her nothing. He will hear this Rosary prayer because to it Mary has attached the promise that it will be heard. Lord, hear my prayer through our Mother.

God answers all prayers, but this does not mean He complies with all requests as they are stated. We would not give a razor blade to a child, even though he cried for it. In prayer be sure to keep the will of God in mind, as there are things we seek which we shall have to attain by praying for strength to carry a burden, rather than by having it taken away. Three times St. Paul asked to have the "sting of the flesh" taken away, and God told him: "My grace is sufficient for you." Whatever this affliction was, St. Paul bore it with patience. Today there are many who have given up their faith because they wanted that "sting" removed, and would not take anything else. They don't wish patience. They desire to have their own way. If we all had our burdens removed the earthly Paradise would be here again. God closed that to our first parents and has not opened it since. This is a world of sorrow, a vale of tears for many of us. Generally speaking, when a burden is removed from one person it settles down on another. It is better at the outset to pray for strength than to pray for relief. There is nothing wrong in praying for relief, but one should not be resentful if God has other plans.

The above simple prayer that states its purpose and acknowledges the will of God, and the intercessory power of the Blessed Mother take less than thirty seconds to say, yet elevates the entire act from what may be mere mechanics to something closer to real prayer.

The world of the supernatural operates through the world of nature. Grace uses nature. In prayer, then, we may well make use of any device which enables the will to keep control of the natural processes of the mind that must take place while we pray. Prayer is not something that happens to us from outside. That belief is passivism, or Quietism. This was

Some Practical Helps 57

an heretical movement that attempted to operate within the Church in France in the seventeenth century, with great damage to the Church. Quietism is the counterpart of the false belief that prayer works its own answer by calming the mind to accept the good things that are waiting for those who are wise enough to "tune them in."

I have no concern here with attempting a scientific definition of prayer. That is outside my province; but there are some things related to what prayer does, and how it operates that are within my experience. These I feel I should point out to the wayfarer who has had troubles with prayer. Prayer is lifting the heart and mind up to God. It is, in a real way, speaking to God. If we speak to other men we take some care to know what we are about, what impression we wish to leave, and what we want as a result of our conversation. I will not say that all men go to this trouble in practice; there is entirely too much random talking (and writing) done. A lot of us go about our business and social contacts without enough deliberation. Now, God is not moved to hear our prayers in the same way a prospective customer is moved to sign an order for merchandise, but the preliminary work we are willing to do to prepare the mind for prayer shows how *important* we consider prayer to be, and has a lot to do with the faith we bring to the prayer. A mind in great agitation and trouble will not be able to go about these preliminaries clearly and calmly, so that unless there is some orderly method as an ideal, prayer becomes practically impossible, or at least very difficult in times of stress and danger. But when the mind is heavy with care there is often no more one can do than to sit heavily in a back pew and look at the tabernacle, and no words will come to the mind. God will supply for our defects in our needs, but God cannot be expected to compose prayers and hand them to careless and lazy people. Let's do some praying before we get into trouble.

CHAPTER 6

The Prayers of the Pendent Beads

MOST likely the rosary you have has a crucifix at the end of the pendent beads. If it does not, get one and put it there. The crucifix represents the most important thing that ever can happen to the world. It makes an especially fine introduction to the Rosary. Take the crucifix into your hand and after you have said a short prayer to clear the mind of side issues you have brought along with you from the affairs of this world, stop and look down on the crucifix there. This is the symbol of our redemption and should recall to our minds this most important event. This is the great sign that the God-man, Jesus Christ, loved us enough to hang on this brutal instrument of torture until He died. He still loves us enough to listen to our prayers and to our troubles. He will either lift those burdens or give us strength enough to bear them, if these burdens are "our cross." Christ told us: "He who will not take up his cross and follow Me, is not worthy of Me." From this we may well learn that this is a world of crosses to be carried, and not too much of having crosses taken entirely away. Christ accepted the bitter things the Father gave Him to do. Remember that we do not live in the terrestrial Paradise. Sin closed that to us, and the Father has not willed to restore it. This is the one thing that Christians should make clear to themselves nowadays, of all times.

Prayers of Pendent Beads

This is a world in which there is, and has always been, and will always be evil, and evil men who will put unjust burdens on others. Often when we pray that God will remove evil from us we are really asking Him to cut down evil men in their sin. God will usually not do this. He will generally not cut down evil men as they are about to commit evil, any more than He has cut us down as we reached out for the evil of sin. Other men may have been praying for our destruction as they asked God that their burdens be lifted. We can be thankful that many prayers were not answered that way. Be patient—but not weak and passive—under sufferings imposed by evil, and let God have His opportunity to keep offering His grace to convert evil men to where they will freely turn from evil to do good. It is not hard to see how those who saw St. Stephen stoned to death might have asked God to destroy not only the ones who hurled the stones, but to destroy also Saul, who stood by holding the coats of those who threw the stones in this evil murder. Did St. Stephen pray that God should strike his enemies dead so that the valuable work of the Church, done by Stephen, could go forward? No, Stephen prayed for his persecutors and thereby made himself *Saint* Stephen. If God had struck Saul down by force at Jerusalem, there would have been no Saul to have been struck down by grace on the road to Damascus. Saul could not have risen to go on forward until he, too, sealed his teachings in his blood and became St. Paul who was, perhaps, the greatest single influence in the entire history of the Catholic Church. God forbid that anyone should take from these words the conclusion that we should not pray that evil be overthrown—we do as a matter of fact pray for this whenever we say in the Our Father, "deliver us from evil." In this age of small faith we pray too much for the childish things that tickle the nervous system and fail to pray for the big things we could be granted.

Let us not be too strenuous to pray God to unload burdens, sufferings, and difficulties from ourselves. If we had enough generous people who would pray that God would take away the burdens from other people, God would more readily grant this, because it would be backed by charity. If enough persons become affected by such a spirit of charity the favors of God will get around to a lot of us who are now going to work out our destiny in penance, because we do not have love enough to be trusted with favors without becoming proud. By our unremitting prayers we can move God to overthrow evil by grace, but perhaps the very first evil that needs to be overthrown is that which is now too prevalent. That is the frenetic desire of our age to get away from burdens of all kinds.

We are the channels that God has chosen in which to operate His providence. Through God will come from our labors and sufferings all conversions and reforms. It may well be that our patience under difficulties will convert some new St. Paul whom God has designs upon. We can be sure of one thing: God will not destroy evil by means of destroying the freedom of any will He has created. If God had it in His plans to overthrow evil thus by force, He would surely have destroyed Lucifer at the moment when His own angels rebelled against Him. If God held it to be a lesser evil to permit Lucifer to live on as Satan instead of killing him before the Father of lies could have touched our first parents, and so set off the long train of ruin that brought even the Son of God to a cross; if God sees greater good in permitting evil, if God permits sin—although the very slightest sin is more serious than the physical destruction of the entire universe— then we have gone astray, if we approach the problem of evil any other way than through the eyes of God.

Any promise to do away with all human sufferings and to remove all ills from man from without (for man can, from within, do much to remove wrongs and evils); all promises to bring back the terrestrial Paradise are from Satan, who simply repeats over and over again the first rash promise he made to our first parents: "You shall be as gods, knowing good and evil." The knowledge promised was not mere information, but superiority over good and evil. The same boast came from the mad brain of Nietzsche who wrote a book called "Beyond Good and Evil." Present day Communists are heirs to the same tradition, because to them "good" is what helps Communism dominate the world, and "evil" is what keeps them from destroying civilization. In fact, all Utopian schemes since Adam's day have been attempts to redeem that original foolish promise. One does not like to use the term "foolish" in connection with the greatest of all created intellects—that of Satan's—but it does go to show that only God can solve the problem of good and evil, and if we are sometimes puzzled by its operations we can remember that Satan has not solved it either. All we need to do, then, is to develop our faith, hope, and charity, and leave the rest to God. He will work things out. Thus we can possess our souls in peace and this will destroy Communism to its roots, for Communism is also from Satan, because it, too, promises that a day will come when all men shall give without stint according to their abilities and take only according to their needs. Somehow through killings, torture, treachery, and all the other Communist "virtues" they expect to bring a day when there shall be no more sickness, no more sorrow, no greed, and the world will again be Paradise. While these promises are very enticing to sorrow-laden mankind it just happens that these promises are not true, and cannot be true.

These promises are not true although man has, and perhaps always will run after these will-of-the-wisp theories, because man does not like to suffer, and can be wooed away from the prospect of suffering by promises to remove his ills. The end of these false promises is always a thousand times as much suffering than if man had simply girded himself for his day-to-day sufferings, in a world marred by original sin. The sight of the crucifix as we hold it in our hand will bring back the reality of suffering brought about by sin.

But think, too, how much suffering has been blotted out from this sin-laden world by the sufferings of Christ, and how much the penetration of the hearts of men by the merciful message of Christianity has relieved the heavy lot of human kind. There are those who pretend that Christianity has fostered suffering and is indifferent to it. The truth is that those who rant most about abolishing suffering cause the most of it. Consider how terrible the world would have been without Christ. When we think of all the horror of the Communist world, we imagine it to be something never before heard of; but any study of the ancient world makes it clear that this was pretty much the daily life of all men in the ancient world before Christ.

There is no need—nor even desirability—to make the preliminary prayer of our Rosary very long. Neither does it have to be in any set words. We want only to set up some personal relationship between ourselves and that mystery of evil which besets the world, but which will be made clear to us thinking in our hearts of Christ, and Him crucified. The world has been seeking answers to pain and suffering every place but in the one spot where it can be found. We invent drugs and then they are put to use to twist men's minds to where they will tell lies about themselves. We invent explosives to clear the land for expanding food resources, and the explosives end up in the war-head of a torpedo, or in an artillery shell. Psychology advances to teach men how to get along with each other and it is turned aside to teach men to hate each other. No *thing* will bring peace. Peace belongs only to men of good will. We see this but we are infected more than we think by the spirit of the world. We must find the answer to evil and to suffering in the crucifix, and all these material things that plague us will be turned into blessings.

THE APOSTLES' CREED

We now consider the preliminary prayers of our Rosary. First we recite the Apostles' Creed. We say it with close attention, because it is a kind of overture to the entire prayer, where, as in the symphony, the theme is stated for later development. Here we see the work of the Trinity: Father, Son, and Holy Ghost. To the Father is attributed the work of creation, including the creation of the divine humanity of His Son. To the Son, appearing among us as the Godman, Jesus Christ, is attributed the work of our salvation. When the Son returned to His Father the Holy Ghost came among us to remain, and so to continue on earth through the Catholic Church the work of Jesus Christ. The Holy Ghost is the Sanctifier.

We must not attempt to meditate at any length on the articles on the Creed, since the mysteries themselves will expand this material. Simply give this prayer the direct, close attention that has been mentioned before, as the kind of attention one gives to a good book, or to an interesting speaker. There will, of course, be great profit in going over the Creed point by point, apart from the saying of the Rosary. We learn the Creed at an early age by rote, and usually grow up with no particular added study being given to it. We suggest as a beginning to divide the Creed as we outline immediately below, and then go over each point carefully. When we say the Rosaries afterwards we shall be enriched by this study, as the lessons of our holy faith will be called more readily to mind.

I believe in God the Father	Almighty Creator of Heaven and earth (and in)
Jesus Christ, His only Son	Our Lord Who was conceived by the Holy Ghost born of the Virgin Mary suffered under Pontius Pilate was crucified

died and was buried.
He descended into hell (and)
the third day He arose again from the dead
He ascended into heaven
sitteth at the right hand of God the Father Almighty
Whence He shall come to judge the living and the dead.

I believe in the Holy Ghost the Holy Catholic Church, **the communion of Saints**
the forgiveness of sins
the resurrection of the body (and)
life everlasting. Amen.

THE OUR FATHER

The preliminary or pendent beads represent the only opportunity in the Rosary of paying exclusive, undivided attention to the beautiful vocal prayers. During the rest of the Rosary they will only furnish a backdrop to the meditations. The Our Father is the most perfect of all prayers, since it was composed for our needs by our Lord Himself. It is, above all other prayers, "The Lord's Prayer." It is made up of seven petitions, with an act of adoration to the Father and submission to His holy will. This is one of the very few prayers we address to God the Father, without seeming to go through Jesus Christ, our Lord. Most prayers, even those to the Holy Ghost, are directed "through Jesus Christ, our Lord." Jesus Christ told us that no man goes to the Father except through the Son, but here we go direct to the Father because our Lord told us to do so. Give a few thoughts to this prayer.

Our Father—Christ willed to point out to us that God is a real father, not only because He brought us into being, but because He watches over us, and has a care for us in our bodies and in our souls, which He has lifted up beyond the deserts of our own nature, to give us through sanctifying grace a share in His own divine life. We who live in a world of stress need to remember this; but when we can see that Christ did not say *"my* Father" but *"our* Father" much of the trouble of this world will pass away. We hear much about the "brotherhood of man," but we may just as well speak of a "brotherhood of dogs" if we are to forget the Fatherhood of God. If God is *our Father* all men are our brothers. Without a Father of us all it will always be "each man for himself and the devil take the hindmost."

Who art in Heaven—St. Paul reminded us that "you have not here a lasting city, but must look for one that is to come." The false teachers of today tell us that we must look for any heaven we may hope for in this world, and then set out to make the kind of world we have today as an example of the only sort of heaven they can make for us. There is no man so foolish as to believe that he is happy. The false philosopher who prates of an earthly happiness is trying to bolster his own position, which he sees to be hopeless. It is as the series of the broken-down Five Year Plans that have been following each other in Communist lands. "If something didn't go wrong they would work," we are told after each succeeding failure. It has been going on since 1925, and still we see no heaven on earth. Some one is blamed for failure so as to cover the dictator's embarrassment, because a dictator's plans must never seem to go wrong. Someone pays for the failure in blood, and suffering and the plans for "heaven here and now" go chasing after each other as a dog chases its own tail. Something went wrong a long, long time ago, and time will not cure it. Sin has marred the world and only eternity can cure it—an eternity with God in heaven.

Hallowed be Thy Name—If there is no reverence for God's name there can be no respect of man for man. In that case no man can pursue his work with peace of mind when he is away from home, nor will he find it any better when he returns to the bosom of his own family. If men do not respect the name of the Father of us all, how can they respect the earthly father, or respect the authority of the laws of the land? As the prophet Jeremias says: "It is an evil and bitter thing to have left the Lord." It is this bitterness we are all tasting, for even those of us who have not left the Lord have become careless, as we saw those around us drift away. We call it "broadmindedness." This is the first petition, and the most important. It is the way back to peace for men of good will. Our troubles do not spring from something that God has done to us; they are what we have done to God.

Thy Kingdom Come—God must reign as king over all of us. Much of the disturbance around us springs from the yearning for "religious democracy," whatever that may mean. The term is used, but it has no meaning. It comes back to the promise of the Serpent: "You shall be as gods, knowing good and evil." We are so accustomed to democracy in government that the idea applied to religion seems quite reasonable to us. Democracy can be reasonable only amongst equals, but this cannot apply even to a family between a father and his infant children; nor can it apply to our Father in heaven and His children. On earth Christ left His teachings to be kept intact until He returns as Judge of the living and the dead. Jesus Christ said to Pilate that He was a king, and He left Peter and his successors to rule the kingdom of Christ on earth, promising to ratify in heaven what Peter and his successors would bind or loose through the Catholic Church on earth.

Thy Will be Done on Earth as It Is in Heaven—We become saints by doing the will of God; we sin only by opposing His will. In heaven all is harmony and all is happiness, because the angels and saints are happy to the degree that they reflect the divine will. Man thinks, too often, that this must be a weak and supine existence, and he thinks that a man can be strong only if he tries to work out his own will, even where God has said that he may not. Once in heaven the will of God was not done when Satan rose up, imagining the glory he saw upon himself was from his own nature, and said: "I will not serve." And too often Satan has succeeded in getting man to defy the will of God on earth, as he did to his sorrow in heaven. Heaven rejected him, and so restored its harmony and peace. If we reverse this Satan-born discord we can restore even here on earth some of the harmony of heaven.

Give Us This Day Our Daily Bread—The providence of God is always watching over us and providing for us, but let it be remembered that generally God wills to act out His care for man through other men. There is a typical Communist trick to poison the minds of the young which causes them to bring in children who are hungry; and usually those who are hungry through Communist bungling or their lust for conquest. The children are told to pray to God for food, and see if God places food on the table before them. God has already provided the food in the annual miracle of growth, where man sows, and God gives the increase. However, these men who have food which belongs under the providence of God to these children, hold it back until they have gone through a blasphemous ritual to destroy the faith of the children of God. The Communists then ask the children to pray to Papa Stalin, or to some other local Communist deity, and when they do the food is immediately brought forth. In this caricature of providence there is a lesson for all of us. God has provided for all of us and will provide—but not in a dull socialistic equality. To one in superabundance; to another dull wits, poverty, and bad health. But woe to the man to whom it has been given if he does not regard himself as the agent of the dispossessed. We do not have to give up all we have, but we had better give up some of it, not entirely through charity, but partly as dispensers of the good things of God.

And Forgive Us Our Trespasses as We Forgive Those Who Trespass against Us—This is the real test of practical religion. Anyone who imagines that Christianity is a collection of soft, weakling devotions should look into the strictness with which we are held accountable for our forgiveness of our enemies. To hate a man one needs only to let his emotions run wild, and after a while he will find that he still hates, but will forget entirely what his quarrel is about. Satan hates God and he wants us to hate our fellow man, who is an image of God. It is the spirit of hatred carried to a national scale that is the cause of war, and it can be shown that some of these senseless hatreds have been prolonged for more than a thousand years. Communism always moves in on existing hatred and wrongs. (How could the Iron Curtain have clamped down so easily on most of eastern Europe, had there not been a preliminary preparation of dislike among Slav, Magyar, and Teuton?) Too many of us are out to punish someone for wrongs, real or imaginary. How many times have we heard the statement: "I could forgive, but I have to get even first." There is no use of our turning to God for forgiveness for ourselves if we exclude others from our hearts. "Vengeance is mine; I will repay," says the Lord. Vindictiveness imperils our eternal salvation. "How can your heavenly Father forgive you, unless you forgive every man in your heart?" This ought to be the sovereign reason for giving up grudges; but a world weak in faith has to run to "advantages" and cultivate only those who can do something for us. This is a counterfeit forgiveness, and it will not work for Christians, because the grace of God does not go with it. Any man who wants peace should keep the peace himself, and attempt to be at peace with those who are of no use to his social advancement. When we can make the effort of forgiveness as God wants it done we have helped set the world on the way to peace.

And Lead Us Not into Temptation—St. James tells us that God does not tempt anyone, and He is not a tempter to evil. I remember when I was a boy one of my associates came up to me during a mission at the parish church and said he had a question for the box. It was, of course, the old one: "How can God lead anyone into temptation?" It did not take long to find out that some petty, local atheist was behind the question, thinking, no doubt, to upset someone's faith, if only he could catch him young enough. The missioner demolished the question, of course, but it showed the need for a living authority to interpret the petition of the Our Father in comparison with the denial of St. James. Since evil is an attempt to overthrow God, we cannot so much as imagine God promoting His own destruction. But this is a world of strife, and we must pass all our days in a place that abounds in trials and temptations. If we are humble enough to see our own wretchedness and weakness, and if we will ask God for His graces, He will give them to us. We can ask God to keep us so that we shall not have to come too closely in contact with the evil around us as we go in search of our daily necessities. If we will not ask for help, grace will avoid us and we shall find ourselves crowded in by the world and easily overcome.

But Deliver Us from Evil—God permits evil but He gives us His grace and strength to overcome all the evil that besets us. As God told St. Paul: "My grace is sufficient for you, for strength is made perfect in adversity." God will not help us by destroying evil men, because "God desires not the death of the sinner, but that he be converted and live." Since we have already prayed that God's will be done we must also pray to be delivered from evil, in the way that God wills it. God may even visit us with physical difficulties and handicaps in order to draw out from us the power that will sleep as long as we are not called on to struggle. Our struggles in patience may also gain graces for those who are at war with God. When they are converted the evil they have done will largely disappear. Let us pray, then, and have patience.

Amen—This is a sign of ratification. It means in Hebrew, "So let it be." Christ always used it to introduce solemn teachings and to impress His hearers that He spoke the literal truth, and wished His words to be taken just as He spoke them. Thus, "Amen, amen, I say unto you, unless a man be born again he cannot enter the Kingdom of heaven." Or, "Amen, amen, I say unto you, unless you eat the Flesh of the Son of Man and drink His Blood, you shall not have life in you."

FAITH—HOPE—CHARITY

As we move on to the three Haily Mary beads in the pendant we encounter a rather old devotion which is only now becoming widespread: that is the custom of offering these three Hail Mary's for an increase of faith, hope, and charity. Naturally, such a prayer is praiseworthy and highly laudable. It is, perhaps, all too true that we do not make enough of the practice of deliberately praying for the simple, basic things we need. We receive faith, hope, and charity as free gifts at baptism. We receive an increase in confirmation. In worthy confession and communion our store of these virtues is added to; but still more deliberation and definite seeking of these three virtues will make it easier to accumulate them in greater measure. There is no upper limit that we may dare set on the acquisition of faith, hope, and charity during a lifetime, as long as we try to go forward; but when we think we have done just about enough, there is danger that our feet may slip down hill again.

The rule is to foster acts of piety whenever they may be done, without endangering other acts of piety. One must watch not to get such a load of prayers worked into his daily program that it becomes a heavy burden, and causes us at length to regard a lot of religious exercises as irritations. If the adding of any intention to these three Hail Mary's causes distractions and disturbs the main flow of meditation on the mysteries of the Rosary, by all means drop the side issues, and stay to the main purpose of the Rosary. Yet there are some who may be actually benefitted by this short, added devotion, as it may form a prelude to the meditations on the mysteries and turn the mind more readily away from distractions. These prayers now are non-essentials to the Rosary and may be dropped out without the slightest misgivings.

Yet, there is something engaging about the intertwining of the virtues of faith, hope, and charity with the mysteries of our holy religion, as they are brought out in the Rosary. When we think how much damage was turned loose on the world by the confusing of faith and hope by our unhappy tormented brother, Doctor Martin Luther; and when we recall that we are again going through a phase where there is a lack of hope, either through the presumption of those who say there is no such thing as moral right and wrong, or the despair of those who feel that the world will never be "right" again, we may regard it as providential that some deliberate attention to the fundamental virtues of faith, hope, and charity is attaching itself to the Rosary.

FAITH

In faith we encounter a mystery of religion which is basic to all other concepts in the spiritual life, because without faith we cannot save our souls. Do not confuse this with the unfortunate statements of the proud of heart, that this means that no one can attain to God without first having been given a membership, outwardly and formally, in the Catholic Church. If we had been born to live in the depths of the Amazonian jungles or on the burnt wind-swept reaches of the Gobi desert, it would still be true that we could not save our souls without faith, and without baptism, since God extends to all the gift of faith in some saving form which men may grasp dimly in a dim light, but must grasp fully in full light. There is baptism of desire for those who will never know the baptism of water or blood. God makes no one for hell, and when we get to the heavenly home we have set out for, we shall be surprised at the ones we see there, and at the ones we shall not see there. God is just, but His mercy outruns His justice.

Faith is a gift. It is the entry into the spiritual life we can never attain to by our nature, because it admits us to a supernatural life which is no part of human nature. Faith is no less than an invitation from God to partake in His life, and through its action we arrive at conclusions which would remain always beyond us if left to our own intellects and wills. We have all seen those who have fallen away from the faith they were raised in; who offer as excuses for their conduct the fact that they "found it impossible to believe in the Real Presence of Jesus Christ in the Eucharist." They explain that they cannot understand it, and thought they had better just quit the Catholic Church. Generally they have been manipulating the marriage contract, or by sharp business contracts have removed their neighbor's property. No one understands the mysteries of our faith with unaided intellect, but this does not trouble the soul in the state of grace. One will always find mortal sin before faith grows dim. The soul has turned its back on God first, and has stopped praying for His grace. Even if we do not meditate at any length on what faith really is, it is good for us to give a fleeting thought that faith is a gift, not something we have earned; not something we can capture with great learning; nor something we deserve more than our neighbor, who is groping towards the light. A man who has thrown the gift of faith back at God may regain it, but I think it is only through a greater miracle than being raised from the dead. Let us with great deliberation do something to gain the grace to hold tight to our faith. It can be lost, but not by the man who prays.

HOPE

Hope is probably the most misunderstood of all the virtues. It is only through hope that we can avoid the sin against the Holy Ghost, for we must neither take the stand that we are infallibly sure of our salvation and have no need to hope —this is presumption—nor must we ever feel that God has no care for us, and that we are lost—this is despair. Against presumption the Scripture says: ". . . man knoweth not whether he be worthy of love or hatred, but all things are kept uncertain for the time to come, because all things equally happen to the just and to the wicked, to the good and to the evil. . . ." Against despair we have the psalm which Christ quoted as He hung on the Cross (the twenty-first in the Catholic version, which begins: "My God, my God . . . why hast Thou forsaken Me?") Here we read, ". . . in Thee have our fathers hoped; they hoped and Thou hast delivered them. They cried to Thee, and they were saved; they trusted in Thee and were not confounded."

In the virtue of hope we can make up for the uncertainties that surround our last end, for we know infallibly that if we hope in God and do the things we can, He will help us with the things we cannot do, and will never let us be tempted above our strength. It was at this point that Doctor Luther went off the path. He was worried about his salvation, and not seeing clearly to the end, thought that if he threw himself in *faith* on the mercy of God he would be sure of his salvation. If he had only seen that it is in hope that we cast our cares upon the Lord, all would have been well. We have no need to fear unduly about our last end if we will strive manfully from day to day; not taking our sufferings and temporal setbacks as signs of divine displeasure, for God causes the rain to fall both on the just and the unjust. The "fear and trembling" in which we work out our salvation is fear of the instability of human nature.

Among the soul-chilling doctrine of Calvin that we must seek the predestinated among those who are blessed with this world's goods, and the bitterness of the cynics who have abandoned all hope of getting rich and powerful through the favor of heaven and have decided to get what they can for themselves, and the Communists who teach that the only heaven there will ever be is on earth, and they will bring it to pass after all other systems have been destroyed, the simple ones of this world must be in turmoil. They are poor, they reason; therefore they think they are not the favored ones of God. They have no power nor ability to seize what they want, for others can keep them away from it. They do not see many advantages to themselves in a life of slavery under Communism for the sake of a far-distant generation which will come into all these good things after their own pain-racked bones have whitened in some ditch, after a life of digging canals or mining uranium for a small master-race that does not have to wait for this distant evolution to do pretty well for itself.

Without God, and the hope of His promises, there is nothing left but despair. A few years ago those without God lived in presumption, but there is not too much of that left for the millions upon millions who have had their lives torn up by the roots by the disasters of the past twenty years, or more.

Apart from those who have suffered real disaster, there are many of us who are well-fed and well-housed who still have lost so much of our hope that we distrust the providence of God to keep us from day to day, and we wonder at the inequalities that visit upon us so much care and suffering. What we need more than anything else is a visit to a refugee camp. But supposing we do have some suffering, do we not complain too much about it? My experience is that there is more wailing over a headache than there is over a brain tumor; more resentment over colds than over tuberculosis. Exaggerated, perhaps, but something to mull over. Nevertheless there are in this world many quiet heroes who carry burdens for years without complaining; but these are usually the ones to whom the restless and the irritated point as "ones who never seem to have any trouble; not troubles like mine, anyhow."

Hope and suffering are closely allied, and many a man who dragged on his life in exhaustion and discontent has taken on a new life when he sees in his sufferings a larger purpose than just "somebody trying to make it hard for me." God does not impose suffering on us to no purpose. God doesn't *impose* suffering; He permits it; and the world, the flesh, and the Devil will take care of the rest. Suffering may be visited upon us as a warning to the wayward that this is not our eternal home, as an indication that the good things of this life are not the sign of God's favor. We are all too willing to believe this. A well-known multi-millionaire once said: "God gave me my gold." Many a person who has become a canonized saint has made a painful introduction to the spiritual life, and being stripped of honors, wealth, or health has kept hope alive in misery, and so reached his goal.

Suffering may be expiatory for the sins of others, but this usually comes by invitation to become a chosen "victim soul." Some more generous souls have even asked for suffering to be visited upon them to protect those who may not be able to withstand their own temptations. Such was the whole life of the Little Flower. However, such immolation is to be taken up only with advice and the consent of a prudent confessor. Sufferings in this life will also shorten our purgatory, if we accept them with a spirit of resignation and docility

Most suffering, I dare say, comes from the evil in men around us. If we do not collapse in the face of evil and compromise with it to save ourselves trouble, we do very well. However, we shall have to put up patiently with much evil. We can remember that God desires not the death of the sinner but that he be converted and live. It will take patience and prayer on our part to act as we should, as the instruments of the providence of God. St. Monica prayed and waited for twenty-eight years for the conversion of her son. When finally he turned away from error in belief and immorality in his personal life, the change in him was so great that he became St. Augustine—one of the four great western Fathers of the Church. It takes a lot of skill and patience to know when to be silent and when to strike back. We must hate evil, but we cannot hate evil men. Pray much for an increase in hope, and God will help us in working out a better destiny here and hereafter, not only for ourselves but for the world at large.

CHARITY

Charity is the queen and crown of all the virtues. for we shall see faith dissolve in knowledge; hope will pass over into possession, but charity must remain forever. Through charity we love God for His own sake, and we love ourselves and our neighbor for the love of God. In charity we begin our heaven, even here on earth, for this is what puts us into the state of sanctifying grace. St. John says: "He that loveth not, knoweth not God, for God is Charity."

For centuries we have been assaulted by the doctrine that God is off at a distance, and that man is the measure. In many cases God is not loved; or He is loved only for the sake of what He may be able to provide in the way of temporal advantage. Love of neighbor has come to mean the cultivation of "the right person." Love of self has taken on the cultus of "self-development." How far is the cry of seeking out those who can do us some good temporally from the injunction that we are to love all men—even our enemies. Think of all the heart-scalding, pulling, and hauling that goes on to rise above one's neighbor, just to show forth more diamonds piled upon our wives' fingers; just a little longer wheelbase on an automobile, and a wider spread across the front of our houses. There is plenty of room for self-development in a correct sense. Every one should remember the gospel injunction of the proper use of talents. Talents should be developed to the utmost by giving back to God in an immolation for a greater good. Let us place the practice of charity around obedience to God's will; both to His will of good pleasure, wherein we accept all that happens willingly and cheerfully as coming from His hand, and to the signified will of God, by obeying His commandments, and as far as we can, His counsels. Peace is not far from a generation that loves God.

We have, then, our intention of praying for an increase of faith, hope, and charity on the three Hail Mary beads of the pendant. There should be no need of extending this intention beyond a mention of the purpose of the prayer. Yet, we must make little acts of faith, hope, and charity during the day as aspirations. If it will not interfere with meditation on the mysteries, a short prayer such as "My God, I believe in Thee, because Thou art Truth itself; My God, I hope in Thee because Thou art kind and merciful and faithful to all promises. My God, I love Thee, because Thou art infinitely good; and I am sorry for having offended Thee," would be in order here. Or, we may insert the prayer of the Angel of Portugal which he taught the children of Fatima: "My God, I believe, I adore, I hope, and I love Thee! I beg pardon for those who do not believe, nor adore, nor hope, nor love Thee." Our Lady did not ask that this be added to the Rosary; but there it is, to leave out or to put in at choice.

THE HAIL MARY

The three Hail Mary beads in the pendant will give us an opportunity to pay close attention to this prayer, given to us from God Himself. It was the Archangel Gabriel coming as an ambassador from God, delivering God's message to Mary, who gave us the opening phrases. It was Elizabeth, "being filled with the Holy Ghost," who continued it. It was the Catholic Church defining its constant teachings about the Blessed Mother from a general council at Ephesus, who declared she was the "Mother of God." From the daily teachings of the Catholic Church on the meditation of the Blessed Virgin we obtain under the inspiration of the Holy Spirit, the final part of the Hail Mary. In the Our Father we have a summary of our spiritual life in regard to God, and in the Hail Mary the summary of what God has told us about the Blessed Virgin. Let us, then, develop a few thoughts about the Hail Mary.

Hail, Mary—We know that "the Virgin's name was Mary," but it is the nature of the salutation that interests us most. Through all the range of the Scriptures we encounter the meeting of men with angels sent by God. In many cases the angels concealed their identity under the guise of men, but when they came with the glory of the angels those to whom they were sent usually fell down to the ground, willing to worship the apparition as God Himself. No one had ever before received the salutation of respect, "Hail." Now if Gabriel, one of the bright spirits whose place is before the throne of God, uses language of deference to Our Blessed Mother, we shall do well to remember that there must be a very good reason for it.

Full of Grace—Our Blessed Mother was not only a woman whom God looked on with favor, but the *one* human being who had been chosen for the most exalted office that could come to anyone. In order to save the human race God had seen fit to have His own divine Son be united to a human element, in such a way as to make it possible for His Son to suffer as man, so that the actions of that man would have the value of the actions of God Himself. If there was to be a

God-man there was going to have to be a human mother; but before the process leading to motherhood was begun there was need of the free consent of THE WOMAN God had so chosen. It is obvious that no ordinary person could fulfill such a destiny; in fact, no possible human talent or endowment could attain such heights. Only the grace of God could bridge such a gap between God and man, and the amount of grace needed would have to be so much as to make the chosen person "full of grace."

The Lord is with Thee— If the Lord is with us who can be against us? This is true of all of us if we be in the grace of God—more correctly, if we are in the state of grace. God is with us only to the extent that we participate in His life in the supernatural. No power can win this support from God; no amount of learning can make a man worthy of it. Grace alone will do it; and since Mary was full of the grace of God she was in His friendship as no other person has ever been. I know from this that I can turn to Our Blessed Mother for answers to my prayers, because through her God answered the most earnest prayer of the world since our first parents left Paradise: i.e., that God would send a Redeemer.

Blessed art Thou amongst Women— This blessing was twice announced: first by the Archangel Gabriel, and then by Mary's cousin, Elizabeth. Here, God's first promise made to man was being redeemed in the woman at whose hands, or rather "heel," the serpent was being defeated. The Savior, born of woman— born of THE WOMAN— was at hand and deservedly she had conferred upon her both by angels and by men the title of "Blessed." Was not she the one who could make the coming of the Savior possible? Not only is she blessed but of all women she is the most blessed, as Mary's cousin, Elizabeth, under the inspiration of the Holy Ghost saw her as the "mother of my Lord." Mary, in all humility, took up the refrain under the inspiration of the Holy Ghost and prophesied: "From henceforth all generations shall call me Blessed." Thus Catholic hearts of all ages have called her the "Blessed" Virgin. Those who think that by degrading the Blessed Virgin they are better honoring Christ should remember that the Sacred Scriptures show that from the direct inspiration of God Himself comes her title of Blessed.

And Blessed is the Fruit of Thy Womb—Christ was blessed in a different sense from that of His Mother, because, being God, He was the source of all blessings, but as man He was blessed and full of all graces. His was not an ordinary birth, and the Holy Ghost inspired the use of the term "blessed" to both Son and Mother to set them apart as singular and unique among all births. This will not detract from the honor due to Jesus Christ, because He is blessed in His own right, but to Mary blessedness is derived from her association with Christ. Any Catholic child knows that, but our friends outside the Catholic Church still say, "Too much Virgin Mary." However she will never permit the blessedness of Christ to be submerged below that of herself. She has one joy, and that is to lead men to Christ. The words she uttered under the inspiration of the Holy Ghost still guide her: "My spirit has rejoiced in God, my Savior."

Jesus—There has been a marked falling off of cursing and swearing among men in the past forty years, since the reestablishment of the Holy Name Society in the United States. Anyone whose memory goes back several decades will remember that the use of obscene language was more common then. "The gentleman of the old school" who marked his manhood by the length and vigor of his oaths has not survived. Either he has gone on, or he is looked upon as a survival beyond his time with grudging tolerance. In an earlier age the same sort of blight had fallen upon society, but mainly from Dominican and Franciscan influences there came the first Holy Name Society, canonically erected under

Prayers of Pendent Beads 81

Dominican auspices. A movement was set afoot by the Dominicans to introduce the Holy Name of Jesus into the Hail Mary, which then concluded with the words of Elizabeth. To make the practice more enticing, all members of the Confraternity of the Most Holy Rosary who piously pronounced the name of Jesus at what was then the end of the Hail Mary, would receive an indulgence of five years and five quarantines. The rest of the Hail Mary was not said in the western Church until about the time of the Reformation, although for centuries the Eastern Church had been using the Hail Mary much as we say it today.

Holy Mary— We call that "holy" which is in any way related to God. Thus, Moses was told to remove his shoes as the ground upon which he stood was holy: made holy by the presence of God. An object is called "holy" when it is set aside for the service of God. A human being is holy when he does the will of God, and as the work that God gives him to do is more difficult and exalted; that person is most holy who carries out his mission most faithfully. What person in all the world does this describe if not the Blessed Virgin? When we think of her mission and how well she carried it out, we may exclaim in the words of the Litany of Loreto: "Virgin Most Holy, Pray for us."

Mother of God—This title which has brought on bitter controversy among men of ill will, was formally bestowed on Our Blessed Mother by the Council of Ephesus. It was given to her not so much for her own honor as for the honor of her divine Son. We find that attacks on the mother usually spring from bad thinking about the Son. Such attacks are as old as Christianity itself. The form the attack upon this prerogative of the Blessed Mother generally takes is: "How can a mortal human being ever be called the mother of an eternal God, who was before all creatures?" The next step is the statement that the Blessed Virgin is made a goddess, as Diana, whose cult flourished in this same city of Ephesus. But, No, we say. We realize as much as anyone that God is eternal; that no one could ever be called the Mother of God in any sense as this. But notice that further argument against the office of the Mother of God is an attack on the true status and nature of Jesus Christ. Mary was the mother of Christ, as no one denies. But Jesus Christ was united to the second Person of the Blessed Trinity to form *the Person,* Jesus Christ, God and man. In becoming a mother, a woman is not merely the mother of a lifeless body into which God infuses a soul. She is the mother of the human *person,* although the principle of life, the soul, is created directly by God. No human mother ever has anything to do with the creation and infusion of a human soul. Neither did Mary have anything to do with the infusion of the human soul into Christ, nor did she have anything to do with the union of the divine Son of God with Christ's human body and soul. But this union in Christ formed only one *person.* Mary was the mother of that *Person.* Unless we keep the human and divine united in Christ there could have been no divine merit in the sufferings of Christ. Unless Jesus Christ is a divine Person there could be no more benefit to our salvation from His suffering and death than from those of any other human being. The sufferings of Christ had to have this unique value that would attach to them the infinite action of God. So then, when we call Mary the Mother of God, we are really defending Jesus Christ.

Pray for Us Sinners—We can all pray for ourselves and for others. God has promised that He will hear *all* our prayers as far as they are directed to our best welfare, and insofar as our requests do not interfere with our eternal salvation. If God will hear sinners who pray for themselves, how much more will He hear the prayers of our Immaculate Mother who was without sin, all of whose prayers are directed in charity to the welfare of others? To the hypocrites who would have stoned the woman taken in adultery to entrap our Lord—for the smug deceivers had already let go the equally guilty partner in sin, who also should have been stoned—Jesus replied: "Let him who is without sin cast the first stone." This was to silence them as He well knew that those who were really without sin would not be casting stones at anyone. Neither will Our Blessed Mother cast stones at us poor sinners, but she will make continual intercession with God to gain mercy for us. Christ is our mediator with the Father since all things belong to Him who earned them on the Cross. But Mary is our advocate, our Mediatrix with Christ; for He came to us through her and we must go back to Him through her. He worked His first public miracle for her, even though He protested to her that it was out of time, and on the Cross He gave her to us through St. John to be our Mother. She will not see any of her children fall into hell if there is a possible way she can win us for Christ. She will not see the precious blood of her divine Son spilled out in vain; in vain for the poor sinner who finds himself lost at length in hell.

Now and at the Hour of Our Death—We need the graces of our daily living, but most of all we need the grace of final perserverance. Only God can give us graces, and God rains these down upon us, yet not so as to force them upon us If we want graces we must pray for them, and not wait for them with pride and presumption, expecting God to offer us what we may feel we do not need. In truth, most of us do not make the best use of the graces that God has showered down upon us. Many times we get graces we have not earned, nor even asked for, but our Mother petitions for us and grace comes down to us, drawing us back to God when we had rather wander afield. Graces are to be prayed for, so we must keep on asking for them in person, through the souls in purgatory, through the saints, but most of all through Mary Immaculate, our Mother. We need help now, and we shall need it as our senses and minds grow dim and death swoops down upon us. The Serpent will save some of his wiles for us in that hour, but THE WOMAN is still the enemy of the Serpent and will help us to overcome him. Pray now, pray often that we shall be all worthy to have Mary present at our deathbeds.

THE GLORIA

The prayer, "Glory be to the Father, and to the Son, and to the Holy Ghost, as it was in the beginning, is now, and ever shall be world without end. Amen," is used to mark the end of various prayers and psalms in the Divine Office. Since the Rosary is an office among the Dominicans, this prayer serves the same purpose here and is now in general use even among those who do not employ the Dominican method. Since the Rosary is Our Lady's Psalter, the decades are as groups of psalms to be ended with the same doxology. It is a beautiful act of faith in the Trinity, and should be sounded always with a note of joy and adoration.

SUMMARY

1) Make a deliberate act of attention to the task before you. It is only asking for distractions to pull out the beads and begin without excluding the tumult of thoughts that are always coursing through one's mind. Say something like this: "I am going to say this Rosary for such or such an intention" (Name your intention as clearly as possible). "This prayer will be heard, because to the effect of prayer are also attached the promises of Our Blessed Mother. If I do not get the answer I think best, it is because God knows that something else is better for me."

2) Look at your crucifix for a few seconds with the thought that this was the measure of God's love for us. Sin brought Jesus Christ to Calvary's Hill—your sins and mine. Ask Our Lady to bring home to you the lessons of the Rosary you are

about to say, in such a way as to make these lessons effective in repaying in some way the love of Christ for us. Too often prayer is just a way of asking for a temporal favor we want just now; but we can well spend a second or two in opening up our hearts.

3) Say the Apostles' Creed slowly enough to catch some of its meaning, but do not spend a great amount of time tryin to expand any of the points. Do not say the Creed in such a way as to attempt to memorize it; let the points sink down into the mind and disappear from consciousness. The effect will not be lost.

4) Say the first Our Father with attention, dwelling on the petitions, but again not so as to extend the consideration at any length. Let the points as they arise sink down again into the mind. Do not attempt to hold them in consciousness.

5) Make a brief intention of asking for an increase in faith, hope, and charity without arousing discussion in the mind on what these virtues may be, or how they can be gained. They are gifts of God; you can't earn them directly. They come as graces from the right performance of acts of religion; from Mass and the sacraments; from a right intention towards others; from prayer, including the Rosary you are about to say. Short acts of faith, hope, and charity will not be amiss here; but if this impedes the saying of the Rosary, make a simple intention and go ahead with the Rosary.

6) Then say the three Hail Mary's slowly, and with the same attention you gave to the Our Father above. After this do not attempt in any way to carry forward a consideration in detail of any of the vocal prayers. The mind cannot span this. Above all do not worry about what happens to the vocal prayers, even when you seem to be quite unconscious of their succession.

7) Conclude the preliminary prayers with the Glory be to the Father. You may most certainly give some study and care to the vocal prayers, to learn their meanings in depth, but do it apart from the saying of the Rosary. In all vocal pray-

ers the pattern and formula are set for us, and you may be sure that you are praying in a real sense as long as that form of prayer is said without willful distraction.

CHAPTER 7

The Development of the Rosary Meditation

WHAT IS MEDITATION?

WE NOW treat of the Rosary proper, where the meditation of the mysteries begins. Meditation frightens a lot of people away from attempting any improvement in their methods of saying the Rosary, and it deters more from attempting anything at all in lifting their saying of Rosaries out of the ordinary. There are, of course, degrees of meditation and we are not all called to be adepts at meditation or of mental prayer. As for those of us who live in the tumult of the world, we may never reach the heights of mental prayer, but spiritual writers say that God will reward any earnest soul with progress in prayer, even though he be most simple and unlearned. St. Teresa of Jesus said that a nun of her convent was raised by God to a high degree of prayer, though she could never do more than say the Our Father with attention to its meaning. Too much emphasis cannot be placed on the fact that we are children of God, raised to a spiritual life where the rewards are not always to the most learned and to the most distinguished. Start where you find yourself; you can make as much progress as you permit God to give you His graces. Perhaps what this beleaguered world needs right now is a great number of men and women who can give a touch of the spiritual to the secularized paths along which we must all move.

It is the secular spirit which is stifling men today. We cannot hope to overcome Communism if the very men who are charged with the task of defeating it have a materialistic point of view. That, after all, is what is wrong with Communism. It seeks to effect changes by exclusively material means. A university group that maintains that religious training is a divisive force in America is an intellectual brother to the Communist who thinks that such training is a divisive force behind the Iron Curtain, and who insists that all education should be a state monopoly. No matter how much a secular-minded person protests that he is "on our side," and prates about being anti-Communist, what opposition can one of his frame of mind give to the onrush of Communist ideologies? The Communists have been helped by a few deliberate traitors, but they are getting much more benefit from those who have nothing to propose in opposition to them except the washed-out idealism of the nineteenth century, which planned to have everything in the world run without God. They called themselves idealists or liberals, but they were secularists who denied that God was the measure of things, and some of them were quite violent about it, too. Viviani, in France, said when they closed the Catholic schools in France about the turn of the century: "We shall tear God down out of the heavens." The Communist is the brain child of the nineteenth century liberal. The idea that a liberal philosophy can hope to overthrow Communism is pitiful to contemplate. It is as though a man grown old should try to overcome his own son, grown to strength and vigor, by tricks and devices he himself taught the boy long ago. Only a new point of view can stop this steady advance of secularism and materialism. That is the spiritual outlook we can gain through meditating on the mysteries of the Rosary. Many of us have been affected more than we think by the pervading spirit of secularism. The Prophet Jeremias lamented long ago: "With desolation is all the land made desolate, because there is no one to think in his heart."

That, in its simplest form, is what meditation is—"thinking in the heart," or considering how to bring about the things we desire. Meditation in this sense can be secular as well as religious. It is the laying of plans that we have a will to bring to successful conclusion. Anyone who can think at all has done some meditating. There are those who do not really think about anything. They run after sensations, and drift with the current into trouble and out of trouble, but never cause the slightest difference in the direction the world takes. Usually a few determined souls have directed the affairs of this world upwards or downwards, according as the men of strength stood with or against God. However, if there would come forward large numbers of simple people who had some thought of what they wanted this world to be, the so-called leaders who drag it their way could make no headway. Our Lady wanted millions upon millions of simple unknown persons to say the Rosary every day so as to give the world a spiritual outlook. Herein lies our salvation, both in this world and in the next. It is not difficult to see in the saying of the Rosary the fulfillment of Mary's prediction that if we say the Rosary there will be peace; if we do not say the Rosary great evil will come upon the world. The reason is, of course, that the secular spirit is so widespread that even persons of religious bent have been tainted.

God does not will to visit punishments on His people, but unless the heart is pure the soul turns away from God of its own accord. How can we obtain any of the promises held out to us by God if we go in directions where He may not be found? Thus God promised to His chosen people a land flowing with milk and honey, but when they left Egypt they kept the memory of the flesh pots of Egypt in their hearts. And so they wandered in the desert for forty years, and those who had come out of Egypt had died almost to the last man before the Israelites could cross the Jordan into the Promised Land. We, too, shall wander in the desert; and it may be a very real desert if we unleash the full fury of our material might against each other; we, too, can enter the Promised Land only when we learn to think in our hearts. Peace is only to men of good will.

Distraction will undoubtedly plague one who attempts to penetrate into meditation, but there are many aids at hand to help control this activity. We can listen with more care to the reading of the Epistles and Gospels at Mass; we can improve our attention to sermons and lectures, and we can even get much these days from radio and television. If we do this we do well, for, as St. Paul says: "Faith comes by hearing." An earnest soul no matter how brilliant and learned he may be is always well employed in listening to the word of God, even when it is announced by voices not as eloquent and learned as we may wish for. The Holy Ghost may speak to us through the very simple, and we in all humility should listen. Do not have the slightest hesitancy about borrowing any turn of thought or expression that may develop. Borrow anything that will be of help in the saying of the Rosary; there should be no shame about using the labor of others in this regard. They have worked up their thoughts so that we can have the benefit of them. We don't have to be original in prayer. All we *must* do is to love God.

In due time our own thoughts will begin to flow; haltingly at first, muddy as the spring was at first at Lourdes; but these thoughts will clear up, too, and flow clear and full. Meditation applied to religious subjects is the door that opens the way to mental prayer. It is called the doorway because meditation is not by itself prayer. However, as it is applied to the saying of the Rosary according to Our Lady's wishes, and the purpose she had in mind, meditation will enter into the domain of prayer, since it will lead to certain acts of love which grow out of what we learn in meditating. Moreover, it will demand of us certain resolutions when we see what has been done for us brought out in the mysteries of the Rosary. In thinking of the Annunciation we do not stop at the fact that the archangel Gabriel came to tell the Virgin Mary that she had been chosen to be the Mother of the Redeemer. We shall press on to ask what is the import of such a message. We shall see that God, who has no need for man, wills to lift man back to a state from which he has fallen of his own free act. We can only echo St. John in paraphrase: We should love God because He has first loved us. We then consider that Mary had a free choice to accept or refuse. The first Eve, also, had a free choice and turned away from God. A new Eve turns to God so that the new Adam can come and repair the damage the first Adam wrought. Seeing this do we have any resolutions to make? We merely wish to delve into the simple gospel story. Communism cannot live in that atmosphere.

Communism, secularism, materialism—all seem to be driving down on all our traditional concepts of a Christian civilization. Can we rush into the breach millions of men and women who have a spiritual viewpoint; who look on all those things that gratify nature with the desire for moderation, such as St. Francis taught and left for his children to follow in the rule of the Third Order? In print, over the radio, and now by almost actual sight over television comes a constant solicitation to buy things, things, things. Most of these are good for us in some real way, and most of them are useful for lifting burdens. No one, surely, wants to see his brother bending under brutish burdens until sheer labor forces out of him all semblance to the God whose image he is. In things there is convenience, but the danger comes in seeking the new leisure for its own sake, as an end.

It is all a matter of restoring the balance where the motive is the important consideration and "things" are just a tool. If this comes out of our Rosary meditations we can win the world for Christ. No one wants to abolish, for example, the automobile, but the truth is that many use the automobile more as a weapon than as a tool. As a very simple person remarked to me recently: "A lot of folks drive them things like they was mad at them." For a homely example think how much an improvement it would make in public morals if just a smaller group of automobilists were to stop being pushy, as though every one who tried to make a crossing ahead of them was a deliberate enemy who wanted to cheat them out of some right. What if, in one city, driving would take on a tinge of Christian charity and a fair number would drive as though others had a few rights in the matter, and allow others to get ahead of them or to beat them to a crossing? In a short time the red and green lights would start to come down; the police would not have to stick so many pins in the "death corners" on the maps, and everyone would get to his destination sooner.

Let us begin to build a simple method that everyone can follow in learning how to "think in his heart," and at the same time not have to wait for a period of study to be ended before the saying of the Rosary can commence. So, then, do not have any regrets at what you may be pleased to call your shortcomings, and do not be sorry that you cannot do any better. Least of all, never have great disturbances come over distractions in praying. The time will, perhaps, never come when you do not have distractions of one kind or another. Unless you bring on a distraction by your own deliberate act there is no fault of any sort. If you do bring in another line of thought while praying you have simply stopped praying, and you can always start over again. As long as you live in the world you will have to take care of things that arise in your daily life. Suppose you do have to interrupt your prayers from time to time during the day? You have all day to finish the Rosary and you need only say one decade at a time. Sometimes it is better to interrupt the saying of the Rosary. At times thoughts will crowd in so fast it is almost impossible to make any headway. Or at another time you may be praying for an answer to some problem. It may try to come while you are praying the Rosary. If you get disturbed at the foreign line of thought trying to intrude itself, and insist on calling it a distraction, the solution may sink

Development of Meditation

down below the level of consciousness and be lost. What would be wrong with stopping then and there and taking out the note book to jot down the solution you have been looking for, and then returning to your prayer?

A METHOD OF MEDITATION

Be very certain that you know perfectly the names of all the fifteen mysteries of the Rosary in their proper sequence, and in their division into joyful, sorrowful, and glorious mysteries. Most of us know these, but I have found out by asking around that there are many who do not have complete facility in giving a full name to each of the mysteries.

If the extent of your meditation is the naming of the mysteries you will find it a help to get a set of Rosary picture cards from some religious supply house. These are located in the larger cities, but the nearest Catholic church is in touch with them and the pastor can give you an address. These sets are quite inexpensive and are a lot less trouble than trying to get together the fifteen scenes from various sources. However, if you prefer you can find reprints of paintings by the masters reproduced in colors. There are many companies which make such reprints in various sizes. Almost any book store or public library can furnish you with the address of such a publisher of these pictures, but ask for them simply as small art reproductions of the masters. You may want to go to the trouble of getting such pictures if you are of a more artistic turn. I found that certain pictures of the Agony in the Garden did not bring out what I sought to find, so I kept on searching for such pictures until I came upon the treatment I was looking for. Study these pictures of the Rosary mysteries until you have in your mind a definite mental image of the scene called up by the mere mention of the name of the mystery. Words sometimes do not evoke any response, especially when we get used to the words as a part of a formula we have heard many times. We do not make much progress in mental prayer until our affections are involved in the prayer. Thus the mention of the words "the Crucifixion" may not move our sympathies, but when we have looked upon a representation of Jesus Christ actually hanging on His Cross, and when we can thereby call up a picture of what Christ suffered for us, we are by this simple device entering into meditation. Then when your meditations grow "stale," as they will do, you can refresh them by studying the pictures for new thoughts.

When we tend to keep the content of the mystery too much on the word-level there is danger that it will fail to make a deep enough impression as to what is going on, so that we shall not make progress in our prayers through the Rosary. When we can see the mystery as a picture, and what is better, when we can insert ourselves into the picture so that we go along as spectators or participants, the scenes of the Rosary story will have a much deeper personal meaning for us. Words often do not move us to action because they get too fixed for us in a formula. This is true even of our vocal prayers. For that reason we have tried to get those who would improve the effectiveness of their Rosaries to "work over" the way they say the vocal prayers, so as to take them out of the flat level of routine and formula.

Since words do not always move us, the Church fosters the cultus of the saints, of the Blessed Virgin, and even of devotions towards our Lord Himself through pictures and statues. Some of our separated friends still have suspicions that there is some idolatry going on here, yet they do not see anything wrong in cherishing pictures of their beloved ones; nor do they hesitate to display images of national heroes for public veneration. Of course there is nothing wrong with the picture method of recall; there is nothing amiss with having parades come up the street with wreathes to lay at the feet of statues of heroes. This gives a sort of sense of participation in the life of the hero. Thus, too, when St. Francis devised the crib to bring home to a careless age the story of

Christmas, he put himself into the scene. When Fra Angelico painted his frescoes of the Rosary he put St. Dominic into the pictures. Pictures, participation, and deliberation will give a great impetus to Rosary meditations. In the times of my difficulties in saying the Rosary I found it a distinct help to use the Rosary pictures while actually saying the Rosary, looking at each picture in turn as I recited the vocal prayers. Once I used a little note book with some simple Rosary thoughts on one side of the page and the picture on the opposite page. After some effort to work the thoughts evoked into the scene depicted I would go on with the vocal prayers. Thus, simple and primitive as the device may have been, it brought some thoughts and resolutions to bear on a mystery of the Rosary, and that, dim though it may have been, was in the direction of meditation.

Despite what has been said of the supposed unfamiliarity of Catholics with the Scriptures, it is hard to imagine a Catholic who is not, to a great extent, familiar with the mysteries of the Rosary, at least through listening to the cycle of Epistles and Gospels throughout the year. He would be bound to encounter most of the Rosary mysteries year after year. From what I found out about the way many say the Rosary, I am certain they do not bring over this knowledge into the Rosary as a meditation. The human mind does not relish the work of reorganizing knowledge gained in one way to use it for another purpose, and so the Rosary is said at a prosaic level while all the time the person has at his disposal much better thoughts. Hence the study of pictures relating to the Rosary is not as childish as it may seem, and if it is childish, we must become as little children to get to heaven, so that anything that helps get Rosaries said and brings us to heaven is useful. Besides, picture-study may form the basis of a Rosary project to teach children, early, how to meditate.

You can say Rosaries profitably by considering the pictures successively through the mysteries, making an act of love or calling up a resolution in return for all the labors that were endured to open up for us the gates of salvation.

When each mystery is clear and stands out as a picture in the mind you will find that there is a tendency to make a little summary of what is happening in each of the mysteries. This tendency should be developed. Most of the shorter books I have seen on the Rosary go no further than this. This will turn out to be a sort of summary of the physical happenings at the mystery. For example, "The Second Joyful Mystery: Our Lady goes to visit her cousin, Elizabeth." Or again, "The Third Glorious Mystery: The Holy Ghost comes down as tongues of fire upon the apostles, and upon the Blessed Virgin." This is hardly more than naming the mystery, but as the summary gets intertwined with the picture it will be an improvement. Many a Rosary you will say when you are just too tired and cannot find consolation or pleasure in prayer, and so it will be well to have something like this to fall back upon, as we need prayer most when we are least in the mood to use it.

The critical stage in Rosary meditation comes at the next step. We must make some kind of determined effort to penetrate into the meaning behind the mysteries. The main thing we must overcome is the habit of saying only prayers that were composed for us. These we recite from memory, or read from a book. There is nothing wrong with this. The prayers of the Mass are thus set down with great precision. So is the Divine Office. These prayers are official, and are said in the name of the Church rather than mainly for the personal benefit of the one saying them. There are also whole books of prayers composed for many, many purposes, most of them for private devotion. No one wishes to do away with these familiar prayers and substitute for them long rambling ex tempore prayers. Vocal prayers will always have an important place, but we must make application of religious lessons to our own lives, and for this we shall have to do something on our own account. So it becomes absolutely necessary to round out our information. The habitual knowledge and

Development of Meditation

recollection that most of us have about the Rosary mysteries are more than we should be led to credit ourselves with, but the human mind is made in such a way that no matter how well one may know a series of facts for one purpose, he still has considerable organizing to do when he comes to apply his knowledge to another purpose, and to recall it in a different sequence.

If we are going to get full benefit out of the Rosary we shall have to take out the family Bible, or some other sources, and read the chapters that have to do with the Rosary mysteries. For convenience we have collected all these episodes in Part Three. We shall have to use the Rosary mysteries as a sort of storehouse, if we are to keep our own meditations from falling into a formula. As for myself, I try to read everything I can lay hands on that has to do with the Rosary and have thereby kept my saying of the Rosary fresh and interesting. Please note that some Rosary mysteries are found in only one of the Gospels, while others are in two, three, or four of them. Where the story is in more than one place we have made up "harmonies" to give a continuous narrative. For my own purposes, I needed these combined forms very much, especially in working out the exact sequence of happenings on the first Easter morning.

If we are going to meditate we shall have to know what has happened, and what it means to us that this has happened. If we are going to make use of the Rosary lesson it will have to be through observing what our Lord and His Blessed Mother did during their lives, as shown in the Rosary mysteries, and then we shall have to apply those lessons to our lives.

Many historical notes and observations will come from reading appropriate Bible texts to add fullness and richness, but it is still true that the Bible is not a self-interpreting book, and its pages are full of details of life and customs that the evangelists took for granted that a first century hearer or reader would be familiar with. However, many of these are meaningless to us unless they are explained by some sort of commentaries on the Scriptures. In the same chapter where the Scripture passages are given at length we have also added comments which may prove of value in looking for meanings.

For example, it will profit us greatly to read and study the Finding of our Lord in the Temple, but we may be somewhat mystified at His conduct in regard to His Mother and to St. Joseph, until we learn that a Jewish boy became of legal religious age at twelve years. Therefore, even an ordinary youth would have had some rights in staying behind in the Temple to discuss religious matters with the doctors. As God Christ's rights were paramount, of course. The meaning is that God has His rights which are above the rights of man.

There is also the incident of the stone rolled before the door of the tomb of Christ. This stone was cut as a huge wheel, two or three feet thick, about the height of a man or even higher. It rolled into place along a groove, and when it was before the mouth of the tomb it dropped down some inches into a scooped out trough, which helped to keep it in place, and prevented any despoiling of the tomb and its contents. It was very difficult to move it. Besides this the seal of the Empire was on the stone and a guard, furnished to the High Priest by Pilate, stood on watch before it. We can see, then, what deep promptings of the Holy Spirit must have sent the holy women out at the first break of dawn to attempt the almost impossible task of gaining access to the—as they thought—dead body of Christ. Their faith made them the first witnesses of the Resurrection.

When we consider the carrying of the Cross, it helps us to feel the brutality of this journey to know that the streets mostly sloped upwards towards Calvary. At the destruction of Jerusalem in the year 70 A.D., the rubble made by pulling the houses out into the streets in order to level the city to the ground, actually changed the grade of the streets that were later laid on top of the old ones. The Cross, we know, was of a local pine wood. It was not rubbed smooth as the crosses that represent the Cross of Christ in our devotions. This Cross was rough-cut from the tree with mallet and wedge, and then chopped to dimension with an adze. The weight has been calculated at about 200 pounds. Now in meditating on the fourth Sorrowful Mystery one can almost see himself in the mob along the way, watching the heavy end of this beam knocking against the rough cobblestones with every step, rubbing its splintery edge over Christ's back and shoulder cut and swollen by the scourging.

In searching the historical aspects for material for meditation, it is sometimes very helpful to work a comparison and make an application in terms of today's problems. Thus, to give a homely example, we can take something like the following and make a whole meditation on a mystery out of it. In the second Joyful Mystery, we may wish to make an application of Mary's act of charity in terms of today. Think how Mary laid aside all consideration of the great honor that had just been given her, and thought only of Elizabeth's need for her before the birth of John the Baptist. Nazareth was to the north of Palestine, and El Kharim, where Elizabeth dwelt with Zachary, was in Judea, as Zachary had to be near the Temple which he served as a priest. This meant a journey of about ninety miles over rough, unpaved roads. Mary and Joseph were poor; it may be she had to walk. The roads were dangerous from robber bands that infested the way, as the Romans had not completely subdued the country. Now think how easily we are turned away from acts of charity because of lesser difficulties.

It will not be necessary to attempt to exhaust the meaning of any of the mysteries. As a matter of fact you can spend the rest of your life on any one of them and not exhaust it. Remember that there are religious orders devoted to a single mystery of the Rosary. For example, there is an order now existing only in England, France, and Belgium which was founded by St. Jeanne de Valois, Queen of France, that of the Annonciade. The principal task of meditation of these nuns is that of the Annunciation of Our Lady.

Each of the mysteries is related to some fundamental religious principle, or to one or more of the virtues. From them we must draw lessons for ourselves. In the sorrowful mysteries there are exemplified in the conduct of those who beset Christ in His Passion, vices that are dangerous to us, and from these we can learn salutary lessons. In the Visitation the important thing to bring out is the charity which impelled Mary to drop everything and hasten to the home of her cousin. To get there she had to make a dangerous journey of about six days if she went afoot, or somewhat less if she rode donkey-back. From Mary's charity came the opportunity of Christ to sanctify St. John the Baptist, and from Mary and Elizabeth came, under the inspiration of the Holy Ghost, great revelations.

We must take what we see in the mysteries and apply them to our own lives, problems, needs, and conduct. Thus to pursue the thought in the Visitation a bit further, we see how God uses our works to bring about His providence. Christ willed to remove original sin from St. John the Baptist, but He willed it to be done only with Mary in the presence of Elizabeth, within the sound of her voice. Christ could, of course, cleanse John even if they had remained ninety miles apart; but He willed that Mary should first answer to the prompting of the Holy Ghost in charity. Let us seek our lessons in the Rosary by bringing back to our own lives the examples given by Christ and His mother. Only thus can we start the transformation of our own lives, and then the reformation of society. The world can improve only when the gospel is put back into daily life.

Be sure to ask for something out of each Rosary you say. As a mystery is meditated upon it is simple to see whether we are lacking in the particular virtue we see exemplified. Ask for temporal favors; ask for spiritual favors, but ask, ask, ask, always and without ceasing. It is pride for us to think that we can make headway against the world, the flesh, and the Devil without constant help from Christ and His Mother. There is no virtue in imagining that we do not need to pray, nor that there is something wrong with us if we ask for all we need.

Make an examination of conscience often while saying the Rosary. We are always in great danger of falling into pride when we first start meditation, as though that were some sort of guarantee of our goodness, but any comparison of how we have responded to all the pain and trouble that was put out for us should bring us back to size. When we begin to read the lives of the saints we may be struck by their deep convictions that they were the worst of sinners. We may feel that they were badly mistaken; we thought we were pretty much all right, and therefore the saints could have given themselves a little more credit than they did. Later we realize that the saints had a little more insight into the nature of God and into the nature of sin than we have. Thus they alone could see how far all of us are from the perfections of God. Since they are saints they would apply the lessons of this vast astronomical gap to themselves. Those of us who are not saints may be tempted to apply to others whatever we see of this difference. I remember the comments of a young man who once made a closed retreat: "He sure gave those lads a going-over." I had a certain fondness for this young man. There was not a thing wrong with him that a few well-considered Rosaries could not have corrected. It never seemed to occur to him that there was anything else to do with time outside of working hours except "have a good time." This is sad, because it takes much more effort to "have a good time" than it does to be moderate, even apart from any damage done along the way. He never made another retreat; that might have cracked his shell and revealed to him that there was more to it than "having a good time." He ate and drank too much, but he was far from being a glutton or an alcoholic. The fat lumped around his heart; one day he sighed and just stopped breathing. The mercy of God reaches far but it is safer for us to possess a little contrition that grows out of examination of conscience. There is no more fruitful place for this than in the Rosary.

Naturally when a person says his Rosary he cannot go into all the points we have dwelt on in the foregoing. Ponder the mystery; what it means; and what we ought to do about it. Do not follow the outline slavishly but strike out on your own train of thought as anything else occurs to you. As the habit of attempting meditation grows there will be more and more ease in its use. It is not at all difficult if we remember not to attempt great feats of prayer at the outset, and just be humble. After all, we only seek to bring to mind the gospel story in such a way as to make it a part of our daily lives. A little deliberate thought will do it. The human mind tends to wander, so be content with a few crisp thoughts directed to the subject of the mystery with a practical application growing out of it.

In working up these notes I have tried to keep in mind that I was writing for those who, like myself, have earthy tasks to do in this world. It would be utter presumption to address myself to any who are devoted to a life of prayer in religion under competent directors, while following an approved rule of life. I have tried to keep the same approach I have used to teach the idea behind the Third Order. All of us cannot leave the world and follow a rule, but we can take a rule and use it to measure the activities of our lives in the world. It cannot be too strongly insisted upon that piety does not consist in running away from our prosaic duties to external works of devotion, no matter what they be and how they attract us. The Rosary will sanctify life with its little duties and its big duties, and those duties have to be performed.

There is no advantage in stretching out the Rosary meditations. If you find that you do not get the Rosary said in the time at your disposal after you have performed the duties of your calling, you may soon conclude that the Rosary is not

Development of Meditation

for you. You will then tend to swing back into the habit of merely mentioning the name of the mystery, or you may abandon saying the Rosary at all. Our Lady said she wanted the Rosary said every day by everybody, and that *it was to be meditated upon.* I believe that she meant this literally. These notes are the result of my attempt to respond to that invitation in the face of real difficulties which are now surmounted. In the past ten years or so, the beads have slipped through my fingers thousands of times while driving, walking, working, or what not. Sometimes I even wake up at nights and say a decade before dropping back to sleep again.

DANGERS TO AVOID

There are a few more practical suggestions as to ways of getting the Rosary said, and then we shall summarize the points in the method of meditation we have just been over, to show how they may be applied to the saying of the fifteen decades of the Rosary. However, the general rule will be not to attempt to put all the points of meditation into any one Rosary that we say, as this is too much material to try to get over each day. One good thought on a single point brought to mind by a sincere effort to "think in one's heart" will do much more good than any amount of rushing through several points under pressure. I know, because I have also tried to get all the points of meditation into each decade of the Rosary, and it does not work out satisfactorily. After a few days of making time to get this extra meditation done, the affairs of the world begin to press in, and meditation is hurried up a bit until all that is being done is the repetition of a formula that is memorized.

There are two main reasons why the Rosary is not said with unfailing regularity, day after day without letup, even by those with the best of intentions. Enthusiasm prompts us to take in too much ground in our meditations when we begin; we soon let down, since we cannot get over the same material day after day and do it justice. Or, we slight the essence of meditation and soon we are merely repeating a dry formula without trying to apply the meaning and lesson of the decade to our own lives and problems.

To get and keep a balance always name the mystery, and extend this to a short phrase that takes in what is happening. Then strive for a compact expression of the meaning of the mystery. The other points can then come and go, now one, and again another. At another time omit these points altogether when thought will not flow. There will be times when you will have to be content with the bare mention of the name of the mystery. If you cannot meditate at all, you do not have to do so. If you cannot meditate at a given time because of pain, worry, sickness, or fatigue, you do not have to meditate at that particlar time.

However, we should always try to get at some of the essential meaning of the mystery, and also make some resolution concerning what is before us. Be patient; never mind perfection in meditation. Begin where you find yourself right now and don't give up. If you say the fifteen decades twice a week, that gives you one full day a week when you can omit saying the Rosary, and you can still go through the cycle of the gospel story in the Rosary more than a hundred times during the year. With practice you carry your thoughts forward better—but the way to begin *is to begin*.

Another hint: as you begin each decade after saying the "Glory be to the Father" repeat the name of the mystery with great deliberation, turning your attention upon the words as you say them. For example say: "The Second Sorrowful Mystery: Jesus is Scourged at the Pillar." Pause a fraction of a second and let the words sink in. "Scourged"—does the word "scourging" convey anything to you? If it does not there is no reason to keep the usual wording of the mystery. You may put it: "Jesus is beaten with leaden-tipped whips." Does that do it? Can't you almost hear the swish of the flails as they swing, and the dull hollow sound as they

Development of Meditation

strike? Can you see the angry red welts raise as the whips pull back for another blow? Then ask: "What does this mean?" It means that you have sinned and I have sinned, and that Jesus Christ has not sinned—yet He is being whipped because we have sinned. From this you can put a worthy resolution together.

While this takes place the fingers are holding the Our Father bead. Keep them there until you have quite finished the point of meditation. Then say the vocal prayers. Do not make any further conscious efforts to hold the meditation in mind while saying the vocal prayers. There will be times, however, when the vocal prayers will fade back in the mind, but the meditation will remain sharp and clear; or again the subject of meditation will appear to go right out of mind and we shall become keenly aware of the sequence of vocal prayers. Suffer it to be either way and go ahead saying the vocal prayers.

It does no harm if the subject seems to drop out of consciousness. The creative touch that comes to thought has always seemed to me to occur below the level of consciousness. The human mind is a living entity, a power of the soul, and it knows what to do with thought according to its own nature. It is only the shortsighted materialistic theories that worry about what happens to thought when it leaves consciousness. We know that the living, substantial soul takes thoughts as they come in, and relates them to other thoughts in a way we cannot follow. Who of us has not fallen asleep over some problem and waked up in the morning with the solution all worked out?

Thus we direct a few pointed thoughts towards some of the mysteries of faith in the Rosary and let the thoughts sink down and into our souls. It will not be long until thoughts about God and His mercies will envelop thoughts about our daily secular tasks, and all become tinged with the supernatural. That is all it will take to remake the whole world. Do not make a great task out of this process. We do not have to take all we learn and fit it painfully together with what we already know. It does take an effort to organize knowledge gained in one way for use in another way. That is why we had to set up a method to get any results from meditation. However, once we have mastered the meaning of the mystery and given it direction and purpose, the very nature of the mind will carry the process forward.

If thinking is to be of effect it must be, as a process, as easy as walking. When you try to think about your walking as you walk across a room, see what happens to you. Thinking about walking breaks up walking, and thinking about thinking impairs thinking. Many are deterred from meditation because they think they have to carry the whole subject of meditation at a conscious level. This is not true. The best advice that can be given on this subject is: "Leave your mind alone."

Our Lady showed herself to be an excellent psychologist when she taught ordinary mortals to master the difficult art of meditation simply by combining the mental with the vocal and the manual. To use a homely example, it promotes thought to whittle on a stick, or to walk up and down a pathway, or to talk a thing out with one's self. The effect of the side occupation is to keep us from thinking about our thinking. We think for a few seconds on some great truth of our faith and then let it sink down in the mind under the influence of the recurring vocal prayers. It is also true that there is a soothing reaction in the engaging of the fingers in counting out the beads. This occupation keeps the mind from wandering. Thus all the powers of the person are engaged, and the soul is set free to absorb the lesson before it. Have no fear about your ability to meditate on this basis. Just do what is asked in the method and the results will take care of themselves.

CHAPTER 8

Suggested Outlines of Meditations

THE JOYFUL MYSTERIES

LET US refer back to what our Holy Father, Leo XIII, has said about the joyful mysteries and the simple virtues of every day life. It was true in his day and is much more true today that there is a general forgetfulness of the simple lessons of poverty, and many of us tear our hearts out over the complex living that is supposed to end in wealth and fame. Too often we believe there is no importance to our lives unless the headlines and the applause of the multitude go with it. In the joyful mysteries, seeing what God did for us, we may take heart, perceiving the inherent dignity of human nature; there is in man a touch of divinity put there by Jesus Christ in raising us to the supernatural life, to a share in His life. If the world holds us of no importance, we can go forward as best we can, remembering that we are not to hide our talents; but if we do not reach a goal we think is due us we can offer it up to God, as it is evidently His will that we remain obscure and unknown. There is only one time we need fear being unknown: that is to hear the sentence from the lips of Christ: "I know you not."

The First Joyful Mystery:
The Annunciation

The Archangel Gabriel comes to tell the Blessed Virgin Mary that she has been chosen by God to be the Mother of the Redeemer.

This was the most critical instant in the history of the human race since our father, Adam, turned his back on God to go his own way. For thousands of years God has been ready to repair that damage. He willed to send His only-begotten Son to be joined with our human nature to reopen heaven for us. This needs the cooperation of someone who will become the mother of the man who will also be God. God has been ready and now in Mary He finds man ready to cooperate. What if Mary, like Eve, had refused? It was only through her free consent that God could work this plan to send Jesus Christ into the world.

God is always willing to take back the sinner, whether it be the entire human race or an individual. God is mercy and we can always turn to Him. From Mary we learn that the will of God should be sought in all things. When Mary did not see how the Angel could be from God, she held back; when she saw that here was the will of God she consented.

The sinner, who may lean towards despair of the mercy of God need have no fear when he sees what God has already done for us. God always seeks out the sinner and showers him with graces to return to His favor. From Mary we can learn that we should test all spirits to see whether they be from God. One crime of this age is the running after wonders; the seeking after private revelations; the attempting of the immediate experience of God instead of living by faith. Another plague is the demanding of our wills over that of God. With fine balance Mary avoided both sins and assented as soon as it became plain to her that the will of God was at work.

Ask God to give us the grace to cooperate with His will as He has ordained it for us. We all have work to do in this world; work for ourselves and for God. If Mary had refused to cooperate it would have been a greater catastrophe than the Flood. Our failures to serve will not be of such great consequence, but many of the strains and sufferings of the world stem from the ordinary failures of everyday people.

How much are we affected by the teachings of the world that man is the measure of things? The world must continue to spiral into the pit as long as this state of mind prevails. This is just the promise of Satan which cannot be fulfilled: "You shall be as gods, knowing good and evil." Let us search ourselves from day to day to see how and where we pull against God.

The Second Joyful Mystery:
The Visitation

Our Lady goes in haste on the long dangerous journey to help her cousin, Elizabeth.

This event grew out of personal charity. Our Blessed Mother knew that Elizabeth was advanced in years and could expect difficulties at the birth of St. John the Baptist. Our Lady did not idly presume that since God had favored Elizabeth with this child that He must also remove all other possible complications. She went with haste to give her own help out of her personal charity but under the inspiration of the Holy Ghost, and God elevated this to a great act of public revelation. He made Elizabeth recognize in Mary the "Mother of my Lord," although the conception of Jesus was still unknown even to St. Joseph. God here revealed to us the mediation of the Blessed Virgin as she carried Jesus to John. Jesus freed John from original sin, and it was at the sound of Mary's voice that the unborn infant leaped for joy. Here Elizabeth took up the message of the Archangel Gabriel and repeated his words: "Blessed art thou amongst women."

Mary responded with her prophecy: "From henceforth all generations shall call me blessed."

The great lesson for us in this mystery is one of charity towards our neighbor, with a marked illustration of how God accepts our efforts and works through us His providence. We also see how Mary was not of a mind to rest on the great dignity that had been conferred upon her, but hastened out into the hill-country with what help she could.

Our neighbors also look to us for charity of one kind or another. Many think there is no need for personal charity nowadays because the charitable agencies can do the work so much better; but there is work of many kinds to do in person-to-person contact that no amount of efficiency can ever replace. Be on guard that no man will ever be drawn away from God through any act of ours.

We should examine our conscience to discover if we feel that our duty to a neighbor is discharged in full when we have made a donation to a fund for charity. Do we tend to look down on those less fortunate than ourselves and withhold from them the charity of our kindness?

The Third Joyful Mystery: *The Birth of Our Lord*

This is the story of Christmas. God comes to man in a most helpless and humble form. He could have come as a great conqueror, in all richness and power. If He had done so He would have loved us just as much and would have done everything for us He has done; but how could the poor, the weak, and the downtrodden have any hope for themselves amid such power and display? Since that day of all days when Christ was born no man can call himself worthless, no matter how mean his surroundings. The kingdom of God is within. We are so blinded by the world that we may forget that really every day is Christmas, and every day the great gift of God Himself can be ours.

To save any number of worlds, it would have been enough for Christ to have made any act of reparation to His Father. All that the sufferings and degrading death of Christ added was wholly for our benefit. The thing that causes us unceasing wonder is why God should have expended all His love on an ungrateful human race. Sinners have been turned into saints in pondering this thought.

So much labor and pain expended upon us! Let us ask for a heart of gratitude that we may repay in a small way what God has done for us. We ought to love God, for as St. John said: "He has first loved us."

The message of the angels on the first Christmas was: "Peace on earth to men of good will." Great sinners upset the peace of the world in a great way, but a lot of us small sinners upset the world's peace in small ways, in a great many places, and maybe do more harm in the aggregate. We cannot excuse our ill-will by saying that our actions cannot do much harm.

The Fourth Joyful Mystery: Jesus is Taken to The Temple

Jesus was Lord of the Temple and His mother was the Virgin Most Pure. He had no need to go through a ceremony of redemption nor did Mary need to be purified. Our Blessed Mother did not exempt herself from the requirements of the Law because she had been given so great an honor, and so again her humility gave the providence of God an opportunity to carry out the promise of the Holy Ghost to Simeon that death would not claim him until he had beheld the Savior of the world.

The Presentation exemplifies for us faithfulness to duty. Jesus and Mary performed their religious duties simply because it was the Law of Moses. In Simeon we see a patient waiting for years for the sight of the Redeemer that was promised to him. If he had absented himself once, it might have been on the very day that Jesus was brought to the Temple.

In a world that seeks to escape from unpleasant tasks it is difficult to find one who stands up faithfully day after day to drab and humdrum duties. We should see to it that we, also, are more careful in performing our religious tasks.

Pray for patience; it takes a long series of doing small daily chores to build up the habit of being faithful to uninteresting routine.

It is so easy to excuse ourselves from what is unpleasant that a man is often considered foolish who stands his ground at a sacrifice to himself. We can see where others fall short, but it takes a sensitive conscience to take our own measure.

The Fifth Joyful Mystery:
The Finding of The Child Jesus in The Temple

When Jesus was twelve years old He had attained His legal majority. Thus He chose the earliest possible moment to begin His mission. No doubt Christ wished to call the attention of the elders and leaders of the people to the prophecies about the Messias. Jesus, always kind and considerate, did not spare the feelings of Mary and Joseph to teach us that where the things of God are concerned we must not allow human feelings to interfere.

Zeal for the things of God consumed our Lord. We have become soft, and often sentiment guides us where the call of God's vocation should be followed.

We must not put any obstacle in the way of those who want to serve God, and if God should call those who are near to us we should not consider our own feelings—God must come first.

Ask God to help us see things in their true light. God is the measure of all things.

There are many ways to fail in this besides turning others away from their vocations. Zeal for the things of God includes the spreading of His word in all ways. Do we conceal our faith when the interests of God bid us speak up?

THE SORROWFUL MYSTERIES

In these mysteries we are introduced to the riddle of suffering. It is precisely on the reactions we make to the ills and setbacks that are visited upon us that our faith stands or falls. Many a Christian has been stalwart in faith, only to fall away when trouble comes. It is not always the deliberate fault of one affected, since the air is full of the false belief that the favor of God is shown in the prosperity of His children.

The present-day world has got so far away from the true meaning of suffering that it has become the only evil the world wants to take into account. Suffering is truly an evil. It is a physical evil, uncomfortable to the nervous system. Certainly there is no reason why men should not try to avoid physical sufferings through the exercise of human ingenuity. There are no sane reasons for condemning heating systems, air conditioning, anesthetics, labor saving devices, or any of the thousands of other things that take burdens off our shoulders. But these things have a way of taking over the direction of our lives, until they appear as the only important things, and we come falsely to believe that all else that removes us from material comforts must be the only evil to avoid.

How foolish a life of toil and renunciation appears to the generality of mankind! How can we ever get to them the message that suffering is not merely something to be stoically endured until we become powerful enough to push it off on another, who is not so far up the ladder of success? How can we get men to see that the actual seeking for suffering on the part of such as St. Thérèse, the Little Flower, has real value, and is not the utmost in lunacy?

Perhaps we can best start by studying more carefully the

sufferings of Jesus Christ. Surely no one who is at all worthy of calling himself a Christian would dare to presume that the sufferings of Christ had no value. Consideration of His agonies will help us be more patient when confronted by sufferings, setbacks, frustrations, sickness, and the train of ills that carry us away from the road we should like to follow. It is small wonder that so many crack under the strain of toil, under obstacles for which they see no use. On the other hand man is elevated and strengthened no matter what the odds against him in the world; no matter how much he suffers, if he can only see himself as a part of God's plan; if only he can understand that God takes all these things into account. All this is made clear to us in the sorrowful mysteries of the Rosary.

The First Sorrowful Mystery: *Jesus Enters into His Passion in The Garden of Olives*

Jesus instituted the Blessed Sacrament and intertwined it with His approaching death. He strengthened His apostles and then went into the Garden for His agony. All His sufferings confront Him. All the sins of men from the sin of Adam to the sins of those who will be trapped by the end of the world, come before Him. He is sickened by so much sin so close to the Sinless One. With the picture of sin is linked the ingratitude of men who do not seem to care whether Christ loved them or not. Something in His agony so revolted our Lord that He besought His Father to remove it, but only subject to the will of the Father.

Jesus allowed His human nature to have sway while His divinity withdrew, but it is blasphemy to say that He was asking to be permitted to escape His passion and death. Everything that Christ ever did led up to the Cross. So much sin so close to Jesus Christ would have slain Him, had He not been sustained by His divinity. Sin is an attempt to kill God, but only God can look on sin as it is, and not die. These thoughts made Christ sweat His precious blood, but He endured it all because it was the will of His Father.

What causes our sufferings is not the sight of sin as sin really is; this we could never endure. What we must endure are the external effects that sin has left on this world. We cannot get away from these; we must stay and overcome evil with good. By enduring evils around us we help to restore the balance set up by God, but this takes patience and acceptance of the divine will.

Ask for a great depth of patience to bear the burdens of this world. Ours is a world of suffering, under the best of circumstances; unless we are running out on our share of responsibility we shall encounter soul-trying difficulties. Pray for strength to bear your "agony"—in the original meaning of a contest or trial. Patience is needed to live in this world where the contest is spread out over so many years.

If we could only get through our heads and into our hearts what Christ undertook for us in His passion and death, we should all be saints. The world gets so close to us that we forget the prostrate form of Christ in the deep shadows of Gethsemane, faced with our sins. If we remember this picture we can reach back over the centuries and lift some of that burden from the back of Christ by not sinning any more.

The Second Sorrowful Mystery:
Jesus is Scourged Beyond Mercy with Roman Whips

Pilate knew that Jesus was innocent and he wanted to set Him free. Pilate, however, feared what the leaders of the Jews could do to him at Rome. They had already forced him to remove pagan emblems from the Temple. He was faced with the necessity of upholding the truth and suffering for it, and like so many others he could see no virtue in suffering. "I will scourge Him and let Him go," he said, hoping thus by reducing Jesus to a pitable condition to satisfy the blood lust of the leaders of the Jews. Through disgrace and pain he might have become St. Pilate, but instead he is the type of all official cowardice.

There is always a danger that those in possession of position of any sort will try to hold onto it at the expense of conscience. There is always "an easy way out," which ranges all the way from a simple shifting of blame to an innocent man to avoid losing some advantage, to the terrible mass murders at Lidice, perpetrated simply because Hitler wanted a "victim," and it was easier to order every man in the whole village murdered than it was to admit that the secret police had been unable to find the killer of the "Gauleiter."

It is sometimes very hard to see justice done, especially when the unjust verdict would be popular with an excited mob. This is the special task of those in authority. In all abuses of justice Christ is again scourged. If we can only remember that all power comes from God and that we are acting merely as His agent, it will be a lot easier to be just.

Pray always for a sense of fairness and justice. The big thing wrong with the world is that millions upon millions of people are oppressed by abuse of power. Pray that we in the "free" world will reform ourselves, so that God may use us to liberate those who are in the slave world.

To hold power is one of the greatest dangers to which we can be exposed. Anyone who has authority in home, factory, office, or government has to keep a firm check upon his motives. It is easier to favor the powerful against the weak for the sake of avoiding trouble. It is dangerous, too, for of such Christ will say at the judgment: "Whatsover you have done to one of these my least brethren, you have done it unto Me."

The Third Sorrowful Mystery:
The King of Kings Receives a Crown of Thorns and is Ridiculed as the King of Fools

The soldiers were using Jesus as a means of "getting even." Pretenders like Barabbas had been rising against the Roman invaders and had been trying to get the people to accept them as king of the Jews. They knew that the prophecies had foretold that a king of Israel was soon to come and reign forever. The pretenders thought, reasoning backwards, that if they could be accepted as king, they would inherit the rightful title. These men gave the Romans a lot of trouble. Jesus had said that He was a king, and for that the soldiers were venting upon Him the spite they held for the pretenders. They did not care that Jesus was innocent of stirring up the people. He was helpless, and He was in their hands. See, then, how they mocked Him; spat in His face; gave Him a reed for a scepter. See how they pushed Him; slapped Him; ridiculed Him. Then they jammed the platted mass of thorns into a circlet of rushes and pushed it down on the sacred head of the Savior. Jesus wore this painful crown until He died.

There is hardly anything closer to the hatred of demons than the bitter lust to "get even." Even where the offense has not been malicious the self-imposed payment for wounded pride is always full of malice. When revolution strikes, those who engineer it always turn the mobs loose upon anyone they wish to cut down in revenge. There are always enough of those who hate to disrupt the old order of things.

Human pride is the hardest of all tendencies to curb, and it is always pride that battles these real or imagined wrongs for which men want to see the "score evened up." It would, perhaps, not upset the course of the world if men were satisfied with taking "an eye for an eye and a tooth for a tooth." In a more primitive society where the administration of justice had to be in private hands this could be permitted; but where do we see a person in the act of "getting even" who is not set to inflict much graver damage than he has sustained? If we are to stop the development of revenge in ever-widening circles, someone has to forgive.

We have to pray without ceasing for a spirit of forgiveness. Whoever says that Christianity is for weaklings does not realize how foolish he is until he makes some sort of an attempt to forgive one who has really harmed him. Forgiveness is really that good will which alone can bring peace to the earth.

There is a balance we have to maintain between a real and genuine defense of our honor and property, and a spirit of revenge which we have to keep looking into to be sure we are free from guilt. A person cannot allow everyone to use him as a footstool. He has to put up a reasonable defense of his person, his family, his country, and his God. Yet he must have a care to follow the injunction of Christ: "Do good to those that hate you, and pray for them that persecute you." Give thought to the difference between justice and revenge, and if you must fall, fall to the side of mercy.

The Fourth Sorrowful Mystery: *Jesus Drags a Rough and Heavy Cross through the Streets of Jerusalem*

The Cross that Jesus bore from Pilate's hall to Calvary was not His own. It belonged first of all to Barabbas, who was to have been crucified with the two thieves. The Cross really belonged to all of us, for it was our guilt that made Jesus Christ undergo all His sufferings and death. The Cross was heavy; it weighed about 200 pounds. It was rough-cut and splintery. When we consider that the sweat of blood had made the skin sore and sensitive, and that Jesus had been whipped until He was cut and swollen over His entire sacred body, the pain that the Cross caused as it rubbed back and forth over His shoulder is beyond imagination. It was not for mercy that Simon the Cyrenian was made to bear the Cross for Jesus, but because His tormentors were afraid He would die along the way.

Our Lord has made the tortuous journey of the way of the Cross a symbol of the longer journey of life. Of this He had said to His disciples before they knew what He was referring to: "He who is not willing to take up his cross daily and follow Me, is not worthy of Me." This is a world of difficulties that have to be surmounted, and they are compared by Christ Himself with the bearing of this terrible instrument of torture, the cross. He knew that life is not easy, but He gives His grace to make it possible.

If we could attain sanctity at a bound we might all become saints, but the road on which we recover the integrity lost at the fall of man is along the way of the Cross. We elevate ourselves a little at a time. At first when the call of Christ comes it is as a bid to take up the cross. We are like Simon of Cyrene. Usually we are at the task of making a living or building up a career, when circumstances we cannot control push us over to the cross and we are told: "Carry it." We had not planned it; we did not want it that way. Yet carry it we must, for upon the cross depends our eternal salvation.

A few chosen souls can earnestly pray for the grace to receive crosses and burdens, which are offered up to Christ in union with His own Passion for the sins of men. Other souls recoil at the mere suggestion that they should be called upon to suffer poverty, disgrace, failure, or the other ills that befall men. Meanwhile there are a lot of people who never seem to be troubled deeply during their whole uneventful lives. God has His plans and whether it be honor or dishonor, health or sickness, wealth or poverty, let us look at Christ toiling up the slope towards Calvary for us, and pray for the strength to accept whatever He may have in store for us.

We can, most of us, examine our consciences with confusion because most of us do not accept what comes along with any show of good grace. No one says it is easy to accept bitterness from the hand of God. Only the few can turn this into sweetness, but we can all try to achieve resignation.

The Fifth Sorrowful Mystery:
Jesus is Crucified and Dies on the Cross

The most tremendous happening in all human history took

place on the hill of Calvary. Until the world sees in Jesus Christ and in His sacrifice the fact of a fundamental change in every other human being, there can never be peace on this earth. Christ literally hung on mangled and frayed nerve-endings, until cramping muscles of arms and chest pulled tight and tore His heart asunder. When Christ died, there died with Him every "natural man" in all the human race. From His death came a new race of supernatural men, men who can hope to partake of the divine life of God Himself. Let us free ourselves from the world that would cheat us of such a destiny in the name of rational freedom of man from God. We can never understand why Christ endured so much to bring to us such great benefits, for which we give so little thanks in return. He gave Himself then, and He perpetuates His gift every day in the Holy Sacrifice of the Mass and in the sacraments, through which we can become more and more like Him.

This is the test of God's great love for man. From the first promise made at the closed gates of Paradise down through the patriarchs, the prophets, and the Chosen People who were prepared for this great day, there was never an instant when God was not looking forward, so to speak, until He could bring back man to His favor. Through Mary's consent God could perform the creative act which would generate the body and infuse the human soul of Christ to make Him become man in the pure womb of Our Blessed Mother and there, through union with the second Person of the Blessed Trinity, give to us the Man-God, Jesus Christ.

The fruits of the passion and death of Jesus Christ are ours if we only give back to God a little of what He has first given us. When we love God, He has first given us the grace to love Him. When we first believed in Him, He had given us the gift of faith.

Not everyone for whom Christ died will save his immortal soul. Our constant prayer should be that the blood spilt on the Cross may not have been shed for us in vain. There were two sinners very near to Christ when He hung on the Cross, but only one of them accepted the graces given him. Soldiers were grouped around the Cross, but only Longinus, the Centurion, saw in Christ the Son of God. The Cross of Christ must become very personal to each of us to do us any good. Let our petition be: "Lord, that I may see."

Perhaps every time we say the sorrowful mysteries of the Rosary, we should examine our consciences to see whether, since the last time we said the Rosary, our lives have meant more consolation or more suffering to Jesus Christ. God does not act by killing the sinner in his sin, but patiently waits the sinner's return. While He waits, the sinner's added sins cause Christ more and more suffering. Are we the ones who bring more pain to Him?

THE GLORIOUS MYSTERIES

The glorious mysteries deal with the application of the fruits of the passion and death of Jesus Christ and with the promise of our future glory. There is too much overlooking of the fact that Christ, as He promised, did not leave us orphans, but sent the Holy Ghost to remain with us, to sanctify us and to draw us to the things of God through grace; and also to remain as the guide of the Catholic Church until the end of time, to preserve all the things that Christ had taught during the three years of His public ministry.

When religious unity was broken in the sixteenth century many thought that the Holy Ghost was to be the individual guide of each person in turn, to tell him what Christ had taught. Now that it is becoming transparent that the bewildering array of beliefs is proof positive that our Lord did not promise personal infallibility to each man, disbelief and despair are making headway. In truth, all that is needed is a return to the unity that Christ set up, through the Holy Ghost in the apostles and their successors in the Catholic Church.

The world has fallen into a despair at the sight of the material disaster around us, as though this were the end and aim of all human endeavor. There is no patience in pain and adversity because they are looked upon as time lost, and not as a deferred payment of what is to come after death. It is not only the pagans who fret and fume under material chastisements. There are even Catholics who seem to disdain eternal reward for the present satisfaction. When they are closely questioned they admit they have no such pagan beliefs, but the world does press in on all of us, and it will not harm any of us to restate his beliefs from time to time to keep the proper proportions.

The First Glorious Mystery:
Jesus Christ Rises from the Dead, Glorious and Immortal

The Resurrection was the seal of approval that God put on the teachings of Jesus Christ, because only He can bring the dead back to life. His followers had seen Him die the most disgraceful of all deaths. They had buried Him. For them nothing remained but a few decencies connected with His burial that they had not time to perform on that Friday that killed all their hopes. Never had a man appeared so thoroughly defeated. Christ had claimed the authority and power of God Himself, but it now seemed that God had turned away from Him and left Him helpless in the hands of His enemies. Then the women burst into the upper room with the word: "He is risen." He is truly Life itself, and death could not hold Him any longer than He willed to be held.

God is always faithful to His promises, but He has said: "My ways are not your ways," and God has ways we cannot follow; He has purposes that do not match our desires. We sometimes look upon the apostles with critical eye because they fled from their enemies and lost confidence in Christ; but do we not do the same thing, who now know better? The Resurrection was for us. It was proof so strong for the divinity of Christ that no man of good will can any longer turn aside from Him.

The Resurrection is for us the quiet assurance that in Christ we can conquer death and hell. This is the promise of Christ, and since He could effect His own Resurrection, He can effect ours at the end of time. The world will press about us; death will at last claim us. But we can go forward with trust that in Christ we shall live again—and forever.

When God leaves proof of His truths for us, He does not make them so compelling that they force the will, in spite of itself. God's proofs are always for men of good will. Ask, then, for the good will of integrity that we may not be hardened in heart against the works of God. Pray for the grace to triumph over sin and death; for grace to remain tranquil and with peace of soul amid the turmoil which surrounds us. In Christ we can triumph over the world and its attachments, for He has said: "I have overcome the world." Pray to be so detached from the world that we shall not stake eternal salvation on the amount of this world's goods that we can lay hands on.

We must examine ourselves often to see whether we have made our standard of values Christ or the world. We are impatient when our plans do not come to instant fruition. So were the apostles downcast, terrified, and defeated, when Christ bowed His head and died on the Cross; but there was a victory ahead for them greater than if He had never died. We may blame them because they should have known better. We should know better, too.

The Second Glorious Mystery:
Christ Returns to His Glory, to Prepare a Place for Us

Christ could have returned to the Father as soon as He rose from the dead, but He remained to prepare the apostles for their great mission. He instructed them; He gave them power to forgive sins; He confirmed Peter as the head of His Church; He appeared time and again to His disciples, and even to others, to make it utterly certain that He had returned from the dead in the truest sense of the term. When He had prepared all for the coming of the Holy Ghost He was taken from their midst from the top of Mount Olivet, the spot He had chosen long before as the place of the last judgment.

Our Lord showed the deepest consideration for His followers in staying with them until they were ready for the work He had given them to do. He had said before He died: "I will not leave you orphans." So He remained with them, to build up their shocked minds and devastated faith until they were ready to carry the glad tidings to the uttermost corners of the earth.

We may not have the responsibility of teaching formally, but every one of us must teach by word or example, either in the home, or in the office, or factory. Often we are unaware that we are teaching by example, but we may be sure that what we do often has a most profound effect on others. As Christ was faithful to us in pointing out the way, we can be faithful to Him in following the way. St. Paul tells us: ". . . if you be risen with Christ seek the things that are above where Christ is sitting at the right hand of God." Many a Christian has driven seekers of truth astray by acting as though he lived only for this world.

We must pray always that while we are in the world we shall not be "of the world." We cannot generally solve our economic problems as Benedict Joseph Labre did—by turning our backs on them. A good solution to adopt is the economic program of the Third Order of St. Francis: "To commit no sin of head or hand for goods of fortune." We must strive to resist the temptation to compromise our principles, even to make a strike that will help make us economically independent for life. It takes continued graces to keep swimming in the flood when land is at hand, and grace comes only by prayer. Pray for a spiritual sense.

The world crowds around us so closely, and the next world seems so far away that we can easily become infected with the spirit of the last hundred years; a spirit which implies a promise of a heaven on earth. It was a false promise and deep hatreds have grown out of the resulting disappointments. Against these twin evils we must be ever on our guard.

The Third Glorious Mystery:
The Descent of the Holy Ghost upon the Apostles and upon the Blessed Mother

As long as Christ remained upon this earth there was, of course, no one who would dare to take upon himself the government of the faithful. If our Lord had gone away and left the apostles to themselves, human error would have crept in and marred His teachings. His teachings must remain pure; if they were added to or taken away from, the passion and death of Christ would have been in vain. Men would not have known how to apply to themselves the merits of Jesus Christ. Christ knew that only God, the Spirit of truth, could preserve truth over the long course of centuries, so that the twentieth century and the thirtieth century—if it comes—will be just as secure in faith as the first century, that received truth from the very lips of Christ. The Holy Ghost came to abide until the end of time with the Catholic Church, to teach and guide so that error will never be taught by the Church of Christ. The Holy Spirit dwells in our souls and makes us strong in the faith so we can see the truth.

Christ could have willed that each man would have to make a painful search for truth, but what would have become of the millions upon millions who have no time, nor talents, nor opportunity for such a search? God is faithful to His promises, and Christ who made the work of salvation necessary for every man, had to make it possible for men to find this rock of truth. Our lack of zeal has slowed down the spread of the truth, but that is our fault—not God's. God will protect those who could not come to the truth by their own faculties when it was not brought to them.

In charity we owe it to our brothers to give them an opportunity to hear the word of God. The work of Christ will not be complete upon this earth until all men have had an opportunity to come to the truth. This calls for an apostolic effort on our parts. To some it will be as a call to the mission fields, as priest or nun; to others it will be the support of those who bravely go out to work. It may even be an apostolate to our next-door neighbor whose call to the truth may be destined by Providence to take place through us. Whatever the ways we are to help, the spread of the truth of Christ falls upon all of us.

Pray for the missionary spirit, no matter how God in His providence has decreed it to come to pass. Pray for those to whom God has entrusted the protection of the deposit of truth; our Holy Father, the Pope, the bishops over all the world. Pray for priests, and brothers, and nuns; for all those who teach; for lay apostles such as in the Legion of Mary. Pray that the Lord of the harvest will send laborers into the fields. Men are hungry for truth as never before. If we pray enough, Christ will come into His own.

Men of ill will have from the very beginning made it harder for the reign of Christ to begin upon the earth. The Holy Ghost came down upon the apostles to enlighten them and to guide them. The pride of Satan has entered into men of every age to challenge this primacy of teaching. Most of us never go so far as to make a complete break with the Catholic Church, but do we not at times put obstacles in the way of the free action of the Church? Do we study papal encyclicals to help bring needed reforms to the world, or do we hold back on the grounds that these are not *ex cathedra,* and we do not have to follow them unless we choose? Do we complain before non-believers, as well as Catholics, about the "terrible things the Bishop wants to put over on us"? The Communists can make better use of a disaffected Catholic than they can of an atheist.

The Fourth Glorious Mystery:
The Assumption of Our Blessed Mother into Heaven

Where there was no sin neither death nor the corruption

of the tomb had any rights, for "from sin came death," and from death the consequence, "into dust thou shalt return." When the Blessed Virgin passed through the gates of death it was not fitting that the body that had brought forth the Savior mingle its substance with the dust of the tomb. In His divine justice God raised her up, in an anticipated rising from the dead, because where there was no disobedience there was nothing for which to punish her. During her earthly life, Mary was the Mother of Sorrows, but now her prophecy comes into its own: "From henceforth all generations shall call me blessed."

God rewards in due season, and in the degree man has merited by cooperating with Him. On the last day we shall rise from the dead and enjoy *our* assumption into heaven, if we persevere to the end. Of His own right Christ was, of course, free from all taint of sin, and the grave could hold Him only so long as it was His will. By a singular privilege the Blessed Mother was free from the smallest shadow of sin, either original or personal sin. All other human beings, even including John the Baptist who was *born* free of sin, have been touched by sin in some degree. Because we are of that group we shall all have to undergo the ravishments of the tomb. We must go back to the original dust until no sign remains of our bodily make-up. On the last day the power of God will gather our dust into a new body to be reunited with its soul, a body over which sin has never had any power. Thus, any victory that Satan may have had over us will be as if it had never been.

Our problem is to make a spiritual use of material things in such a way that the soul will come again into a material body which is glorified. If we meditate on the Assumption it will vitalize our faith in our last end. "I believe in the resurrection of the body and life everlasting." How easy it is to believe it of ourselves when it has already come to pass for one of our own human race. How small the trials of life will seem when we think how she, whose soul was transfixed by a sword, was translated into the highest heaven!

Pray for a tender devotion to the Blessed Mother. Eve was "the mother of all the living," and Mary was made the Mother of all those who live in Christ. We are all members of Jesus Christ in His mystical body, and in this sense, too, Mary is our Mother. Through Jesus Christ we have the means of grace to lead us to heaven, and through Mary we have the means to lead us to Christ. Let us never cease our petition: "Holy Mary, Mother of God, pray for us sinners now and at the hour of our death. Amen."

We become discouraged sometimes—the best of us. Our difficulties seem so very close; our rewards so far away. We are not very far away from a world that was so sure of its independence from God that it claimed that all men are free from sin. We now live in a world that seems to believe in nothing but death and despair; in a world so full of disaster and destruction that we must live carefully so as not to be carried away by what we see around us. Keep always in mind that the victories of disaster and death are only for a time.

The Fifth Glorious Mystery: *The Coronation of Our Blessed Mother as The Queen of Heaven*

In heaven we shall all have a crown of glory. Our Blessed Mother, by her Assumption, is already enjoying her crown, and where shall we place her if not close to Christ? St. John, looking up to heaven in ecstacy, saw THE WOMAN clothed with the sun, and with the moon beneath her feet, crowned with a crown of twelve stars. Mary in her humility said: "Be it done unto me according to Thy will." It is the will of God that Mary be exalted above all the angels and saints, to reign next to her divine Son. "He hath regarded the humility of His handmaid and behold, from henceforth all generations shall call me blessed." You *are* blessed. You are blessed amongst all women. To faithful hearts you will be always as you prophesied, the *Blessed* Virgin. Reign as Queen both in heaven and in our hearts, and bring us safely back to Christ where we may hear from Him: "Come ye blessed of my Father."

With God, everything is in order, and all must come to fruit as He willed it. God has willed to send Jesus Christ to us through Mary, and He has willed that we shall return to Christ through Mary. Mary is Our Blessed Mother and because of her He will give His graces to us. At Cana He performed a miracle for her although His time had not yet come to manifest His power. His time did come as He hung on the Cross on Calvary. There she became our Mother to help and guide us. Jesus Christ could not come into the world as He did until Mary consented freely to become His Mother. There, God decreed Mary as His channel through which He had willed to come. God will not degrade anyone who does His will, as we may be sure that Mary is still the channel as she was at the Annunciation.

We should make a great mistake if we did not use the means set up by God to lead us to Him. Go to Our Blessed Mother with all problems and difficulties. Not only will she help us if we go to her, but she has from the very beginning come to us with warnings, with help, with encouragement, and with the ways to make our road to heaven easier to travel. In countless places she has set up centers of devotion; she has even obtained for us a flood of miracles to build up our confidence in her.

Pray constantly to Our Blessed Mother "that we may be made worthy of the promises of Christ." Be sure that one form of prayer you will never neglect is her Rosary. Pray the Rosary every day.

There is hardly a Catholic in this world who is not devoted to the Blessed Mother, at least in a nebulous way, but there are many who are not careful enough about deliberately cultivating her devotion in a precise form. Have a care always not to be affected by the false doctrine that it is better to go directly to Christ, to the disregard of His Blessed Mother. Do not let yourself be drawn into the error which states that it somehow degrades Christ if we go to His Mother with our pleas. It has always been the teaching of the Catholic Church that Christ wills that all the graces He dispenses be given to us through the hands of His Blessed Mother. If we are not willing to come freely to Mary it may be that there is something in our lives we should root out.

AFTERWORD

With the above suggestions for outlines you can say Rosaries every day without too much difficulty, even in the throes of the cares and distractions of the world. You do not have to say the five decades without interruption; you do not have to go into a church to pray—but if you do you will gain an additional plenary indulgence. If your work takes you over a wide area you can get as many as fifteen decades said during the day, but do not try too hard, since prayers have a way of being set back until they are "bunched up" at the very end of the day when you need a well-earned sleep. This serves to make prayer a source of irritation; a thing not desired by anyone. Remember that work well done is prayer, too. Washing dishes can be a prayer. One of the best prayers is to do without complaint many of the little things that make up a day. Prayer is not meant to be said under strain; it is intended to relieve strain, and bring peace to the soul. If prayer becomes irksome make it shorter. You can do your work and still say five decades of the Rosary every day. It will not take more than fifteen minutes or so to complete this pleasant task, and that will leave ample time for meditation solid enough to fix in mind and heart the message of the Rosary. Anything that is going to be done day after day had best not be begun with a big rush of fervor. It will soon bog down if it starts that way. I know, because I have had this happen to me too often. Get a solid steady pace established from the very outset and you will be able to keep that up for the rest of your life.

The above points given for each mystery are only suggestions. As soon as you can possibly do so get away from them; substitute thoughts of your own which bear on the Rosary mysteries. For example, in the third joyful mystery you have the whole story of Christmas to draw from. Whatever Christmas means to you will provide ample material for meditation on this mystery. At all events stay close to the first and second points for meditation. The first, which simply names the mystery, will not be enough; go on to discover a meaning in the mystery—a meaning that concerns one of your problems.

Remember that prayer is not merely an exercise in psychology, nor is it speech-making to God. There will be times when you can hardly put words together, because of illness or finger-chilling fear of impending disaster. Think how little the poor wretches behind the Iron Curtain "feel" like praying, as they go forward in terror that death or banishment will strike them or their families. It is in such times that we need prayer most. In dire need do the best you can. Get something done about praying in time of need, and in a shorter time than you may suppose the effects of the prayer will make themselves felt. Then your prayer can be expanded. Remember the lesson of our Lord in His agony: "Being in agony He prayed the longer."

All the other suggested points can hover in the background, one or another of them coming into focus from time to time. It will not take away from the effectiveness of the Rosary if one decade treats of a resolution to be made, and another suggests an examination of conscience, while a third simply turns to God with thanksgiving. Attempting too much meditation in each decade is to interfere with getting the Rosary said; one lesson brought home sharply will be of more permanent benefit. If, on the other hand, thoughts refuse to come, you may be forced to fall back on the simple naming of the mystery. In that case, name the mystery and plunge ahead. It may be that something will occur to you during the saying of the vocal prayers. If so, stop for a moment or so and let the thought have expression. The meditations can be made before, during, or after the vocal prayers. The great accomplishment is to say the Rosary each and every day without fail. Do that; have faith in the Holy Ghost and in the God-given powers of your own mind.

There is one more injunction: The lessons of the Rosary should gather depth as you go on. This will depend on yourself and on how much outside effort you are willing to put into gathering information about the mysteries of religion as set forth in the Rosary. God does not desire to turn religion into a study of archeology and dead languages, to be sure. We cannot all find the time and make the effort needed to become scholars of Holy Scripture, but we can all do something, according to our lights and opportunities. Simplicity is not ignorance; yet the greatest scholars do not always have the greatest faith. We must do what we can to improve our knowledge of what our faith teaches.

PART THREE

Meditations for Each Mystery

CHAPTER 9

The Joyful Mysteries

THE joyful mysteries cover the period from the moment when the Blessed Virgin consented to her part in the redemption by becoming the mother of the Savior, until Jesus returned to Nazareth to be subject to Mary and Joseph after He had withdrawn Himself to dispute with the Doctors in the Temple. The joyful mysteries center about the Blessed Virgin.

The First Joyful Mystery:
The Annunciation

Our redemption began with this event. God was always ready to extend His mercies, but man was not ready to cooperate with Him until the time of Mary. Experts may debate whether God could have chosen another way to redeem man; the fact remains that He did not. God's plan was to have this young virgin consent to become the mother of a man who would be united from conception to the Second Person of the Trinity, so as to be both God and man. As man He could suffer, and as God His actions would have infinite worth in the eyes of God, the Father.

God in His wisdom had adorned the young virgin's soul with graces so great that—unlike the soul touched with original sin—she tended always to the good rather than away from it, to such a degree that her consent to the office of mother of the Redeemer would not be withheld, although her consent was still free. Think how great the endowments of Lucifer must have been, yet he could turn his back to the will of God. Consider how much like Mary's, was the original condition of our first parents, but they could still fail in a very slight task. From the prophecies Mary knew much about what the Redeemer would have to endure and what she therefore, would have to go through as His mother. She did not know what God held in store for her as her reward. These matters the prophecies did not cover. Her consent was, therefore, to a bitter task because God had willed it.

God had first promised a redeemer to man at the very time He closed to our first parents the Paradise they had forfeited. Any plan He would extend to man would not include the restoration of the terrestrial Paradise; but notice that all false schemes of saving mankind always promise the return to a state of physical ease, far from sin, crime, sufferings, disease, and whatever else has plagued man since he lost his original innocence.

Through the ages the promise of a redeemer became more and more specific until time, place, and circumstances were well known. There was a time in the reign of Caesar Augustus when for a short period the whole known world was at peace. There was an expectancy over all peoples, even among the pagans. Then God brought into being the Precursor of Jesus, who would go before Him as a voice crying in the wilderness. We begin the story of our salvation with John the Baptist as related in the Gospel of St. Luke.

There was in the days of Herod, the King of Judea, a certain priest named Zachary, of the course of Abia; and his wife was of the daughters of Aaron, and her name, Elizabeth. And they were both just before God, walking in all the commandments and justifications of the Lord without blame. And they had no son, for that Elizabeth was barren, and they were both advanced in years.

And it came to pass, when he executed the priestly function in the order of his course before God, according to the custom of the priestly office it was his lot to offer incense, going into the Temple of the Lord. And all the multitude of the people was praying without at the hour of incense.

And there appeared to him an angel of the Lord, standing on the right hand of the altar of incense. And Zachary seeing him was troubled and fear fell upon him.

But the angel said to him: Fear not Zachary, for thy prayer is heard; and thy wife Elizabeth shall bear thee a son, and thou shalt call his name John; and thou shalt have joy and gladness, and many shall rejoice in his nativity. For he shall be great before the Lord: and he shall drink no wine nor strong drink; and he shall be filled with the Holy Ghost even from his mother's womb. And he shall convert many of the children of Israel to the Lord their God.

And he shall go before Him in the spirit and power of Elias that he may turn the hearts of the fathers unto the children, and the incredulous to the wisdom of the just, to prepare unto the Lord a perfect people.

And Zachary said to the angel: whereby shall I know this? For I am an old man, and my wife is advanced in years.

And the angel answering said to him: I am Gabriel, who stand before God: and am sent to speak to thee, and to bring thee these good tidings. And behold thou shalt be dumb, and shall not be able to speak until the day wherein these things shall come to pass, because thou hast not believed my words, which shall be fulfilled in their time.

And the people were waiting for Zachary; and they wondered that he tarried so long in the Temple. And when he came out, he could not speak to them, and they understood that he had seen a vision in the Temple. And he made signs to them and remained dumb. And it came to pass, after the days of his office were accomplished, he departed for his house. And after those days, Elizabeth his wife conceived, and hid herself five months saying; Thus hath the Lord dealt with me in the days wherein He hath regard to take away my reproach among men.

And in the sixth month the Angel Gabriel was sent from God into a city of Galilee, called Nazareth to a virgin espoused to a man whose name was Joseph, of the house of David; and the virgin's name was Mary.

And the angel came in and said to her: Hail full of grace, the Lord is with thee: blessed art thou amongst women.

Who, having heard, was troubled at this saying, and thought with herself what manner of salutation this should be. And the angel said to her: Fear not Mary, for thou hast found grace with God. Behold thou shalt conceive in thy womb, and thou shalt bring forth a son and thou shalt call His name, Jesus. He shall be great, and shall be called the Son of the Most High; and the Lord shall give unto Him the throne of David, His father, and He shall reign in the house of Jacob for ever, and of His kingdom there shall be no end.

And Mary said to the angel: How shall this be, because I know not man? And the angel answering said to her: The Holy Ghost shall come upon thee, and the power of the Most High shall overshadow thee. And therefore also the Holy which shall be born of thee shall be called the Son of God.

And behold thy cousin Elizabeth, she also hath conceived a son in her old age, and this is the sixth month with her that is called barren, because no word shall be impossible with God.

And Mary said: Behold the handmaid of the Lord; be it done to me according to thy word. And the angel departed from her.

Herod, King of Judea Herod, called the Great, under whose rule Christ was born was the last of the kings of Judea. His

The Joyful Mysteries

claim to the throne was tainted and he ruled only by sufferance of the Roman conquerors; his blood was uncertain; he was more pagan than Jew; but there was still the name of a king on a throne. His son, the other Herod who gave the head of John the Baptist to Salome and who later mocked Christ as a fool was only Procurator of Galilee. It was purely an appointive office in the Roman Empire. The second Herod was no more a ruler than Pilate, who held the power of the elder Herod in Judea. The prophecy of Jacob was fulfilled: "The scepter shall not be taken away from Juda, nor a ruler from his thigh, till He come that is to be sent, and He shall be the expectation of all nations" (Gen. 49:10).

A certain priest named Zachary The priesthood was confined to the tribe of Levi. The services in the Temple were very exacting so that they were divided into twenty-four "courses" of which Zachary belonged to that of Abia, the sixteenth. The priests had to leave their homes during the course of their term of service at the altar. Zachary was on such a tour of duty when the angel appeared to him.

From Zachary we may learn that even when times are bad and men are evil, it is still possible to stand apart and be as he and Elizabeth were, "both just before God, walking in all the commandments and justifications of the Lord without blame." Herod was soaked in vice and murder; the Roman army infested the country; the High Priest and his staff, and the Scribes and Pharisees, used the Temple of God for their own selfish aims, under the protection of the men who were degrading their people and country. In the hills bands of brigands roamed at large, stirring up dissention. Later on, Christ paid bitterly at the crowning with thorns for the trouble these marauders caused the Roman soldiers.

It was a time of evil, as the times we live in. Zachary lived justly amid corruption. Sometimes we look at all the suffering and disasters around us; especially today across the seas at the sad plight of many of our brothers in Christ, and we wonder when right and justice will be restored. It was at such a time as this that Christ came with His grace. "He came unto His own but His own received Him not," and the misery went on until Jerusalem was leveled to the ground. We can put an end to our miseries by being of those who "as many as received Him he gave the power to become the Sons of God, full of grace and truth."

And there appeared to him an angel of the Lord As we find out very shortly this was the archangel Gabriel. He was one of the brightest spirits created by God; one of the seven who always stand before the throne of God. Gabriel was above all the angel of the Incarnation. He had been sent to Daniel the Prophet during the sad days of the Babylonian captivity of the Jews—another time when the Jews appeared to have been deserted by God. But God's grace was at work, and to Daniel God foretold the time of the coming of the Redeemer. He also set the date for the destruction of the Temple and the dispersal of the Jewish people for rejecting Christ. Jesus referred back to this saying: "When, therefore you shall see the abomination of desolation spoken of by Daniel the prophet, standing in the holy place. . . " (Matt. 24:15). Now Gabriel comes to Zachary and will come again to Mary.

. . . . in the spirit and power of Elias The appearance of John the Baptist made it certain to Zachary that the age of the Redeemer was at hand. The prophet, Elias, had been taken up into heaven in a fiery chariot without paying the human penalty of death. Malachias, the last Old Testament prophet, had foretold: "Behold, I will send you Elias, the prophet before the coming of the great and dreadful day of the Lord." The Jews had fixed their minds on a Messias who would come with great temporal power and majesty;

drive out the Romans and set up a great earthly kingdom. So they rejected Christ who came in humility and poverty.

Many of the Jews who were not blinded by the majesty and power of temporal rule did see in Christ the long-awaited One. After the Transfiguration we see the disciples struggling with doubts as to whether Jesus is the Messias, asking: "Why then do the Pharisees and the Scribes say that Elias must come first?" Jesus answering said to them: "Elias indeed shall come and restore all things. But I say to you that Elias is already come, and they knew him not but have done unto him whatsoever they had a mind. So also the son of man shall suffer from them. Then the disciples understood that he had spoken to them of John the Baptist."

At the first coming of Christ John preceded Him in the spirit of Elias. At the end of the world, when Jesus appears in power and majesty, His coming will be dreadful. Elias will then appear to save a remnant of the Jews and lead them back to Christ. The Jews expected Christ to come down from the Cross in great power as a sign of His office. They could not understand a suffering and humble Messias. When Christ hung on the Cross He called attention to a prophecy about Himself in His *Eli, Eli, Lamma Sabacthani*. Some of the bystanders said: "This man called Elias." And yet others said: "Let be, let us see whether Elias will come to deliver Him." How blind the human heart can be when it wants to be. John in prison sent two of his disciples to Jesus to ask Him: "Art Thou He that is to come, or look we for another?" Jesus made answer to them: "Go and relate to John what you have heard and seen. The blind see, the lame walk, the lepers are cleansed, the deaf hear, the dead rise again, the poor have the gospel preached to them. And blessed is he that is not scandalized in Me." Here Christ is sending His hearers back to Isaias, since all these signs pointed to the Redeemer.

Fear not, Zachary Note that when Zachary saw the angel

"he was troubled and fear fell upon him," before the angel said anything to him. Mary, when greeted by the angel with "Hail, full of grace . . ." was also troubled, but only because she did not understand the nature of such a salutation. To both the angel says: "Fear not." Zachary is then reassured because his prayer for a son has been answered; Mary, because she has found grace with God. To both is announced the birth of a son: to Zachary by ordinary generation, but Mary is told that her Son "shall be called the Son of the Most High."

Both Mary and Zachary demurred to these annunciations. Zachary doubted because of Elizabeth's advanced age. Mary did not doubt; she merely did not see the possibility of such an event because of her vow of virginity. This vow was unusual among the Hebrews, but it was legitimate and was accepted by God. She simply could not understand how the message could be from God, as it contradicted her vow.

Zachary was struck dumb until the birth of John, as a punishment. Gabriel said: "Because thou hast not believed my words . . ." To Mary the angel merely explained that Christ's generation was to be the direct creation of God, and that her vow and state of virginity were to be preserved.

There is a grave lesson for all in these parallels of Zachary's and Mary's responses. Zachary did not believe, although from the Scriptures he should have known that before God shortened the life-span of mankind to three score and ten, great age was no bar to conception. God could have released him from the fetters of age, as He had done for Abraham.

Mary's response was one of great prudence. St. Paul advises us to test all spirits to see if they be from God. Much misery can be caused when people run after wonders; they imagine that such are from God, when a simple precaution or two would show they contradict the known law of God. The devil has appeared in false guise to many a saint to tempt him to relax the works and vows he had undertaken for

The Joyful Mysteries

God. The devil also gets his work done cheaply by those who would attempt to discourage the good who wish to serve God, ridiculing them or telling them: "You can be good, but you do not have to be a fanatic."

He shall be filled with the Holy Ghost even from his mother's womb Mary brought about the fulfillment of this prophecy at the Visitation. This was the beginning of her function of bringing Jesus to us. John was one of the few who were freed from original sin before birth. The prophet Jeremias is supposed to be another so favored, because he was a figure of Jesus in his teachings, especially in his forgiveness of his enemies, and in his violent death at the hands of his own people. This is not the same as the great privilege of the Immaculate Conception of the Blessed Virgin who was never touched by original sin. These others were stained by original sin from conception, until they were cleansed of it sometime before their births.

The angel Gabriel was sent from God . . . to a virgin . . . and the virgin's name was Mary God was about to redeem the oldest promise He had made to the fallen human race. THE WOMAN who was to crush the serpent's head through her divine Son; THE WOMAN who would cooperate with God was here in this world. Man's long exile was about over. A means will be given to him to repair the damage which his sin had brought about through the malice of Satan. That means will be the atonement of Jesus Christ, God and man, of whom Lucifer had said: "I will not serve." Now, "how art thou fallen from heaven, O Lucifer, who didst rise in the morning! How art thou fallen to the earth, who did wound the nations" (Isaias 14:12). Jesus is about to come.

There remains only the obstacle of winning the free consent of a fifteen-year-old girl, a virgin by nature and grace. Unless God had revealed to His court the outcome of this embassy, all heaven must have awaited it with breathless awe. If the vast concourse of souls who lingered in the shades of Limbo were told, they must have hovered around this spot to see if their long centuries of exile were over. The moment for which the whole Hebrew nation was founded had arrived. For this Abraham had been called forth from Ur of the Chaldees to found a mighty nation. God had elected to make man free and could not destroy his freedom without degrading him to the animal level. The cow, the dog, and the lion can be said to have wills of a sort, but the wills they use are not their own. They blindly follow the pattern set for them by Him who made them. But it is not so with man. Through grace God solicits human wills to follow the good, and grace goes with man every second of his life. Grace can draw man to what God wills from him, but grace does not destroy his free will.

Hail, full of grace To Mary was given grace above that given to all men, because hers was the most difficult and exalted of all vocations. "Without Me you can do nothing," said Christ. We do not try to make Mary a goddess whose power is in her own right. She has her grace and power through God, the same as the rest of us, but in a far greater degree. But, although we need grace to do good, we can still turn aside from grace. St. Paul says: "We helping do exhort you, that you receive not the grace of God in vain." Mary corresponded to the graces she received. For that we honor her.

Thou shalt bring forth a Son, and thou shalt call His name, Jesus Mary did not consent to this decree at once. She did not turn away from grace, but she tested the Spirit "to see if it be from God." Does it occur to us that no one asked the consent of Jesus Christ to His Incarnation? Mary *was* asked, because this was the only way to make it possible for Jesus to come. This is her title to a share in the mystery of the redemption. She was "full of grace," and so did not think of refusing God whatever He asked; but clearly, she did hesitate at first, as we see in what follows immediately.

How can this be, because I know not man? In effect this was as much as saying: "How can I be the mother of Jesus, the Son of the Most High, when I am under vow not to be the mother of anyone?" Thus we know that Mary was free to refuse. We also know that she must have had a solemn vow of virginity, otherwise, her words would not have an intelligible meaning. If Mary had intended marriage with St. Joseph in the ordinary sense of the term, the interpretation which she must have put on the angel's words would have been that a son would be born to her in the ordinary course of events. This is what the angel's message conveyed to Zachary.

But since Mary had an understanding with St. Joseph that they were both to preserve virginity, she did not know how the angel could have his prediction fulfilled. She must have considered that if this messenger were really from God, he should know all these circumstances. All those who rush into what they think are revelations from God, would do well to pray to the Blessed Mother to get for them from God the prudence which she showed in this mystery.

The power of the Most High shall overshadow thee This resolves for Mary an apparent contradiction. Jesus will have no human father, but God Himself will create directly in her virginal womb the element of conception. The Blessed Virgin will then be a mother in a true sense, and she will preserve her virginity in a true sense.

Behold thy cousin Elizabeth: she also hath conceived a son in her old age Thus Mary received the urging of grace to go to the aid of her cousin, and so she cooperated with God again. Here began her work with God, a work that will not end until the final soul that is to be saved has safely reached heaven.

Be it done unto me according to thy word Jesus can now enter upon His mission. Mary hastened to do the will of God as soon as it became clear to her that the message of the archangel Gabriel was really His will. How often do we seek our own wills, even when it is clear to us that God has set a path for us to follow?

We must not neglect to thank the Blessed Mother for giving her consent to the coming of the Savior. What if she had refused? Many men of ill-will have tried to make it appear that she was forced into submission by God, and that her position is not that of a free agent. As a matter of fact, Mary did refuse until she was convinced that this was what God willed. Thus she followed the call of grace which, after all, is the highest sanctity. Lucifer was endowed with all graces; he was the greatest of all created intellects, and yet he could say: "I will not serve." Eve was "born" with an analogous "immaculate conception"; Adam had talents and graces without any pull of sensuality to drag him down; yet all these refused their graces.

With what terrible labors would man have had to struggle back to God without the Incarnation of Jesus Christ through Mary. God would have worked another plan, to be sure. But when? And how? Would it have brought us far below our present position, as we are below Adam and Eve in Paradise? Who can say? In His infinite knowledge God foreknew the outcome of the Annunciation. Across the centuries prophets had prepared man for this moment; but Mary's consent was still free and for that we must thank her without ceasing, and love her with a boundless love, second only to the love we have for Jesus Christ.

The Second Joyful Mystery:
The Visitation

In this mystery are unfolded the first effects of the coming redemption. In essence this mystery means that Mary did not climb upon a pedestal when she received such a signal honor, but went to help Elizabeth when it became known to her that her cousin needed help. Elizabeth was an old woman; how old we do not know, but obviously beyond normal childbearing age, and hence she was in some danger. Mary could have said to herself that since God had brought it about that Elizabeth was to have this son, He should see to it that nothing went wrong. That would have been presumption, because no one knew, then, what God had in store for Elizabeth. But grace works through nature, and in the nature of things Elizabeth should look for some difficulty. Mary knew this truth, which takes some of us many hard pains to learn. God does not drag wonders in from nowhere. When He answers a prayer, that answer comes in the working out of the day-to-day events of our lives—generally not as something totally outside all expectancy. When He does go outside expectancy that is a miracle, and miracles are only for the sake of something beyond. He who looks for miracles to pull him out of the difficulties he has created, invites Satan to come and work a cruel deception on him, to the consequent damage or loss of faith.

Mary's was an act of personal charity. God elevated it to a great public revelation. We have seen that John was to be filled with the Holy Spirit, even from his mother's womb. Mary's visit brought about the possibility of bringing Jesus to John. Note, however, that it was Mary who brought Jesus; that it was at the sound of Mary's voice that the unborn infant leapt for joy. Mary brought Jesus to John and she will bring Jesus to us. This story is from the Gospel of St. Luke.

And Mary rising up in those days, went into the hill country with haste into a city of Juda, and she entered into the house of Zachary and saluted Elizabeth.

And it came to pass that when Elizabeth heard the salutation of Mary, the infant leaped in her womb. And Elizabeth was filled with the Holy Ghost and she cried out with a loud voice and said:

Blessed art thou among women, and blessed is the fruit of thy womb.

And whence is this to me, that the mother of my Lord should come to me? And behold as soon as the voice of thy salutation sounded in my ears, the infant in my womb leaped for joy. And blessed art thou that hast believed, because these things shall be accomplished that were spoken to thee by the Lord.

And Mary said: my soul doth magnify the Lord and my spirit hath rejoiced in God, my Savior, because He hath regarded the humility of His handmaid: for behold from henceforth all generations shall call me blessed. Because He that is Mighty hath done great things to me; and holy is His name.

And His mercy is from generation unto generation to them that fear Him. He hath showed might in His arm; He hath scattered the proud in the conceit of their heart. He hath put down the mighty from their seat; and hath exalted the humble. He hath filled the hungry with good things and the rich He hath sent empty away. He hath received Israel His servant being mindful of His mercy: as He spoke to our fathers; to Abraham and his seed forever.

And Mary abode with her about three months; and she returned to her own house.

And Mary rising up . . . went into the hill country with haste When she received the 'sign' of the coming of John the Baptist Mary went to help her cousin Elizabeth. "With haste"—with no delays, deliberations, nor debates. Charity is for today. The poor and the oppressed cannot wait. "Who gives quickly, gives twice."

Today we do not fear the difficulties of a ninety-mile trip, especially in this country where everyone seems to be on wheels. But then Mary's journey had to be trudged on foot, or at the very best on some such animal as the lowly jackass, since the noble horse was only for the rich. No one would

The Joyful Mysteries

dream in those days of starting out alone. Arrangements had to be made to travel in a caravan, because robber-bands swept down from the hills on the unwary. When Christ told the parable of the Good Samaritan there was nothing strange in the thought of a wayfarer who "fell among robbers."

To go from Nazareth to Judea below Jerusalem, a wide swing was made across the Jordan River, so as to avoid going through Samaria which separated the two parts of the then existing Jewish nation. The Jews and the Samaritans were enemies, and generally travelers would not risk going through Samaria. Our Lord later went there, of course, as we read in the story of the Samaritan woman. The Samaritans were mostly Jews with a heavy overlay of eastern pagans who stayed behind from the Babylonian conquest, and corrupted the religious beliefs of this people.

When Elizabeth heard the salutation of Mary, the infant leaped in her womb and Elizabeth was filled with the Holy Ghost The angel had told Zachary that the infant would be filled with the Holy Ghost even from its mother's womb, and here it had come to pass. It must be carefully noted that Elizabeth received her inspiration and John his sanctification when Mary saluted Elizabeth. Mary, of course, did not bring all these things about, because that is the work of God. But she did bring Jesus, and Jesus used Mary's charity as the occasion of His action. This is more than pure coincidence. Jesus could have worked the purification of John from original sin from any place in the world, but He did not do it that way. He employed the good offices of His Blessed Mother, just as He wishes us to go to her and through her for favors from Him.

Blessed art thou amongst women This was a part of the salutation of the angel, and its use by Elizabeth was a direct inspiration of the Holy Ghost. Thus, we have the same person twice given a blessing direct from God. We, too, can do no less than to hold her "blessed."

. . . and blessed is the fruit of thy womb Elizabeth had no way of knowing that Our Blessed Mother was going to be the mother of Jesus. This was the inspiration of the Holy Ghost. Such a mother of such a Son was blessed above all others. Those who deny a blessing to the Mother, soon forget to bless the Son.

. . . that the mother of my Lord should come to me? Here Mary's most exalted title is used for the first time, under inspiration of the Holy Spirit. In the Scriptures the word "Lord" always means "God." The Jews could not utter the Holy Name of God lest they use it in vain. Only at four stated times during the year could the High Priest stand in the Holy of Holies, in the Temple, and pronounce the name of God, "Yaweh." The Name was so written in the Scriptures but it was read as "Adonai," or "Lord." There is no doubt about it. Mary was addressed as the "Mother of God."

And Mary said: *My soul doth magnify the Lord . . . to Abraham and his seed forever* This is the beautiful prophecy which brings to a climax the action of the Visitation. Not only has Mary visited Elizabeth, but here is a great public revelation that God has visited His people, and that Mary herself is blessed for her part in it. This prophecy came to fulfillment when John saw her crowned Queen of Heaven: "A WOMAN clothed with the sun, and the moon under her feet, and on her head a crown of twelve stars."

Have charity in all things because God works His providence through us. Jesus will save the world through the Blessed Sacrament, bringing His graces to all men. But in this sacrament He has no hands, no feet, no tongue. *Our* hands must be used to do His work. *Our* feet must carry his message from place to place, and *our* tongues must sing His praises. As Mary carried Jesus still helpless (humanly speaking) to John, so it must be our task to make His influence reach all men. God intended the poor to be helped, but we must do it for Him. He will not strike us dead if we fail Him. He will wait for our return, just as He waits for the return of all sinners. But if we fail God, the poor will suffer and all manner of ills will stalk the earth, as is happening today. The Reds make tremendous inroads into human society because there is so much injustice. Evil powers always try to turn men against God and persuade all to rebel against Him.

Often it is we who call ourselves "the good," who do the damage for the bad ones to exploit. Let each put his own house in order; do his charity as it may be found around him, and much of the evil in the world will disappear.

And Mary abode with her about three months These words do not mean that Mary went back home before St. John was born. St. Luke touches upon the matter with delicacy, and passes it over, but the Church celebrates the feast of the Visitation on July 2, the day of the circumcision of John the Baptist. We may be sure that Mary's charity was not half-hearted.

The Third Joyful Mystery:
The Birth of Our Lord at Bethlehem

This is the story of Christmas. The heart of this mystery is the great love that God bore for man, granting man peace and reconciliation with Himself if he will turn aside from his own ways and do the few little things that God asks. Man cannot pay God back in any sense of the word. Even when he tries to turn to God it is the grace of God that prompts him, helps him, and keeps him in the pathway. All that man can do of himself is to sin. Even to sin man still needs to use, or misuse, God's gifts. Of himself man has nothing.

Despite all this the great labor of the Incarnation was undertaken. Christ could have returned home to His Father a split second after the Incarnation, and thousands of worlds as sinful as Sodom could have been redeemed. The long years of toil and suffering leading up to the shameful death of the Cross were all endured to win back from us a little response for the great love of God for us.

Christmas is the greatest day in all human history. For thousands of years God led up to it, making the day of His coming more precise and definite as centuries unrolled, so that He even sent Gabriel to Daniel with an announcement of the time of His coming, over four hundred years before His birth.

When the Wise Men came looking for the new-born King it was well enough known to the priests and the elders that Christ was to be born in Bethlehem, and Herod was sure enough of the time to order the killing of all male children of two years and under. Such was man's first response to the coming of Christ to save him, and that resistance and rejection have continued until today.

Put the Wise Men into the Christmas story, for they are the symbols of the acceptance for redemption of those of us who are not of the House of Israel. That was the Christmas of the Gentiles.

An ancient tradition tells us that the Wise Men themselves experienced persecution for seeking out this new-born King of the Jews. Their relics have been venerated for centuries in Cologne, in Germany. We are told that none of them was ever permitted to return to his kingdom.

In the Gospel we have the story of the birth of Christ and the adoration of the shepherds (Luke: 2), and that of the Wise Men (Matt. 2).

And it came to pass that in those days there went forth a decree from Caesar Augustus, that the whole world should be enrolled. This enrolling was first made by Cyrinus, the governor of Syria. And all went to be enrolled, every one into his own city.

And Joseph also went up from Galilee, out of the city of

The Joyful Mysteries

Nazareth into Judea, to the city of David, which is called Bethlehem, because he was of the house and family of David.

To be enrolled with Mary, his espoused wife, who was with child. And it came to pass that when they were there, her days were accomplished, that she should be delivered.

And she brought forth her first-born son, and wrapped Him up in swaddling clothes, and laid Him in a manger: because there was no room for them in the inn.

And there were in the same country shepherds watching, and keeping their night watch over their flock.

And behold an angel of the Lord stood by them, and the brightness of God shone round about them; and they feared with a great fear. And the angel said to them: Fear not: for behold I bring you good tidings of great joy, that shall be to all the people;

for this day there is born to you a Savior, who is Christ the Lord, in the city of David. And this shall be a sign unto you: You shall find the infant wrapped in swaddling clothes and laid in a manger.

And suddenly there was with the angel a multitude of the heavenly army, praising God and saying:

Glory to God in the highest and on earth, peace to men of good will.

And it came to pass that after the angels departed from them into Heaven, the shepherds said one to another: Let us go over to Bethlehem, and let us see this word that is come to pass, which the Lord has showed to us. And they came with haste.

And they found Mary and Joseph and the Infant lying in the manger. And seeing they understood of the word that had been spoken to them concerning this child. And all that heard, wondered, and at those things that were told to them by the shepherds.

But Mary kept all these words, pondering them in her heart.

And the shepherds returned, glorifying and praising God

for all the things they had heard and seen, as it was told unto them (Luke 2).

When Jesus, therefore, was born in Bethlehem of Juda, in the days of King Herod, behold, there came wise men from the east to Jerusalem, saying:

Where is He that is born King of the Jews?

for we have seen His star in the east, and are come to adore Him. And King Herod hearing this was troubled, and all Jerusalem with him.

And assembling together all the chief priests and the scribes of the people, he inquired of them where Christ should be born.

But they told him: In Bethlehem of Juda, for so it is written by the prophet: And thou Bethlehem the land of Juda art not the least among the princes of Juda: for out of thee shall come forth the captain that shall rule my people Israel.

Then Herod, privately calling the wise men, learned diligently of them the time of the star which appeared to them: and sending them into Bethlehem said: Go, and diligently inquire after the child, and when you have found Him, bring the word again, that I also may come and adore Him. Who, having heard the king, went their way: and behold the star which they had seen in the east went before them, until it came and stood over where the Child was. And seeing the star they rejoiced with exceeding great joy.

And entering into the house, they found the Child with Mary, His mother, and falling down they adored Him: and opening their treasures they offered Him gifts; gold, frankincense, and myrrh.

and having received an answer in sleep that they should not return to Herod, they went back another way into their country.

And after they were departed, behold an angel of the Lord appeared in sleep to Joseph saying: Arise and take the Child and His mother and fly into Egypt: and be there until I shall tell thee. For it will come to pass that Herod will seek the Child to destroy Him.

The Joyful Mysteries

Who arose, and took the Child and His mother by night, and retired into Egypt: and he was there until the death of Herod. That it might be fulfilled which the Lord spoke by the prophet saying: Out of Egypt have I called My Son.

Then Herod perceiving that he was deluded by the Wise Men was exceeding angry: and sending, killed all the menchildren that were in Bethlehem, and in all the borders thereof, from two years old and under according to the time which he had diligently inquired of the Wise Men. Then was fulfilled that which was spoken by Jeremias the prophet:

A voice in Rama was heard, lamentation and great mourning: Rachel bewailing her children, and would not be comforted, because they are not (Matt. 2:1-48).

... there went forth a decree from Caesar Augustus that the whole world should be enrolled Rome had recently overcome her internal enemies. Her power had spread to England, to Germany, across all Egypt, and as far as Arabia. It was now time to consolidate those gains. The world was at peace so the confusion attending moving numbers of people back to their native villages could be undertaken. The Emperor now needed an accounting of his far-flung holdings. Some of the census sheets still exist from many of these widespread censuses which took place each fourteen years after this, the first census.

This enrolling was first made by Cyrinus Unbelievers had long claimed that Cyrinus, or in Latin, Quirinus, was governor of Syria at an earlier date and that St. Luke did not know the facts. But it is now certain that this official served two terms of office; one as civil and one as military governor. In 1899, a construction crew, levelling a right-of-way for an electric interurban line, uncovered a boundary stone bearing his name and office with the date, which was at the time of the Augustan census.

And all went to be enrolled, every one to his own city Documents have been uncovered in Egypt relating to the Roman census prove that it was necessary for families that had been scattered abroad to return to the city of their birth to be counted. Amongst the Jews especially this was necessary as they all counted themselves as stemming from one of the twelve tribes. Further, in the case of those who like Mary and Joseph counted their descent from David, the King, it was wise on the part of the Roman Emperor to know those who might form the rallying point to set up a King of the Jews. Thus Providence brought back from far off Galilee the mother-to-be of Jesus and caused her to be sent to Bethlehem, the City of David for the birth of the Savior who was to be born there according to the prophecies.

Before we go further we remind the reader that the calendar we use was set up about the sixth century of our era. Before that the years were counted locally by dynasties, or by the year of the Olympiad, or as in Rome, from the founding of the city. The monk who devised our calendar wanted to make it for all the world as it has become, and he wanted it to begin from the birth of our Lord. However, he made a mistake of a few years in his calculations and we now know that we must put Christ's birth a few years earlier than the calendar indicates. Our information of documentary sources is better than in much earlier ages. The first census of Caesar Augustus was made about the year 5 B.C., as our calendar goes. Delays in getting the actual work of enumeration around to a distant province in Palestine were many, and Christ was already born when the numerators got to Bethlehem. Herod the Great died about 4 B.C. Some early Christian writers said they had actually seen the name of Jesus Christ on a census sheet.

And she brought forth her first-born son . . . and laid Him in a manger because there was no room for them in the inn
Thus the Son of God made man came into this world to save us from our sins. He was laid in a manger for a crib in one

of the half-house, half-caves that dot the hillsides near Bethlehem. These were used as shelters for animals. So Christ emptied Himself for us of all wealth and honor. The shepherds had no hesitancy in approaching Christ born in a stable because David had been a shepherd and it was to them a natural place to seek shelter. They could approach this infant without shame for their own poverty. Later the Wise Men would also draw near without hesitancy, because they were not blinded by externals and could see the truth behind this poverty. Both sorts are welcome to Christ; only the shallow are repelled by everything but outward display. Both these types are "the poor in spirit."

. . . for this day there is born to you a Savior, who is Christ the Lord This was the day into which all history leads; out of which all history flows. The Old Testament has as the reason for its existence to point out the Savior who is now in the world. The shepherds did not doubt; they had been waiting for this, as had all the world. It was the great day of freedom. Man must still labor and suffer, since Christ did not will to restore him to his original condition in bodily comfort; but from this day forward man's sufferings will be tinged with mercy. Think back to the condition of the world at the time of Christ. In the great Roman Empire we see all the abuses we look upon with such horror in the Communist Empire. What we see in Communism with such loathing today was the normal way of acting in the ancient world. These are the Empires we have been taught to call "great." Daniel saw them all come in turn, and saw them disappear finally, before the sway of the rule of Christ. Do we want to get rid of Communism? Restore Christ and Communism must disappear. It is as easy as that. As far as Christ is kept from His world so far must Communism prevail. Do we want peace? Peace is to men of good will. Do we want to destroy Communism? Simply welcome the Infant Christ. "There was no room for them in the inn." In modern speech what

is this but the modern conspiracy against infant life? Herod was not the only one who is guilty of the slaughter of the innocents. The corner drug store may have more death to deal out to infants than all of Herod's soldiery; the so-called parenthood clinics fill the city sewers with the unborn and unbaptized.

Glory to God in the highest and on earth, peace to men of good will Non-Catholics use a text which reads: "Peace on earth, good will to men." Of course, it is true that God always has good will towards men, but He enacts His providence through the wills of men. Unless men show their good wills and cooperate with God there can be no peace on this earth.

And they found Mary and Joseph and the Infant lying in the manger When we go to seek Jesus we shall always find Him with Mary and through Mary. The neglected saint is St. Joseph. Those who call on him in their necessities are not sent away with empty hands, for he too, was very close to Jesus and he had the difficult task of protecting Jesus and Mary from danger and distress. The Little Sisters of the Poor who have made of St. Joseph a special provider are never disappointed. The position of St. Joseph shows us, too, that God chooses human instruments for His work as He could have protected Christ without the aid of St. Joseph.

But Mary kept all these words, pondering them in her heart Jesus prayed during His whole life upon earth, and Mary meditated the words of salvation she heard. If only we ponder well the words of the Christmas story and let them have their full effect it will soon make a tremendous impact upon us.

. . . there came Wise Men from the East We know little more about who these mysterious visitors were than that they

The Joyful Mysteries

came to adore a king from a country not their own. Salvation was to have come first from the Jews, but God did not leave His people to work out the years in darkness. This was the Epiphany or the Christmas of the Gentiles. The Magi, or Wise Men, did not know where this king was to be born, as they had to learn that from the Jews in Herod's city of Jerusalem. The channel of redemption was through the chosen people until they repudiated their destiny as they stood before Pilate. This was the first repudiation. Note how quickly the chief priests and the Scribes could tell the Magi where Christ was to be found. It was no surprise to them that men should come seeking the Messias, since the revelation made to Daniel by Gabriel had run its term. The whole world was waiting the Savior. But they did not go out to adore Him.

. . . they found the Child with Mary, His mother . . . and they offered Him gifts; gold, frankincense, and myrrh They, too, found the Child as the shepherds had done—with His Mother, and so shall we find Him. The gifts were gold because they recognized Him as King; frankincense, for in Him they saw God. The myrrh was a bitter drug used in enbalming; also to deaden pain as we shall see when it is offered again to Christ as He hangs on the Cross. But on the Cross the King and the God received nothing but ridicule and abuse. The prophet Isaias saw in vision the scene of the Magi, but he revealed directly only the gold and the myrrh. The frankincense he veiled under the expression "praise to the Lord."

Herod . . . killed all the men-children that were in Bethlehem . . . from two years old and under Herod, called "the Great" because of one of those strange twists of human nature that has given the name of "great" to so many mass murderers was the last of the kings of the Jews. He knew well enough that the prophecies had predicted that when this new Son of David was born the scepter was to pass to Him. As many have done before and after that time he thought that he could set aside the eternal decrees of God by human action. If men will keep their faith in God all that any tryant can do to them is to send them to heaven to an eternal reward. Tyrants must die themselves and if we cannot convert them it is their fault. If we do not even try to convert them we may have some accounting to make to God for that. Keep free from hatreds; we have souls we must save through Christian charity. For others who will not listen, "it is a terrible thing to fall into the hands of the living God."

The Fourth Joyful Mystery:
The Presentation in the Temple

Now Jesus and Mary, His Mother, conform themselves to the precepts of the Law of Moses. Jesus as the Redeemer of the world and as the Lord of the Temple, surely had no need to be redeemed Himself by the payment of two turtle doves, the redemption fee of the poor. Mary, as the Virgin Most Pure, was not in need of purification. But the law was there, and they did not act as many others have done when they judged themselves quite good; they did not hold back and explain that such things are for others—not for them. That is the great lesson of this mystery: there are duties that must be performed faithfully, even though we may feel in our hearts that we have no need to conform.

Too many people today are trying to set up conditions of exemption for themselves, and when enough do this the peace of the world is upset. Really bad people could not do much damage in this world by themselves. They must be aided and abetted by the "good" people, who suffer the bad to prosper so they can have a few privileges they are "too good" to reach out for on their own initiative.

Traffic laws are good for society, but how many are there who will not boast of their ability to "fix a ticket"? Fasting and abstinence are, as all will admit, salutary practices for curbing the very human tendency to let the physical override the spiritual, but some of us believe we do not need such discipline because we can be lax and still be "all right." These are, perhaps, the lesser evils that are permitted in the name of self-dispensation from obligations that bind the generality of men. We need only look about us and read the daily papers to see how serious obligations are cast aside as being for others.

We draw the story of this mystery from the Gospel of St. Luke.

And after the days of her purification according to the law of Moses were accomplished, they carried Him to Jerusalem, to present Him to the Lord: as it is written in the Law of the Lord: Every male opening the womb shall be called holy to the Lord: and to offer sacrifice, according as it is written in the law of the Lord, a pair of turtle doves or two young pigeons.

And behold there was a man in Jerusalem, named Simeon, and this man was just and devout, waiting for the consolation of Israel, and the Holy Ghost was in Him.

And he had received an answer from the Holy Ghost, that he should not see death before he had seen the Christ of the Lord, and he was come by the Spirit into the Temple. And when His parents brought in the Child Jesus, to do for Him according to the custom of the Law, he also took Him into his arms and blessed God and said:

Now dost thou dismiss Thy servant, O Lord, according to Thy word, in peace, because mine eyes have seen Thy salvation which Thou hast prepared before the face of all peoples.

A light to the revelation of the Gentiles and the glory of Thy people Israel.

And His father and mother were wondering at those things which were spoken concerning Him.

And Simeon blessed them and said to Mary, His mother: Behold, this child is set for the fall and for the resurrection of many in Israel and for a sign which shall be contradicted.

And thy own soul a sword shall pierce, that out of many hearts thoughts shall be revealed.

And there was one Anna, a prophetess, the daughter of Phanuel of the tribe of Aser and she was far advanced in years, and had lived with her husband seven years from her virginity, and she was a widow until four score and four years; who departed not from the Temple by fasting and prayers serving night and day. Now she at the same hour coming in, confessed to the Lord, and spoke of Him to all that looked for the redemption of Israel.

And after they had performed all things according to the law of the Lord, they returned into Galilee, to their city of Nazareth.

And the child grew and waxed strong; full of wisdom and the grace of God was in Him.

After the days of her purification . . . they carried Him to Jerusalem to present Him to the Lord After the birth of a child, under the law of Moses, the mother was "unclean" ceremonially and had to be released from the restrictions this imposed upon her. At the same time, if the child was her first-born he had to be presented for redemption. This had all been set forth in great detail in Leviticus, just as God gave it to Moses. "If a woman . . . shall bear a man-child, she shall be unclean for seven days . . . and on the eighth day the infant shall be circumcised, but she shall remain three and thirty days in the blood of her purification. She shall touch no holy thing, neither shall she enter into the sanctuary until the days of her purification be fulfilled." We could well ask why the Blessed Mother was not exempted from this law, but we know that her lot was not one of exemption or dispensation.

Our Lord was to be presented to the Temple, and since

The Joyful Mysteries

He was also the first-born He had to be redeemed. Moses wrote in Exodus: " . . . all that is first brought forth of thy cattle; whatsoever thou shalt have of the male sex, thou shalt consecrate to the Lord. The first-born of an ass thou shalt exchange for a sheep. . . . And every first-born of men thou shalt redeem with a price.

. . . a pair of turtle doves or two young pigeons The customary offering was "a lamb of a year old for a holocaust, and a young pigeon or a turtledove for sin," delivered to the priest. But the Holy Family was poor and was entitled to a further provision made by Moses: "And if her hand find not sufficiency, and she shall not be able to offer a lamb, she shall take two turtledoves, or two young pigeons, one for a holocaust, and another for sin and the priest shall pray for her and she shall be cleansed."

And behold, there was a man in Jerusalem named Simeon . . . The great consolation that we all have is that there are among us, all in obscurity, good people, holy people by whom spiritual force is generated to keep the world in its tracks. We see, too often, the evil that intrudes itself upon us but we should take heart that there are good persons in this world, too. Many of them are living lives of heroic charity under most trying circumstances.

Some time back when I had a more active connection with the Legion of Mary I used to call upon harried pastors as I went around on my own business. Before they realized that this was not to be merely another parish society founded to dwindle and to die, they would be horrified at the thought of another project. "Where could I get such a group?" they asked me. My formula was about the same wherever I went. I would ask the priest if he knew a few quiet young girls who never sold a raffle ticket, nor ran a booth at a bazaar, but who did show up frequently at six o'clock Mass; or a few men who were not otherwise known to parish affairs—

there was his Legion of Mary group. When the work started and succeeded it was plain *who* was behind it. Simeon was one such as these. "The Holy Ghost was in him." How long he had come patiently to the Temple for a glimpse of the Savior we do not know; but having seen Him he was willing to yield up his life to God.

And thine own soul a sword shall pierce The Presentation is considered one of the Seven Joys and also one of the Seven Sorrows of Our Blessed Mother. There *was* joy, for she could offer Jesus to His heavenly Father as a sacrifice, as He will do later Himself on Calvary. It was a joy to be able to look ahead to the salvation of mankind. But Mary's joys were never separated from her sorrows, because she know at what terrible a price that redemption would be effected. If only thoughts would come from many hearts, Mary would count the pain of that sword as little indeed.

And there was one Anna, a prophetess . . . Such is the mercy of God to those that love Him. Night and day Anna had served the Temple, as the Blessed Virgin had done during the time of her service. There was a sort of Temple corps of women who sewed and cleaned up about the Temple, and this must have been a formidable task with thousands upon thousands of visitors coming and going all day long. Most likely Anna knew the Blessed Virgin from the time she had been there.

At last God rewarded Anna, as well as Simeon, with the consolation of seeing the Savior. This should bolster up our patience; sometimes we have to wait and wait, and then we get impatient at what seems to us to be God's delays. God, however, had set the time for the coming of the Savior, and Anna and Simeon had their reward in due course. When it arrived the long wait was no longer long, but during the time of their expectancy it must have seemed stretched out, indeed.

The fourth Joyful Mystery can be extended as far as the Massacre of the Innocents, if we wish to include this part of the divine infancy; or we can go on into the Flight into Egypt. The Presentation came before the visit of the Magi in point of time, but this event fits in so well with the birth of Christ that it is better treated with the third Joyful Mystery.

The Fifth Joyful Mystery:
The Finding of The Child Jesus in The Temple

This is essentially a recountal of the ever-recurring crisis that arises when the claims of man clash with those of God. This world belongs to God, and His will must prevail. Man has put the peace of the world in jeopardy because he seeks his own way in matters beyond him. The great religious revolt of the sixteenth century attempted to give man the "right" to be judge of his relations with God. This was to be a world with "man the measure" of what he should do or believe. The conditions in which we find ourselves are ample proof that man cannot run the world without God. The League of Nations banished God and could not keep the peace. Now the U.N. has yielded to the pressure of the godless and we are daily on the verge of war because of the workings of an exclusively man-made machinery of peace. Peace can be had only by "men of good will" but there is no good will in man apart from God.

The Gospel story is again from St. Luke.

And His parents went every year to Jerusalem at the solemn day of the Pasch.
And when He was twelve years old, they going up unto Jerusalem, according to the custom of the feast, and having fulfilled the days, when they returned the child Jesus remained in Jerusalem; and His parents knew it not. And thinking that He was in the company, they came a day's

journey, and sought Him amongst their kinsfolk and acquaintance.

And not finding Him they returned into Jerusalem seeking Him.

And it came to pass that, after three days they found Him in the Temple, sitting in the midst of the doctors, hearing them and asking them questions. And all that heard were astonished at His wisdom and His answers, and seeing Him they wondered.

And His mother said to Him: Son, why hast Thou done so to us? Behold, Thy father and I have sought Thee sorrowing.

And He said to them: How is it that you sought Me? Did you not know that I must be about My Father's business?

And they understood not the word that He spoke unto them. And He went down with them to Nazareth, and was subject to them. And His mother kept all these words in her heart. And Jesus advanced in wisdom and age with God and men.

And when He was twelve years old . . . At the age of twelve Jesus reached spiritual maturity whereby He acquired some rights, and had to perform certain duties under the Jewish law. Since the age of physical maturity is earlier in the Orient than among us, a twelve-year old had the right to marry and set up his own household. Accordingly, Jesus was within His rights as a human being, apart from those He had as God. In all that He did, He was careful to conform to the law and custom of His day. He did not come to destroy the Law but to fulfill it, as He said to His enemies.

And thinking He was in the company . . . This was a very natural mistake to make, as the men and women walked along in the caravans in separate groups, for reasons of protection, as well as of sanitation and modesty. Sometimes the children went along with the women and sometimes they

The Joyful Mysteries 167

were with the men. Ordinarily the pilgrims left Jerusalem about noon and went on until sundown when they pitched camp for the night. When family groups began to reassemble Mary and Joseph learned for the first time that Jesus had been with neither. It is hardly possible that Mary and Joseph could have gone back to Jerusalem that same night, alone. It was dangerous enough to go back the next day, but they may have had the company of others going towards Jerusalem. This would put them back into Jerusalem during the afternoon of the second day, or even that night. The next day when they started out early to seek Jesus it is likely they would go to the Temple first, as He would scarcely want to be any other place in the city. This would be the third day.

The cause of the mother's grief was not so much the strain of searching for Him as the fear of the possible danger Jesus stood in. Mary knew He would die at the hands of His own people, and now that He was of legal age it could be that this was the time.

Jesus may have dropped a hint to His Mother and His foster-father, but He intended this to be a lesson for us as well. Mary was always to act the counterfoil, when Jesus taught His followers the difference between human and divine love. At the marriage at Cana there was an implied demurrer. "What is this to Me and to thee?" Then Jesus performed the miracle, bringing out the distinction between Mary as His Mother in the family sense, and Mary as Mediatrix.

Then there was the time when the woman in the crowd raised her voice and cried: "Blessed is the womb that bore Thee and the breasts that nursed Thee." Jesus answered on that occasion: "Yea, but rather blessed is he that hears the word of God and keeps it." In other words, it is true that Mary *is* blessed, but it is true more because she obeyed the will of God than because she bore Him and nursed Him. Again when the Master was told: "Thy mother and thy brethren await Thee," He replied: "Who are my mother and my brethren?" Then indicating His disciples He continued, "Behold My mother and My brethren." These were part of Mary's trials. All these occurrences do not prove that the Son does not love her; rather they prove that He loved His Mother very much, and needed to have the one He loved most serve as His example that spiritual love must always prevail over natural love.

St. Francis brought out this same idea very forcefully in the rule of his first Order, where he says that if a mother should love her offspring so much out of earthly love, that brothers in Christ ought to love each other so much the more out of spiritual love.

. . . they found Him in the Temple, sitting amidst the doctors, hearing them and asking them questions Jesus spoke, no doubt, about the coming of the Messias. The leaders of the people should have known that He was in the world. The happenings at Bethlehem made known through the Magi, had focused attention on the King of the Jews who was to come. The time set in the prophecies had run out twelve years before. It was a great mercy for Jesus to open the eyes of the priests and leaders of the people to the events that were about to take place in Palestine. This is a lesson for us: that we must expect disappointment and setbacks while the work of God is being done, but we can be sure that the outcome will be success if we persevere. The temporary pain and sufferings are nothing compared to the end sought, just as the anxiety and sufferings of Mary and Joseph were nothing compared to the work the Lord had set in motion. On the part of Jesus there was sorrow in His Sacred Heart at the sorrow He had to bring to the two persons He loved most in this world. Nothing but His Father's business, which was of the greatest importance, could have made Him bring them any sorrow.

We can picture Jesus calling for a scroll of the Law or of the Prophets and reading therefrom some passage He want-

The Joyful Mysteries

ed to comment upon. In the Gospels we see Him doing this during His public life more than once. This was not so unusual, but in one so young it must have been startling. Was Jesus calling attention to Himself that later He would be remembered by Joseph of Arimathea or Nicodemus? Was He talking to Gamaliel, the teacher of St. Paul, or was He trying to win over an Annas or Caiphas? Perhaps here, Jesus provided Himself with the new rock sepulchre for His burial so that the truth of His Resurrection would be more easily proved.

. . . did you not know that I must be about My Father's business? This is the answer to all the complaints we make to Jesus. The work of God must come first. This is the thing that will bring peace to the world. We may suffer, but all our sufferings will be turned into joy if we do not spend our lives resisting God. We must always realize that Jesus is not lost to us when He is hidden, and that sorrows are not for long if carried with willingness, or at least with resignation.

And they understood not the word that He spoke unto them Mary was not given a full revelation of all that was in store for her. She lived by faith. There would have been no merit for her if she had been told all that was to happen to her at the outset: that she had to gather as she went along. The lessons of God were not lost upon her, because the sacred writer frequently tells us that Mary pondered what she had heard or had seen "in her heart."

And he went down with them and came to Nazareth and was subject to them The rule was that if a young man elected he could achieve adulthood at the age of twelve. If he decided to remain at home with his parents he again became subjct to them, as Jesus did, and the next age of independence was thirty. This is the reason that Jesus did not begin His public work until He was thirty.

And Jesus advanced in wisdom and age with God and man
As God, Jesus possessed all knowledge. As man He did not immediately give evidence of His knowledge but allowed Himself to go through stages of unfoldment, so that one could say that he "grew" as the rest of us.

CHAPTER 10

The Sorrowful Mysteries

THE period covered by the sorrowful mysteries extended only from late Thursday evening until three o'clock Friday afternoon, when Christ died on the Cross. In these mysteries the Blessed Virgin has withdrawn entirely from the scene, though she must have followed Him with her prayers. Christ must tread the winepress alone. Many have speculated on where Mary was during the agony and the scourging. We know she was under the Cross on Calvary, there to become the Mother of the human race. That had always seemed enough for me.

The Rosary has developed in utter silence of all that happened to Christ from the time the Holy Family returned from Jerusalem, until Christ enters into His agony in Gethsemane. Many methods of saying the Rosary have attempted to supply this apparent lack and there is the "read" Rosary of 150 mysteries as we noted above, and there is a Camaldolese Rosary of the Lord of 33 beads in which His whole public life is covered. It is interesting that these latter beads reverse the order of the vocal prayers; saying the Hail Mary on the large beads and the Our Father on the small ones. The Rosary is perhaps, better as it stands. The sorrowful mysteries center about Jesus Christ in all the essential acts of the redemption itself. It has a singleness of purpose that gives it power.

The First Sorrowful Mystery:
The Agony in The Garden

The essence of this mystery is the working out of God's will in the face of the bitterest trial that ever beset a member of the human race. We who believe in the divinity of Christ are prone to be so led by the thought of His being God that we overlook the fact that He was as real a man as any of us. To redeem us Christ had to suffer for us, and need we be surprised to pick up here the evidence of the depth of that suffering? The enemies of Christ have pretended to see in His actions in Gethsemane signs of cowardice and a desire to turn away from the Passion. Nothing could be further from the truth.

We know that He asked the Father to remove some great trial, if it were the will of God; but what was that trial? Some of the Fathers say that He wanted to be spared the great ordeal of the betrayal of Judas, one of the chosen twelve. My thoughts on the Passion have led me to believe that this was also His sight of the malice of all the sins that all men had committed and were to commit, until the last sinner would be surprised in his sin by the splitting of the skies at the crack of doom. In a real way the malice of these sins was to come close to the innocent shoulders of Christ as He paid for them for us. This may well have caused the death of any other but Christ who was sustained by His divine power. A short while ago I read that a bishop in China died of a broken heart because of the horrible charges laid to his name by the Reds. The sheer horror of being so accused caused the poor man to fall down dead as he was led in disgrace through the streets of his city.

The slightest act of Jesus Christ would have redeemed the world and a thousand other worlds more sinful than ours. He always knew the kind of death He was to die; in fact, being without sin, death had no power over Him until He chose to allow death to have its way with Him. Three times on the

The Sorrowful Mysteries

way down to Jerusalem Christ predicted His death and resurrection. "From that time Jesus began to show His disciples that He must go to Jerusalem and suffer many things from the ancients and scribes and chief priests, and be put to death, and the third day rise again" (Matt. 16:21). A little later He repeated: "The Son of man will be betrayed into the hands of men, and they shall kill Him. And after that He is killed, He shall rise again the third day. But they understood not the word and they were afraid to ask Him" (Mark 9:30). Shortly before He was anointed by Mary Magdalen, as He said "for burial," He again said: "Behold we go up to Jerusalem, and the Son of man shall be betrayed to the chief priests and the scribes and they shall condemn Him to death, and shall deliver Him to the Gentiles to be mocked and scourged and crucified, and the third day He shall rise again" (Matt. 20:19-20).

Jesus had just come from the supper room where He had instituted the Blessed Sacrament. There He gave us Himself as a memorial to endure until the end of time. He looked forward from the Last Supper to the Cross, to the Mass, binding all into a unity. At the Last Supper He gave us His body —not only His body, but a body *to be delivered,* to be broken. He left not only His blood, but His blood *shed for us*. The sufferings of His passion were before Him at the Last Supper as much as they were in the Garden. His last discourse is full of forebodings of the passion.

That Christ would be internally tempted to turn His back to the chalice He had just consecrated as the "chalice of My Blood of the New and Eternal Testament," is unthinkable. That He should be filled with loathing at the vision of sin approaching Him as it never before nor again can ever do, is fairly easy to appreciate.

To make the gospel story of the agony complete it needs to be gleaned from all the gospels. We shall not separate for quotations the contributions of each version of the gospel.

When Jesus had said these things, He went forth with His disciples over the brook Cedron into a country place which is called Gethsemane. And He said to His disciples: sit you here till I go yonder and pray. And He taketh Peter and James and John with Him. And He began to fear and be heavy. Then He saith to them: My soul is sorrowful even until death; stay you here and watch with Me.

And He withdrew away from them a stone's throw, (and) He fell upon His face praying and saying: Abba, Father, all things are possible to Thee: remove this chalice from Me; but not what I will but what Thou wilt. And He cometh and findeth them sleeping. And He saith to Peter: Simon, sleepest thou? Couldst thou not watch one hour with Me? Watch ye, and pray that you enter not into temptation. The spirit is willing but the flesh is weak.

Again the second time He went and prayed saying: My Father, if this chalice may not pass away, but I must drink it; Thy will be done. And He cometh and findeth them sleeping for their eyes were heavy.

And leaving them, He went again and He prayed the third time, saying the selfsame word. And there appeared to Him an angel from heaven, strengthening Him. And being in agony He prayed the longer. And His sweat became as drops of blood, trickling down upon the ground. And when He rose up from prayer, and was come to His disciples, He found them sleeping.

And He saith to them: sleep now and take your rest; behold the hour is at hand when the Son of man shall be betrayed into the hands of sinners. Rise, let us go; behold he is at hand who will betray Me.

And as He spoke, behold Judas, one of the twelve came and with him a great multitude with swords and clubs, sent from the chief priests and the ancients of the people.

And he that betrayed Him had given them a sign saying: Whomsoever I shall kiss, that is He; hold Him fast. And forthwith coming to Jesus, he said, Hail Rabbi, and he kissed

Him. And Jesus said to Him: Friend, whereto art thou come; Judas, dost thou betray the Son of man with a kiss?

Jesus, therefore, knowing all things that should come upon Him, went forth and said to them: Whom seek ye? They answered Him: Jesus of Nazareth. Jesus therefore said to them: I am He.

As soon, therefore, as He said to them: I am He, they went backward, and fell to the ground. Again therefore He asked them: Whom seek ye? And they said: Jesus of Nazareth. Jesus answered: I have told you that I am He. If, therefore, you seek Me, let these go their way.

That it might be fulfilled which He said: Of these whom Thou hast given Me, I have not lost anyone.

Then they came up and laid hands on Jesus and held Him.

Then Simon Peter, having a sword, drew it and struck the servant of the High Priest and cut off his ear. And the name of the servant was Malchus. Jesus therefore said to Peter: put up thy sword into its scabbard, for all that take the sword shall perish with the sword. Thinketh thou that I cannot ask My Father and He will give me presently more than twelve legions of angels? The chalice which My Father hath given Me, shall I not drink it? How then shall the Scriptures be fulfilled that so it must be done?

And Jesus said to the chief priests and magistrates of the Temple and the ancients that were come unto Him; Are ye come out, as it were against a thief, with swords and clubs? When I was daily with you in the Temple, you did not stretch forth your hands against Me; but this is your hour and the power of darkness. Now all this was done that the Scriptures of the prophets might be fulfilled.

Then His disciples leaving Him all fled away.

Jesus went over the brook Cedron This brook runs through the Valley of Josaphat at the base of the Mount of Olives. On the side of the mount, or hill, was a garden called Gethsemane, the Garden of Olives. Under the deep shade of the olive trees Christ went into His agony, and in a rocky cave deeper in the shadows He underwent the bitterest part of His agony. Christ ascended into heaven from the top of this mount—Olivet. It is to this spot that He will come again as the judge of the living and the dead at the end of time. When Jesus disappeared from sight the angel said: "This Jesus Christ whom you saw ascending will come again in glory." The Prophet Joel says: "Let them arise, and let the nations come up into the valley of Josaphat: for there I will sit to judge all nations round about." There is something very fitting in the circumstance that the great victory of Christ will come at the very place where He suffered His greatest trial. There He paid for our sins; there He shall judge our sins.

And He said to His disciples, sit you here till I go yonder and pray. And He taketh Peter, James, and John with Him Jesus was about to enter into His Passion, in which His enemies were finally to prevail over Him. So He left His disciples behind Him, lest they be overcome by scandal seeing Him stripped of the strength He had always had. Three were close to Him. Peter bore the primacy. After Christ left this world Peter wore the leaden cloak of authority. James and John were the sons of Zebedee, the "sons of thunder," as Jesus had named them when they would have called fire down from heaven. John was the Beloved; James was his brother. The three of them had been witnesses to the Transfiguration, and the memory of that glory must still have been with them. The Transfiguration was their secret to be held until "the Son of man be risen from the dead." They should have been most able to withstand the shock of seeing Christ in His troubled spirit, and afterward in the hands of His enemies. They felt no shock, it is true, but only because they promptly fell asleep.

And He began to fear and be heavy When one first encounters the story of the agony in the Garden he wonders

The Sorrowful Mysteries

and is upset when he sees the word "fear" applied to Christ. Later should he find himself lying out at dawn on a shell-swept hill watching the second hand on his luminous dialed wrist watch on its final sweep to the "H" hour, it is much plainer what sort of "fear" this might have been. The "soul is sorrowful" at the thought that this is the time for separation of soul and body. It is a very deep sadness, and arms and legs become heavy as lead. If there is panic and cowardice there is no heaviness of the limbs. Cowards just pick up and run.

The man who does not know what he is getting into on his first trip into an advanced area feels that he is off to the "great adventure," but he who goes back a second and third time to the same experience has a kind of foreknowledge of what is ahead. Christ had a very clear foreknowledge of what was in store for Him, and since He was human as the rest of us in all things except sin, with His permission the feeling of oncoming death had sway. Christ could not have His body and soul separated against His will, so there can never be question of personal cowardice raised, as was done by Calvin and others. One writer even went so far as to compare Christ's actions in His agony with the pre-death discourse of Socrates, and then placed the courage of Socrates above that of Christ. As death approached, to be human in all things Christ permitted the sorrow of death to come with even pace.

Christ was no automaton that went through the motions of suffering without feeling, and then bade us to take example from such false actions. When He suffered he felt the pains as much, and more than any of the rest of us, because of the perfection of His physical make-up. This is where we find our example and our courage. Often we are not sure that our reactions to suffering are free from blame; but when we see these same reactions in Christ we can take full confidence that they flow from the very core of human nature. If Christ is said to fear and be heavy, we may be sure that if we feel the same way we are not thereby degraded, as if we had yielded to cowardice. If Christ felt fear we may conclude it was "built into" human nature in such a way as to be antecedent to an act of will. Note that when Christ felt this repugnance His will did not waver; it remained fast attached to the will of His heavenly Father.

If Christ had refused to let nature have its way we could learn nothing from Him. Man cannot learn from the ways of God, "for My thoughts are not your thoughts; nor your ways My Ways, saith the Lord" (Isa. 55:8). That is why Christ became man, so that from what He did we could have an example to follow without hesitation. Men in danger are very suspicious of those who seem utterly free of any signs of feeling the impact of the same situation. I once knew a man who was walking along with the rest of us in battle while machine gun bullets were kicking up dust all around us. He was quite oblivious of his position, and walked along casually smoking a cigar. Finally he remarked: "Look at the dust those field mice are raising." You may be sure he was told what was going on, and the news upset him, as it should have done. A bullet that has hit the ground can be turned into a "dum-dum" and can inflict terrible damage on anything it hits. A person who tries to train himself into a rigid stoicism which will elevate him above human reactions, is in grave danger of cracking up.

The moral test comes at the next step. No physical reaction has any moral weight until the will ratifies it. We may feel the pull of the nervous system but the will can still say, "no."

Abba, Father, all things are possible to Thee: remove this chalice from me; but not what I will but what Thou wilt Jesus saw all the sins of all men heaped upon Him in some way. St. Paul said that He "became sin" for us. The physical sufferings of the Passion were as nothing compared to a full clear view of all the malice of all sins. Many of the sins that

Christ suffered for, were not to be repented; many sinners would fall into hell for their sins with the blood of Jesus Christ upon them. What terrible picture came before Christ that He asked to be spared? Was it the loss of Judas? Was it the fact that the very act by which He saved the world would bring so many into sin (by their own fault, of course), and what was done to save them would bring them to perdition? We shall never know until the end of time; but we do know that however much He felt the pulls of nature upon Himself, He kept His will firmly attached to that of His Father. No one likes disgrace; no one likes deep chronic sufferings. No one has ever asked anyone to *like* these things, for their own intrinsic sakes. Modern psychiatrists who condemn the saints as abnormal because they sought sufferings miss the entire point. St. Francis did not leave his jovial friends for Poverty and Christ because He essentially liked to be in disgrace, but rather because by these sufferings he was set free from the allurements of the world, and could give his every thought and every second to Christ. We read in the Book of Job of this holy man's lamentations because of what had happened to him. We even see him regret the day he was born, but still he clings fast to God. The whole struggle of life is in the will. We either win all or lose all right there. No matter what delights we give up or what pains we endure, the victory will be in the attachments of the will to the will of God.

And He cometh and findeth them sleeping What little help we are to God! He does the work and we sleep. Is it likely the apostles did not realize the terrible struggle going on before their eyes? Whatever they thought, they believed that Jesus would emerge victorious from any contest with the powers of darkness. That is the trouble with the world today. We sleep and think that nothing can hurt the Church, so why should we be in the struggle? This is not the way He wants it, however. God wills to work through us, and Jesus wants our love and our sympathies. We see this in His revelations to St. Margaret Mary. Jesus wants us near Him.

... the second time ... He ... prayed ... My Father if this chalice may not pass away ... Thy will be done. He cometh again and findeth them sleeping Prayer is always a matter of persistence. Sometimes we put in a few half-hearted prayers and wonder why we are not answered without delay. We note that after each prayer of our Lord He went to Peter and the others. Each time He found them asleep. Would not the agony of Christ have been easier if He had had the prayers of His chosen apostles joined to His own? We do not make enough of the effect of our prayers for others. The deep fracture of the sixteenth century is too much upon us all. There is too much of this "every-man-for-himself" spirit at large in the world. In Christ we are all united to one another, and one person's prayers belong in a sense to another, and to us all. If the apostles failed to help Christ *we* can reach back along the centuries and lift some of the burden from the back of the agonizing Christ by refusing to sin any more.

And leaving them He went again and prayed the third time, saying the selfsame word. And there appeared to Him an angel from heaven, strengthening Him At length the prayer of Christ was answered but it was not by taking from Him any of the manifold burdens His Father had laid upon Him. He was answered by an inflow of strength. We tend to overlook this in our prayers. Sometimes we think too much of, and pray too much for plain and simple relief from the burden itself, and it may be that the one situation that causes us so much travail is the one that justifies our having been sent into this world. Think of all the heartbreaks and of all the twisting and straining that goes on in this world to escape burdens, to the edge of insanity and suicide—or, at least, to frustration and cynical defeatism. Christ will always get for us the strength to carry burdens, and with strength the weight of the burden is taken away.

And being in agony He prayed the longer Herein is the main secret of the spiritual life. Let prayer outlast the difficulty; prayer can do anything. We have the absolute promise of God for this.

And His sweat became as drops of blood, trickling down upon the ground This is an actual physical phenomenon which has been observed by competent physicians. Due to a frightful shock from tremendous nervous strain the small capillaries which carry blood to the skin areas actually rupture and allow blood to seep into the sebaceous or sweat glands, whence blood is exuded as a sort of sweat, or it mingles with the violent sweats that come with great pain or intense prolonged strains. This leaves the skin in a very sensitive condition. In the case of Christ it rendered the scourging and the carrying of the Cross on the morrow more painful. But remark that the sweat of blood came after the angel of consolation came to Christ.

He found them sleeping Again, through the greatest agony ever endured by any man, those who might have helped Him were asleep.

As soon, therefore, as He had said to them, I am He, they went backward and fell to the ground Now the betrayal, by a kiss of peace. With Judas, the mob: many of them who had stretched out their hands in the wilderness for bread were now clubbing their fists, crying for His life. Faces once whitened with leprosy were now livid with the rage of the blood lust. The leaders and the people He would have saved had brought with them the soldiers of their deadly enemy to take one man. But all these were not enough. At the sound of His voice all went back to the ground as if dead. Jesus had all His power if He willed to use it. If He had allowed His human nature to make headway in its reactions to His Passion it was because He willed it. If they killed Him it would be because He willed to permit it. So then, after He had shown His enemies that it was not their power that was to take Him captive, He permitted them to have their way.

He would not allow St. Peter to aid Him with a sword. He even performed a miracle to restore the damage done. If Christ had been in need of personal aid His Father would have given Him the unlimited strength of whole legions of angels. His Father's will He would do.

This is your hour and the power of darkness The whole fury of hell was turned loose upon Him; it was this Jesus Christ of whom Satan had said: "I will not serve." Now Heaven had withdrawn its protection and men were permitted to do what they would to Him. We have seen how Christ was tempted in the desert at the beginning of His public life. We may well suppose that temptations were turned loose in force to keep Christ away from His saving mission, now. At this point, all His followers ran away.

The Second Sorrowful Mystery: *The Scourging at the Pillar*

The heart of this mystery is rather in the actions of Pilate than in the physical brutality of the whipping that covered Jesus from head to foot, back and front, with lash marks. Scourging was always a prelude to crucifixion, because its effect was to bring on a high fever. The muscles of the chest would pull up tighter in tetanic contraction to crush out the victim's life with more suffering. It was a diabolical procedure.

But in the case of Jesus He was scourged before He was condemned to death. "He is innocent—therefore I will scourge Him." It was a special kind of cowardice which attacks only those who have the power to do otherwise. Pilate did not wish to condemn Jesus to death; yet he did not desire to override the Sanhedrin, which preserved some judicial freedom. Now they seemed to be giving into Rome on a civil matter by handing over their own King for punishment; then the very next instant it became clear that there was a religious issue of blasphemy at stake. For the latter the Sanhedrin might have condemned Jesus to death by stoning, and had Pilate confirm the sentence.

The Jews wished Jesus crucified for two reasons. First, the sentence of crucifixion reduced a victim to the level of a beast, and so any of His followers who saw Him meet such a death would be repelled from further desire to follow Him. Jesus had said: "Who will not take up his cross daily and follow Me is not worthy of Me." What a horrible memory would now be made of such a saying. "Cursed is every one that hangeth on a tree," they had read in Deuteronomy. This was the second reason for crucifying Jesus, since His cause could never rally from a curse. If He had been stoned He might still be a martyr to the people, as prophets had been stoned to death before by the leaders of the people. Nothing less than utter ruin would satisfy the chief priests, so they set out to upset Pilate and bend him to their will.

Pilate pleaded with the Jews, but they knew what they wanted. But Pilate—weak as his handling of the situation might have been—would do nothing unjust until he conceived the idea of reducing the Lord to a pitiful condition so as to use Him to arouse the pity of the men who sought to have Him killed. Pilate's terrible injustice lay in punishing an innocent man, falsely accused, so as to make His accusers who wanted Him killed be satisfied with less.

The Gospel story that develops the scourging should be read with the Crowning with Thorns, inasmuch as both actions turn about Pilate's weakness in the face of his decision concerning the kingship of Christ. All four of the Gospel stories are here combined.

And they brought Him bound and delivered Him to Pontius Pilate, the governor. And it was morning and they went not into the hall that they might not be defiled, but that they might eat the pasch.

Pilate, therefore, went out to them and said: What accusation bring you against this man? They answered and said to him: If He were not a malefactor we would not have delivered Him up to thee. Pilate therefore said to them: Take Him you and judge Him according to your law.

The Jews, therefore, said: It is not lawful for us to put any man to death, that the word of Jesus might be fulfilled, which He said, signifying what death He should die.

And they began to accuse Him, saying: We have found this Man perverting our nation, and forbidding to give tribute to Caesar, and saying that He is Christ, the King.

Pilate, therefore, went into the hall and called Jesus and said to Him: Art Thou the King of the Jews?

Jesus answered: Sayest thou this thing of thyself, or have others told thee of Me? Pilate answered: Am I a Jew?

Thy own nation and the chief priests have delivered Thee up to me. What hast Thou done?

Jesus answered: My kingdom is not of this world. If My kingdom were of this world, my servants would certainly strive that I should not be delivered to the Jews: but now My Kingdom is not from hence. Pilate, therefore, said to Him: Art Thou a King, then?

Jesus answered: Thou sayest that I am a King: for this was I born and for this came I into the world: that I should give testimony of the truth.

Pilate said to Him: What is truth? And when he said this he went out again to the Jews.

And Pilate said to the chief priests and to the multitude: I find no cause in this man. But they were more earnest, saying: He stirred up the people throughout all Judea, beginning from Galilee, to this place.

And when He was accused by the chief priests and the

ancients He answered nothing. Then Pilate said to Him: Dost Thou not hear how great testimonies they allege against Thee? And He answered him never a word, so that the governor wondered exceedingly.

But Pilate, hearing Galilee, asked if the man were of Galilee. And when he understood that He was of Herod's jurisdiction, He sent Him away to Herod, who was also himself at Jerusalem in those days.

And Herod, seeing Jesus was very glad; for he was desirous of a long time to see Him, because he had heard many things of Him, and hoped to see some sign wrought by Him.

And he questioned Him in many words, but He answered him nothing.

And the chief priests and the scribes stood by, earnestly accusing Him.

And Herod with his army set Him at nought, and mocked Him, putting on Him a white garment and sent Him back to Pilate. And Herod and Pilate were made friends that same day; for before they were enemies one to another.

And Pilate, calling together the chief priests and the magistrates and the people said to them: You have presented unto me this man, as one that perverteth the people; and behold, I, having examined Him before you, find no cause in this man, to those things wherein you accuse Him. No, nor Herod, neither. For I sent you to him, and behold, nothing worthy of death is done to Him.

I WILL CHASTISE HIM THEREFORE AND RELEASE HIM.

Now on the Festival day the governor was wont to release unto them one of the prisoners, whomsoever they would. And he had then a notorious prisoner that was called Barabbas, who in sedition had committed murder.

They, therefore, being gathered together, Pilate said: Whom will you that I release to you, Barabbas, or Jesus that is called Christ? For he knew that for envy they had delivered Him. And as he was sitting in the place of Judgment, his wife sent to him, saying: Have nothing to do with that just Man; for I have suffered many things this day in a dream because of Him.

But the chief priests and ancients persuaded the people that they should ask Barabbas and make Jesus away. And the governor answering said to them: Whether will you of the two to be released to you?

But they said: Barabbas. Pilate saith to them: What shall I do, then, with Jesus that is called the Christ?

They say all: Let Him be crucified.

The governor said to them: Why, what evil hath He done? But they cried out the more, saying: Let Him be crucified.

And Pilate, seeing that he prevailed nothing, but rather that a tumult was made; taking water washed his hands before the people, saying: I am innocent of the blood of this just Man.

And the whole people answered said: His blood be on us and upon our children.

Then he released to them Barabbas.

Then therefore Pilate took Jesus and scourged Him. (Matt. 27).

And they brought Him bound and delivered Him to Pontius Pilate During the night there had been two illegal trials held to condemn Jesus to death. There was a preliminary hearing before Annas and then a hastily gathered meeting of the Sanhedrin. This body was to meet for trials in a special room reserved for them in the Temple only between the hour of full daylight and dusk. The reason behind these violations of justice was that they had not intended to hold a trial to determine the guilt or innocence of Jesus, but were summoned solely to condemn Him to death. The High Priest had decided two weeks before that "it is expedient that one man die for the people" and the only purpose they had in coming together was to pass sentence of death.

There is a peculiar twist to the human mind that makes it seek to hold some sort of a trial, even though the witnesses

The Sorrowful Mysteries

are confined to unproved assertions and there is no defense permitted. We have seen this technique improved upon in our day by drugging the defendant to a point where he can be made to testify against himself, without control over his own mind. We see the process set forth in the so-called trial of Jesus; the false witnesses who tangled up the trial so that no verdict could be given, even when it was known what the verdict had to be. Then the High Priest took over the direction of the trial, asking Jesus point-blank if He were the Christ. Jesus naturally admitted this. If there was to be a fair and just trial this was merely the setting forth of the issues. With great hypocrisy it was made serve as a confession of guilt, and upon this the verdict of "guilty of death" was returned.

There is another circumstance of the alleged trial before the Sanhedrin which needs mention. There have been some who have wondered what Joseph of Arimathea and Nicodemus had done at the trial. We conclude that either they were not present, or that, if present, they did not vote, since there was a provision of Jewish law that if a verdict was returned by a unanimous vote it served as an acquittal. So that if Joseph and Nicodemus had been there and had voted "Not Guilty" they would surely have condemned Him. Their only chance of saving Jesus was to keep any dissenting vote off the record.

As soon as it became daylight another session of the Sanhedrin was called to repeat the process, for two separate trials were needed to condemn a person to death. This was still illegal since the sessions had to be held on two successive days. This was not done, of course, as they wanted to see Jesus crucified on this particular day. On yet another count the trial was illegal, since no sessions were to be held on festival days, and it was just as bad to attempt a Jewish trial as to enter the hall of Pilate for the Roman trial.

It was, then, after these farces of justice that delight those who are out to do injustice, that Jesus was brought to Pilate, trussed up and ready to be condemned to the death of the Cross.

And it was morning and they went not into the hall that they might not be defiled This was a well planned bit of trickery. The Roman trial should have been held in the Hall of Justice where the "seat of judgment" was. By this pretense of not wanting to be defiled by entering the house of a pagan, they not only played up to the mob but also forced a concession out of Pilate which put him at a disadvantage. By trying to hold a semblance of a Roman trial out on a balcony where no witnesses could be examined under oath, there was no chance for a just verdict, and furthermore Pilate had, thereby, broken the Roman law. But the leaders of the people did not want a deliberative trial. They wanted Pilate to take over their sentence of death, but they still had to maneuver the sentence from stoning to crucifixion.

. . . what accusation bring you against this man? Pilate did not see the affair in the same light as the members of the Sanhedrin. If they brought Jesus to him for a Roman trial it could only be as an accused person, not as a condemned criminal who had broken the Jewish law. If the charges were upon Jewish religious grounds, Pilate was not too much interested. The Jews still retained some rights of inflicting the death penalty for violations of the Mosaic law. For this they could stone a culprit to death.

Thus the Jews said they had already tried Jesus and found Him guilty. This can only mean that the charge was religious, otherwise no Jewish group would have dared to hold trial and then tell Pilate they did not wish the Roman officials to take juridiction. Pilate took this to mean that the matter rested within the powers still held by the Jews, so he granted them permission to sentence Jesus, according to the Mosaic law. "Judge Him according to your Law," Pilate told them.

It is not lawful for us to put any man to death This was not true. The Jews put St. Stephen to death; they put St. James the Lesser to the sword and then threw him down from the pinnacle of the Temple. They held St. Peter for later trial at the same time. They put the whip to the back of St. Paul, and Festus, the Roman Governor, was about to have him sent to Jerusalem for trial by the Jews when St. Paul appealed to Rome. If they could do this to St. Paul, a Roman citizen, it must be that they still retained many powers over life and death. They meant it was a festival day and they could not put Jesus to death on that particular day. They could have held Him over the week-end and stoned Him on the following Sunday, but that is not what they sought. This was crucifixion day among the Romans, and they wanted the Romans to put Jesus to death on a cross.

We have found this man perverting our nation, and forbidding us to give tribute to Caesar, and saying that He is Christ, the King What did Pilate care about perversion? He had tried to pervert the Jews by setting up images of Caesar. It had not gone well, and one of these occasions was what brought on the enmity of Herod and Pilate. Pilate bore a hatred for the Jews because of this and was in no mood to give in to them. It must have struck in the throats of the Pharisees to talk about the tribute to Caesar after Christ had so roundly defeated their attempts to embroil Him in Roman law. A direct lie served their purpose very well, but it did not affect Pilate. But what is this about being a king?

Art Thou the King of the Jews? This had the look of a political charge, and Pilate was ready to look into it. It proved a bad mistake, as it set a Roman trial into motion with none of the safeguards of law being observed. So, when Pilate was satisfied that the kingdom of Jesus was not of this world he was determined to turn Jesus free. Up to this point there had been nothing done by Pilate that was gravely unjust. In fact, he delivered the verdict of acquittal! "I find no cause in this just Man."

He sent Him away to Herod   This was Pilate's downfall. Herod had no jurisdiction in Jerusalem, neither did he assume any; but this act of trying to shift his burden to another was Pilate's confession of weakness. Pilate had begun his work with utmost arrogance, but the Jews had been too spirited for him. Twice he was forced to remove Caesar's image from the Holy City, and in this defeat Herod had carried the protest to Caesar in person. Pilate had tried to use Temple funds to build an aqueduct and a riot ensued. It was in this outburst that the infamous Barabbas was arrested, and was now awaiting crucifixion. Pilate seems to have reasoned that if he could send Jesus to Herod, the blame would shift, no matter whether Jesus was freed or condemned. This sort of device has survived today in certain practices of "high diplomacy" by which innocent peoples are shuffled around, killed, starved, or reduced to slavery for a temporary dynastic advantage of an ambitious schemer. Pilate is dead, but his spirit lives on in much that we see about us today.

And Herod, seeing Jesus, was very glad   Herod was in fear of Jesus, for the word had gone about that Jesus was a reincarnation of John the Baptist whom Herod had slain to keep a silly promise. But now here stood Jesus; Jesus who had worked miracles, and had even brought the dead back to life; bound and in the power of Herod; not even opening His mouth. Herod was like any cur dog about to run away howling. As soon as there was no sign on the part of others against him, he felt that he had overawed the man by his majesty. What an opportunity for a shriveled little soul to pretend! How his court must have gasped at the thought of this "mighty" Herod daring to hold as a fool the One who could still the waves and who could make bread multiply itself to the thousandfold. If Christ had so much as looked at him he would have died of sheer fright.

And Herod and Pilate were made friends that same day
When one sees how very devious are the workings of the minds of the children of this world, he can readily understand why simplicity is a virtue. Pilate was trying to involve Herod in difficulty with the Jews, but Herod seeing a chance to strut before his hirelings, was so pleased with himself that he became Pilate's friend. Pilate was at work to destroy all the Jews held sacred; he was an enemy of all that Herod wanted for himself. Yet somehow out of these mixed and devious motives of cowardice and political chicanery was born a *friendship*. God save us from such friends.

I . . . find no cause in this Man . . . No, nor Herod either
Yes, Pilate has an advantage which he is going to press. Herod is now on his side, and if the Jews appeal to Rome they have lost the agent who had upset Pilate before. If Pilate had been any sort of a man he was now safe in releasing Jesus.

I will chastise Him therefore and release Him Pilate knew that the Jews had delivered Jesus out of spite, but he had no idea of the depth of the hatred and the black motives that drove them to the plan to have Jesus crucified. Pilate was still afraid of this screaming mob and considered that if he subjected Jesus to the terrible punishment of a Roman scourging, perhaps that would cool off their spite for Jesus. The mob would not feel that it had been cheated altogether, because a Roman beating with whips was enough to kill a man, when the authorities wanted it to do so. It could, at least, reduce him to such a state of pity that any blood-lust should have been satisfied just by looking at Him. Pilate had no love for Jesus Christ. He didn't care how much Christ suffered, just so Pilate was not upset in his plans. He was not seeking justice. He hated the Jews and sought to turn Christ loose just to spite them; and yet he was willing to harm Jesus enough to quiet the demands of the Jews for punishment. If Jesus died later, that was all right with Pilate. Just so he did not yield entirely to the demands of the crowd, he felt quite pleased with himself. This is not a rare state of mind, especially in dictatorships where innocent millions have been badly treated to keep dictators from punishing their underlings when there are disturbances in such countries. A sop is thrown to the crowd to placate them when things get too intolerable by ordering a fallen favorite to trial for "treason against the people." The spirit of Pontius Pilate still upsets the world.

Will you that I release to you, Barabbas, or Jesus Pilate should have known that Barabbas was a popular favorite with the people, because in the riots on the Feast of Tabernacles Barabbas had acted in a way that could be built up into a defense of his country. Pilate had tried to divert Temple funds into political channels, even for the needed public work of building an aqueduct. The world has always had and still has its criminals who capture the popular fancy and become heroes.

On the other hand the great favor of Jesus with all the people could not have been unknown to Pilate. He must have known about the triumphal entry of Jesus into Jerusalem just the previous Sunday. Pilate also was aware that Barabbas had been set to his task by the same ones who had dragged Jesus before him to be sentenced. He may have reasoned that if he could appeal to the general mob over the heads of the clique that was seeking the life of Jesus, he could still achieve his main purpose of saving Him by outwitting the leaders and by turning the people against them. Pilate could then draw back his offer to scourge Jesus and emerge as complete victor, without having to take a positive stand. What is more, Barabbas, the tool of the leaders, would be dead both by law and by popular demand and Pilate would be at peace.

Have nothing to do with that just Man Was this the call of grace coming to Pilate through his wife, Claudia? Women were strictly forbidden to take any part in political affairs, and that by a direct order of Caesar. Pilate's wife was a pagan, but God is good to all His children and will give to honest souls all the graces they need to come to Him. This must have been, indeed, an urgent call to Pilate through his wife for her to go so directly against the solemn edict that she would even send word through an outsider. It could have had the same effects upon her that disobeying a direct command of the late Red Joe Stalin would have on the wife of a Communist functionary.

Pilate was frightened, and sought to have Jesus released. But he had offered the people their choice between Jesus and Barabbas, and the chief priests moved the mob to choose Barabbas. Rather they had a shouting minority cry down all the others, as good people were still in favor of Jesus. In those days, as today, good people were more timid than bad people and minorities could sway them, or silence them. The world still needs, among other things, a lot of righteous indignation. Too much sheer lack of moral courage still masquerades as virtue. To many of us there comes the urge to do something about the wrongs we see about us, but we can be deterred by the thought: "What will people think of me?" Or if we have more cowardice we get smug and explain: "God will work this out in His own good time, anyway." What *will* people think of us if we try to do something about abuses? They will think we are crackpots, fanatics, meddlers, bigots, and all the rest. What will God think of us if His providence was meant to have operated to clear up some wrong through us? If more of us would get mad clear through a little more often this would be a better world.

A popular way of upsetting the efforts of good people to

bring about improvement is to hurl the taunt: "This is a free country; I can do anything I want." This stops most of us as though there were a constitutional limitation placed only upon those who contend for decency. This is also a free country for those of us who do not think that murderers have any right to kill the unborn or hopelessly sick under pretense of elevating mankind. Why don't more of us feel free to speak up for human rights and dignity?

But they said Barabbas Thus Pilate's strategy tumbled about his ears and he suffered another defeat at the hands of his enemies. Barabbas was now free and Jesus, whom He had acquitted in fact, was still on his hands as though He had been convicted of a crime. Then Pilate went through the motions of washing his hands of the whole affair, but it was still with him for his decision. His efforts had been to secure a decision outside his own will, although he was the only one who had the authority to decide—and he lacked the courage.

Let Him be crucified Pilate was the judge with full and complete power. Yet he turned weakly and asked the accusers of Jesus what he, Pilate, should do with Jesus. What other reply did he expect? This is a common human failing, but since the issues are generally not very important most wishy-washy people do not get so large a share of the world's blame as that reserved for Pilate. So many of us try to work out our life problems through the wills and desires of others, and then expect the conclusions to be what we wished them to be. It is quite clear that these have to be what the others wanted, since their wills were asked to choose. This habit is a rich source of nervous and mental troubles and of moral disaster. Anyone who would make headway against his own troubles has to use his own will, even though he cannot please everyone along the way.

His blood be on us and on our children This constituted a

repudiation of the Messias, Jesus, as King of the Jews. We are at the end of the Old Testament. From this point it is only a matter of hours until the veil of the Holy of Holies is split to show that the Chosen People have made their choice and God has ratified it.

Then, therefore, Pilate took Jesus and scourged Him Jesus was still not declared formally guilty, even though Barabbas has been set free. Pilate will make more efforts to liberate Him but now he kept running up against obstacles he had himself erected. As long as he kept asking the mob what it *wanted* to do with Jesus, the mob would naturally say: "Crucify Him!" That is exactly why they came to Pilate on that one particular day to rush a conviction through him. This was crucifixion day and the leaders demanded that Jesus be crucified. They had already violated their most sacred beliefs to come there; no little pleas on the part of Pilate could lead them to change their minds. Their minds were made up; and Pilate's was not. What a lesson for us when we are tempted simply to let things straighten themselves out. When minds are made up the direction of affairs runs along with those who know where they are going, and what they intend to do if opposed. If there is no corresponding clash of will from the other side the situation perpetuates itself. Today the Reds are attempting to have Jesus crucified all over again. They are getting their way, because the ones supposed to be on the other side do not really know what they want to do, and hope the Communist regime will fall apart from within. A man who is winning without opposition does not easily consider changing his mind.

The scourging given to Jesus was brutal beyond all imagining. There have been private revelations about the scourging which we may accept or refuse, since private revelations are not of faith. On the other hand we cannot just push all these stories aside as though from neurotics. There has come to light of late years the most complete physical evidence of the Passion in the form of the Winding Sheet of Turin. This is a long piece of linen of ancient weave upon which there is imprinted the impression of a man about six feet tall. The imprint clearly shows marks of a scourging; of blood marks encircling the head as though this man had been crowned with sharp objects such as thorns, and upon whose hands and feet there are marks of a crucifixion. Many years of study have been given this winding sheet and everything upon it confirms the conjecture that this is the actual linen Christ was wrapped in at His burial. It was laid over Him and under Him. It is supposed that the aloes that were sprinkled over Him mingled with the death sweat and caused the sheet to be sensitized into an actual photographic plate. The sheet is a photographic negative made before anyone had ever conceived the idea of a negative, and no proper interpretation was ever made of the markings until after photography had been invented. Upon this sheet there are also marks of actual blood that has seeped into the linen.

The signs of a terrible scourging are traced upon this cloth. There can be seen in pairs the outline of leaden tips, looking like tiny dumb bells, with which the Roman *flagrum* was tipped. The whip had two thongs. There are eighty of such marks, indicating a legal scourging of forty lashes. After that there are marks that tell of a lashing with straps, switches, bundles of thorns, and whatever else came into the hands of men who were told to reduce Christ to a state of pity. Every part of His body except His face, hands, and feet are covered with these marks so that the tip of the finger can scarcely be laid any place on the sheet without touching one of them. We hear much of humanitarianism, but there is nothing so brutal as a man who has another man in his complete power, without fear of reprisal.

The Third Sorrowful Mystery:
The Crowning with Thorns

This mystery is so intertwined with the scourging that the

Gospel stories must be read together. The real charge against Jesus by the chief priests and magistrates of the people was that He was making Himself the King of the Jews. They saw in this the end of their profitable and despotic reign over an oppressed people.

The Roman Empire gave them a considerable amount of voice in the handling of local affairs. This they did not wish to lose at any cost. This thought was in the mind of Caiphas when the death of Jesus was first openly decided upon. This was after Jesus had worked the stupendous miracle of raising Lazarus from the dead; a showing of divine power that should have brought them before Jesus on their knees. We read: "But one of them named Caiphas, being the High Priest that year, said to them: You know nothing. Neither do you consider that it is expedient for you that one man should die for the people, and that the whole nation perish not. And this he spoke not of himself; but being the High Priest of that year he prophesied that Jesus should die for tne nation. And not only for the nation but to gather in one the children of God that were dispersed. From that day, therefore, they devised to put Him to death" (John 11:46-53).

Christ was not so old that the memory of the visit of the Wise Men was forgotten. Many of the Sanhedrin must have been in the Temple when Jesus began His Father's business. There can be no doubt that the leaders of the Jews saw in Jesus the true King of the Jews and deliberately repudiated Him for selfish reasons. The "desire of the everlasting hills" had come and the sceptre had departed from Juda in the great refusal: "We have no King but Caesar."

Pilate's part is more complex and weaker. He saw through the envy and hatred of the Sanhedrin. Pilate believed that Jesus was innocent, but by yielding to the terrible injustice of scourging Christ to make the Jews turn to pity Him, he opened the way for the soldiers to crown Him with thorns. When Pilate set up the title "Jesus of Nazareth, King of the

Jews" he gave the first public acknowledgment of the kingship of Jesus. Worse for Pilate—he did not believe that Jesus was an imposter. He finally yielded when Jesus came into discussion or in competition with Caesar. Pilate had dallied too long with injustice; the issue at last became too clear. He could not risk Caesar's wrath against an abstract issue of justice to the helpless.

The soldiers alone were mockers of the kingship of Christ. This outrage seems to have been their own idea, but they had no fear of Pilate since he had turned over to them an innocent man to be beaten into a pitiful condition. This was just one more event; perhaps an afterthought. It was providential, however, as it gave the leaders of the people their opportunity to renounce Jesus publicly.

The Gospel story is mainly in the Gospel of St. John, with some of it in St. Matthew and St. Mark.

Then the soldiers of the governor taking Jesus into the hall gathered together unto Him the whole band; and stripping Him, they put a scarlet cloak about Him. And platting a crown of thorns, they put it upon His head and a reed in His right hand. And bowing the knee before Him they mocked Him saying: Hail, King of the Jews. And they struck His head with a reed. And they did spit upon Him.

Pilate, therefore, went forth again and saith to them: Behold, I bring Him forth unto you that you may know that I find no cause in Him. Jesus, therefore came forth bearing the crown of thorns and the purple garment. And he said to them: Behold the Man. When the chief priests therefore and the servants had seen Him they cried out saying: Crucify Him; crucify Him.

Pilate said to them: Take Him you and crucify Him. I find no cause in Him.

The Jews answered him: we have a law; and according to the law he ought to die, because He made Himself the Son of God.

When Pilate, therefore, heard this saying he feared the more.

And he entered the hall again, and he said to Jesus: Whence art Thou? But Jesus gave him no answer.

Pilate, therefore, said to Him: Speaketh Thou not to me? Knowest Thou not that I have power to crucify Thee, and I have power to release Thee? Jesus answered: thou shouldst not have any power against Me unless it were given thee from above. Therefore, he that hath delivered Me to thee, hath the greater sin.

And from henceforth Pilate sought to release Him. But the Jews cried out saying: If thou release this man, thou art not Caesar's friend. For whosoever maketh himself a king, speaketh against Caesar. Now when Pilate had heard these words, he brought Jesus forth, and sat down in the judgment seat, in the place that is called Lithostrotos, and in Hebrew, Gabbatha. And it was the parasceve of the Pasch, about the sixth hour, and he said to the Jews: Behold your King. But they cried out: Away with Him; away with Him. Crucify Him. Pilate said to them: Shall I crucify your King? The chief priests answered: We have no king but Caesar. Then, therefore, he delivered Him to them to be crucified.

And platting a crown of thorns, they put it on His head and a reed in His right hand The greater part of the crown of thorns still exists in one piece; scattered here and there are individual thorns taken from it across the centuries and doled out as precious relics of the Passion. The circlet of the crown of thorns was given to St. Louis of France. To keep it properly it was encased in a crystal and gold container and the artistic gem, la Sainte Chappelle, which adjoins the Cathedral of Nôtre Dame was built to house it. The French Revolution saw it taken away to be destroyed. However, the Commission decided to preserve it as a bit of superstition and ridicule.

The same learned Commission made a mistake about the

Crown of Thorns, because this particular crown has no more thorns left on it. It is a circlet of rushes, a few inches high, bound neatly with transverse bands to hold it firmly together. The thorns have all been distributed as relics, or lost in one or another of the religious upheavals that have come upon the world. One such thorn was formerly in the possession of the unfortunate Mary, Queen of Scots. That was a double thorn, of which one has been lost and one preserved. According to the evidence of the Winding Sheet of Turin the Crown of Thorns was not a mere circlet, as the band of rushes of Paris, but it was a cap—a real crown that covered the entire head of Christ. A very early representation of the Crown of Thorns survives in the Catacombs. This is shown as a cap covering the whole head. It is quite likely that the modern artist's conception of the Crown of Thorns as a narrow band comes from the remaining part of the Crown at Sainte Chappelle.

It is likely that some one of Christ's tormentors conceived the idea of ridiculing Him as the King of Fools, and platted a circlet of rushes as the crown. The reed was the scepter of weakness. Then some oaf thought it would be very funny if he took this crown, platted a handful of thorns that were in a wood-box for burning in the fire, put the thorns inside the circlet of rushes, and pressed the whole mass down upon Christ's Head. The King of Fools was an ancient character in buffoonery who survived as the Court Jester, and then, after long centuries, became known in vaudeville as the foil or "stooge" who took the butt of all the jokes. This poor unfortunate always appears as he-who-gets-slapped. He is always making up grandiose schemes only to see them tumble about his ears. Then for his trouble he gets his ears boxed as a reward, amid screams and laughter of the audience.

Behind all this ridicule was a deep act of spite. The Romans had not been able to subdue the Jews completely, and every now and then someone arose who proclaimed himself King of the Jews and made trouble for the soldiers. They must have known that Jesus had not done this, but when men are out to "get even" they don't usually ask if they have the right person in their hands. The man they had in their power seemed to be helpless enough to abuse without restraint. He had said His kingdom was not of this world, and even the Jews who said He claimed to be their King had repudiated Him, and wanted Him to die as a slave on the cross. It is a sorry world where the helpless are mistreated.

I bring Him forth unto you that you may know that I find no cause in Him But what of the torture He had just been undergoing? All of this was inflicted so that a bloodthirsty crowd would be pacified. Nothing would satisfy them but the same cause of their bringing Him to Pilate in the first place. "Crucify Him!" Still no cause for a condemnation, but Pilate has exhausted himself and now tried to turn the crucifixion over to the leaders of the people. They could not accept because of the Feast, and because they could not take official part in a crucifixion. Pilate almost outmaneuvered them. Then the true reason for the accusation came out. Jesus made Himself the Son of God, they claimed, and this was punishable with death. Thus the charge swung back to a religious offense, and for this the penalty was stoning, not crucifixion.

Pilate, moreover, was now upset by the new status they have given to Jesus. It fitted in with the message of his wife: "Have nothing to do with that just man." Then Pilate delivered a terrible indictment of himself: "I have power to crucify Thee, and I have power to release Thee." Of course he did have such power. The pity of it is that he did not use the power he had, but tried to work out a solution by compromising with those who had no power to stop him. It was his power; he should have used it—justly.

Pilate had now made up his mind. He would release Jesus. But he had not reckoned with himself and his weakness of character. For all his resolution his motives were wrong, and his method accordingly must have also been wrong.

Many who think that all they have to do to change their conduct is to command themselves to change; that this is all there is to it, are very mistaken, and often find that they have lapsed into sin despite good resolutions. To change our conduct we have to change our motives, our scale of values. We cannot love God simply by saying that we are going to love Him from this time forward, unless we do a little thinking in our hearts and bring out before ourselves a few of the reasons why we ought to love God. Pilate's highest set of motives could not rise above the desire to be pleasing to Caesar. If he could have seen that there is right and there is wrong; that the right must be followed despite the personal advantage that may accrue in following the wrong, there would have been no trouble in coming to a decision about the fate of Jesus. The Jews soon saw their mistake in changing the charges against Jesus so they returned to the old accusation.

Whosoever maketh Himself a King, speaketh against Caesar When these words broke in upon Pilate, grace was lost upon him. What if the Jews were right and Jesus had tried to appear as a king? What if someone told this to Caesar? Jesus had said: "My kingdom is not of this world," but that seemed far away from Pilate's mind. He was a coward at heart, and no coward can win in debate with one who knows what he is after. Why not just give in to them? He would like to spite them, but they might hurt him at Rome again. This man Jesus—who was his friend? What can Pilate lose by giving in?

Shall I crucify your King? Pilate was a waspish sort of a man. He knew he would have to yield, but he could get an underhanded sort of revenge by goading the Jews with the kingship of Christ. He will give them the life of Christ, but they will pay for it in embarrassment. These are the pitiful circumstances in which Juda is to repudiate his birthright.

The Sorrowful Mysteries

We have no king but Caesar To what lengths will not the human heart go when driven by hatred? The leaders of the people were so incensed by the exposures that Jesus had made of their corrupt lives, that they would stop at nothing to ruin Him. Caesar was now their king, but in a generation they were to see what kind of king they had chosen over Jesus. In the year 70 A.D. the Emperor Titus would come down upon them with an army because they had raised the banner of revolt against him, and the Holy City would be leveled to the ground. The Temple would disappear from the world and day after day thousands of the victims would hang from crosses around the beleaguered city.

But God will not abandon them forever. "Therefore speak to them: I will gather you from among the peoples, and assemble you out of the countries wherein you are scattered, and I will give you the land of Israel . . . that they may walk in my commandments and keep my judgments, and do them: and that they may be my people and I may be their God" (Ezech. 11:17-20).

The Fourth Sorrowful Mystery:
Jesus Carries His Cross

This mystery centers about the Way of the Cross. It is for us the great lesson of patience which proves that our eternal salvation is worked out step by step under the burdens which are laid upon us by our wills or against them.

Twice Jesus had used this bitter figure of speech. In Matt. 10:38: "And he that taketh not up his cross and followeth Me, is not worthy of Me. He that findeth his life shall lose it; and he that shall lose his life for Me, shall find it." Again: "Then Jesus said to His disciples: If any man will come after Me, let him deny himself, and take up his cross, and follow Me. For he that will save his life will lose it: and he that shall lose his life for My sake, shall find it" (Matt. 16:24).

Thus the short, painful journey of Jesus from Pilate's Hall to the Hill of Calvary has taken on a symbolism which is nothing less than our entire life-span.

The story of the Way of the Cross is found in all four Gospels.

And after they had mocked Him, they took off the cloak from Him, and put on His own garments, and led Him away to crucify Him, and bearing His own cross he went forth to that place which is called Calvary but in Hebrew Golgotha.

And they forced one Simon, a Cyrenian who passed by coming out of the country, the father of Alexander and Rufus. And they laid the cross on him to carry after Jesus.

And there followed after Him a great multitude of people, and of women who bewailed and lamented Him. But Jesus, turning to them, said: Daughters of Jerusalem, weep not over Me, but weep for yourselves and your children. For behold the days will come wherein they will say: Blessed are the barren, and the wombs that have not borne, and the paps that have not given suck. Then shall they begin to say to the mountains: Fall upon us: and to the Hills: cover us.

For if in the green wood they do these things, what shall be done in the dry?

And there were also two other malefactors led with Him to be put to death.

After they had mocked Him The greatest shame on the memory of Pontius Pilate is the way in which he permitted his subordinates to take over the abuse of the Man he wanted to set free. There are those who decide everything on a basis of personal advantage. These would have turned Jesus over to the leaders of the people with no questions asked. When the innocent get in the way of this kind of powerful individual it is so much the worse for the innocent. Pilate made some attempt to invoke principles of justice, but always in such a way to avoid meeting the issues head on. This is always the fate of those who try to stand aside from the unpleasant decisions of life and wait for external circumstances to "make everything come out right." Things never work out that way. Such an attitude leads to misery.

. . . put on His own garments, and led Him away to crucify Him, and bearing His own Cross He went forth It is said that when the condemned was given his own clothing to wear to the place of his crucifixion he was forced to carry the entire cross. He who carried only the transverse member was stripped of all his clothing. The Jews managed to get the concession from the Romans that condemned criminals should wear loin cloths. Marks which have been preserved on the Winding Sheet show peculiar sorts of creases in the shoulder wound that indicate that Christ wore His clothes on the way to Calvary.

. . . bearing His own Cross The usual Roman law concerning the carrying of a cross by a condemned criminal was suspended for Jews, because crucifixions were generally held on festival days when many Jews were trooping into the Holy City, and so the witnessess to Roman superiority would be greatly increased. But on the festival days it was forbidden to Jews to carry burdens, and as a concession to this the Romans had the crosses sent out ahead.

When Jesus was condemned there was no one to carry His Cross to Calvary. No Jew would so much as touch this horrible instrument, and no provision of military discipline could force a Roman soldier to do this degrading task. Hence the leaders of the people permitted an absolute violation of the Sabbath rest, in order to make sure that on that day Jesus went to His death on the Cross.

And they forced one Simon a Cyrenian . . . and they laid the Cross on him to carry after Jesus It may also be that when the Jews saw Jesus compelled to carry a burden on the festival day they may have set up a murmuring disturbing to the Romans and to the leaders of the people. Revolutions have been started by flagrant and open violations of religious law and custom. Simon the Cyrenian was then forced to take up the burden, since he was a pagan, neither Roman nor Jew. The rough hewn cross weighing, it has been estimated, about 200 pounds, rubbed His raw shoulder and must have been torturing indeed. It was of pine wood; the transverse members had to be long enough to take the outstretched arms of a six-foot man; the upright member had to be long enough not only for the body of Jesus, but also for the centurion on horseback to make the thrust of his lance to pierce Christ's heart—the lance held at a level. St. Bernard of Clairvaux is said to have asked the Lord in an apparition what was the most painful experience in His Passion. Christ replied, according to the story, that the wound in His shoulder was the most painful of all.

Daughters of Jerusalem, weep not over Me, but weep for yourselves and your children These women were most likely a part of the pious group whose work it was to render the terrible pains of crucifixion a little more endurable. Seeing Jesus in such agony who could restrain tears of sympathy, even though these tears may have been officially those of a mourner chanting the funeral wail? Mourners were very important in ancient times, and there was no one to perform the office for criminals except this group. Jesus was referring to the horrifying things that were about to befall Jerusalem, which in repudiating Jesus had laid itself open to destruction, inasmuch as God was no more its protector. Soon the Roman conquerors would come and there would be more to bewail than the redeeming death of Jesus Christ.

Along the Way of the Cross occurred the first public acknowledgment of the kingship of Christ. It was customary for convicted criminals to carry on their chests a placard announcing their crimes. This was set up over their heads after they were crucified. On this board was written, "Jesus of Nazareth, King of the Jews." This, then, was His crime. We, too, must carry our crosses under the banner of Christ, the King. This is the sort of world we live in. We can carry our crosses as Simon did; by having them put on our shoulders; or we can seek Christ out as Veronica did, with willingness. Christ has given our sufferings a value for the salvation of the world, as is expressed in the startling words of St. Paul: "I rejoice in the sufferings I bear for your sake; and what is lacking of the sufferings of Christ, I fill up in my flesh for His Body, which is the Church. . . ." Christ suffered to the death, but we are called on to suffer daily in our duties. Thus we carry our crosses, and thus we help Christ carry His Cross. Attached to His merits, our actions do have value.

The Fifth Sorrowful Mystery: *The Crucifixion and Death of Jesus*

Here is the story of our redemption. Across the long span of the centuries man had struggled; away from the friendship of God, yet in all ages and all places he had kept alive a story handed down from—he knew not where. Away from an infallible guide such as we have today in the Church, the primitive revelation of man's redemption became clouded in myth and fable, but the outlines everywhere preserved—an original innocence, a fall, a redemption. A Redeemer would come and set him free of his oppressors. At length Abram went forth from Ur of the Chaldees, renamed Abraham and was called by God to be the founder of a line of inheritance which would in time bring forth the Savior. From this age forward the time, place, and circumstances of the Savior's coming became clearer through revelations of God, so that at the time of His death on the Cross all men of good will could have seen that this was indeed He who was to come.

That self-imposed blindness, which would not let them see this, was the crime of the chief priests and leaders of the people. They were permitted by the Romans to keep alive their religious observances. These were only the shell of the eternal truth because the priests used their high office for their own gain, and put intolerable burdens on the people. How much this helped upset the peace of the world can be readily understood. Peace could have come to the world then, if Christ had been given His proper place. The same is true today, for what is chiefly wrong with our world is the rejection of Christ by the mighty. There is no more excuse for the leaders of the people today than there was at the time of Christ. The proofs of Christ's place in the world are as clear for him who will pause and think in his heart, as they were when He hung upon His Cross. One who wills to help bring peace to the world can start for himself at the foot of the Cross, seeing there the great love of Christ for us all. Christ does not regret the spilling of His blood; He asks only that we love Him in return, and so bring down on ourselves the effects of His grace.

In the end everything comes back to the foot of the Cross, but the world does not like the lesson of self-denial the Cross teaches. The world today feels the pull of Christ's sacrifice but turns away as the leaders of the people did, attempting to make the Cross, and what it stands for, seem unreal.

All the objectors brought out was the thought that Elias must come first, and this was their excuse for withholding themselves from Christ. Even the disciples of Jesus held the objection, "Elias must come first," but they could see from what Jesus did that this was "He who is to come" and they were not to "look for another." They did not see everything; they had difficulties, but they had good will, and that made the difference.

People today act the same way. They leave the Catholic Church and they stay out of the Catholic Church because of the necessary difficulties that grow out of the unfolding of a divine plan with human agents. Others of good will look past the discrepancies and shortcomings of the human element,

The Sorrowful Mysteries

and as St. Paul says, "though prophecies should be set at naught" they see the hand of God come to it from its blessings.

Sin had so spoiled the world that it took the Cross to restore the balance between God and the world that had defied His law. While He redeemed us Christ also gave us the example of the restoring power of suffering. He could have redeemed us by any simple act of His, for in the union with the Godhead His slightest act would have had infinite value. But this would have given us no example of the road we must follow in daily life. We must endure our crosses with patience every day. The world will try to get us out of its way by imposing suffering on us. How we meet this suffering determines the amount of peace that will come into our souls. and the amount of peace we can radiate out to the world around us by the way we bear our burdens—our crosses.

The gospel story of the Crucifixion is found in all four of the Evangelists. Enough of each story will be given to make for unity of impression.

And they came to the place that is called Golgotha, which is Calvary, or the Place of the Skull, they crucified Him there. And with Him they crucified two thieves, the one on His right hand and the other on His left. And the Scripture was fulfilled which saith: *And with the wicked He was reputed.*

And they gave Him wine to drink mingled with myrrh. And He would not drink.

And Jesus said: *Father forgive them; they know not what they do.*

The soldiers, therefore, when they had crucified Him, took His garments and they made four parts; to every soldier a part, and also His coat. Now the coat was without seam, woven from the top throughout. And they said, the one to another: *Let us not cut it, but let us cast lots whose it shall be; that the Scriptures might be fulfilled, saying*: *They have parted My garments and upon my vesture they have cast lots. The soldiers indeed did these things: and they sat and watched Him.*

And Pilate wrote a title also, and put it upon the Cross. And the writing was: Jesus of Nazareth, the King of the Jews. This title many of the Jews did therefore read, because the place where Jesus was crucified was nigh to the city, and it was written in Hebrew, in Greek, and in Latin.

Then the chief priests of the Jews said to Pilate: Write not, the King of the Jews but that He said I am the King of the Jews. Pilate answered: What I have written, I have written.

And they that passed by, blasphemed Him, wagging their heads and saying: Vah, Thou that destroyeth the temple of God and in three days doth rebuild it; save Thyself. If Thou be the Son of God, come down from the Cross.

In like manner, also, the chief priests, with the scribes and ancients, mocking, said: He saved others; Himself He cannot save. If He be the King of Israel; let Him now come down from the Cross and we will believe Him. He trusted in God: let Him now deliver Him if He will have Him. For He said: I am the Son of God.

And one of the robbers who were hanged, blasphemed Him, saying: If Thou be Christ, save Thyself and us. But the other, answering, rebuked him saying: Neither dost thou fear God, seeing that we are under the same condemnation? And we, indeed, justly for we receive the due reward of our deeds; but this man has done no evil. And he said to Jesus: Lord, remember me when Thou shalt come into Thy kingdom. And Jesus said to him: Amen, I say to thee, this day thou shalt be with Me in paradise.

Now there stood by the Cross of Jesus, his mother and His mother's sister, Mary of Cleophas, and Mary Magdalen. When Jesus, therefore, had seen His mother and the disciple standing, whom He loved, He saith to His mother: Woman, behold thy son. After that he saith to the disciple: Behold thy mother. And from that hour the disciple took her to his own.

The Sorrowful Mysteries

And it was almost the sixth hour; and there was darkness over all the earth until the ninth hour. And the sun was darkened. And about the ninth hour, Jesus cried with a loud voice: Eli, Eli, lamma sabacthani? *That is, My God, My God, why hast Thou forsaken Me? And some that stood there and heard, said*: This man calleth Elias. *And the others said*: let be, let us see wether Elias come to deliver Him.

Afterwards, Jesus knowing that all things were now accomplished, that the Scriptures might be fulfilled, said: I thirst. Now there was a vessel set there full of common wine. And they putting a sponge full of this wine about hyssop, put it to His mouth. Jesus, therefore, when He had tasted the wine, said: It is consummated.

And Jesus, crying with a loud voice said: Father into Thy hands I commit my spirit. And saying this, He gave up the ghost.

And behold the veil of the temple was rent in two from top to bottom. And the earth quaked, and the rocks were rent and the graves were opened; and many bodies of the saints that had slept arose and coming out of the tombs after His resurrection, came into the city and appeared to many.

Now the centurion and those that were with him watching Jesus, seeing that crying out in this manner He had given up the ghost and seeing the earthquake and the things that were done were sore afraid, saying: Indeed, this was the Son of God.

Then the Jews (because it was the parasceve), that the bodies might not remain on the Cross on the sabbath day (for that was a great sabbath day), besought Pilate that their legs might be broken and they might be taken away. The soldiers, therefore, came and they broke the legs of the first and of the other that was crucified with Him. But after they were come to Jesus, when they saw that He was already dead, they did not break His legs. But one of the soldiers with a spear opened His side, and immediately there came forth blood and water.

And he that saw it hath given testimony and his testimony is true. And he knoweth that he sayeth true; that you may also believe. For these things were done that the Scripture might be fulfilled: You shall not break a bone of Him. And another Scripture saith: They shall look on Him whom they pierced.

And when evening was now come (because it was the parasceve, that is, the day before the sabbath) Joseph of Arimathea, a noble councillor, who was also himself looking for the kingdom of God, came and went in boldly to Pilate and begged the body of Jesus.

But Pilate wondered that He should be already dead. And sending for the centurion, he asked him if He were already dead. And when he understood it by the centurion, he gave the body to Joseph.

And Nicodemus also came (he who at the first came to Jesus by night) bringing a mixture of myrrh and aloes, about a hundred pound weight. And Joseph, buying fine linen, they therefore took the body of Jesus down and bound it in linen cloths with the spices as the manner of the Jews is to bury.

Now there was in the place where Jesus was crucified, a garden, and in the garden a new sepulcher wherein no man yet had been laid. There, therefore, because of the parasceve of the Jews, they laid Jesus, because the sepulcher was nigh at hand.

And the women that were come with Him from Galilee, following after, saw the sepulcher and how His body was laid. And returning they prepared spices and ointments, and on the sabbath day they rested, according to the commandment.

They crucified Him It is almost impossible for us to get an adequate idea of what is involved in crucifixion. For centuries the knowledge that Christ had died a death so shameful was hateful to the Christian sense so that no one could bring himself to make a crucifix as we have them now. After some centuries the practice of crucifixion was forbidden and the crucifix appeared, but with a Christ in triumph on the Cross. Once in a while today we see such crucifixes with the figure of Christ garbed in priestly vestments, a kingly crown upon His head, and in attitude of triumph. It was not until the Middle Ages that the crucifix as we ordinarily see it came into use.

Crucifixion was a most shameful death decreed only for slaves and outcasts. A citizen of Rome could not be sentenced to die on the cross except for a very few carefully defined crimes. Thus when SS. Peter and Paul were martyred, St. Peter was crucified (head down so as not to approach his Master too closely) but St. Paul was beheaded, primarily to show his rights as a citizen. (This can be a lesson to over-timid Catholics who are willing to accept the status of "second class citizenship" to keep away from trouble.)

Cicero said that of all deaths crucifixion was most painful and degrading. It was the most shameful because it lowered the victim to a bestial level, and cut him off from all consolation and human comfort. He was not even given burial after death, but customarily was left on his cross until his bones actually fell to the ground. Among the Jews a concession was granted for removal and burial, so that the bodies would not remain on the cross over the sabbath. It was a most painful death because the victim was suspended on nails driven through the heel of his hands—not through the palms as artists commonly show the crucifixion of the Lord.

If you bend your hands towards yourself, palms in, a line will develop at the wrists. With the thumb to the inner surface and the second finger to the outer surface near this line, locate by pressure a spot at about the center line of the hand, where there is an indentation. That is where the nail went through the space in the middle of a small cluster of bones of the hand. Remark the small amount of flesh from the center of the palm to the division between the middle and third fingers. There would not be enough flesh here to support the weight of a man of 175 pounds, the probable weight of Jesus Christ. There is a blood stain on the Winding Sheet of Turin on the back of one hand that shows the impression on the sheet. As the hands are folded, only one shows. Here the stain is at the edge of the wrist but still clearly in the hand.

There are several reasons why the Romans picked that precise spot to drive in the nails. First, the cluster of bones is bound by sinews, which are enough to keep the nails from pulling through the flesh and detaching the victim as he writhed in agony on the cross. Again, there is a broad ligament across the heel of the hand, between the palm and the place of the nail. That gave added holding power. Thirdly, because by driving the nails through this particular place the radial nerves to the hands are completely severed, or rather, torn apart.

Have you ever felt the throbbing pain of a hand injury? The pain impulse is carried up the radial nerve. Can you from that imagine every sensitive spot on the hand being outraged with pain at one and the same time? That would be the effect produced by driving a rough square nail through the large bundle of nerve fibers, and leaving the torn ends of this nerve bundle in contact with the rough iron edges of the nail which was literally pinning the nerve down. Christ suffered like this for hours.

The second diabolic pain of crucifixion was the progressive cramping of the muscles as the waste products of fatigue accumulated in the tissues. After a time this cramping became permanent, and a tetany developed. Sometimes in tetanus a victim is forced into an arch by the pulling of his own muscles with only his head and his heels touching the bed. If a person is nailed to a cross the muscle cramps pull up progressively until the great muscles of the chest actually crush out his life. It may, as happened in the case of Christ, rupture the heart muscles.

The torturers could hasten death or hold it back as they

wished. By properly manipulating the amount of pull exerted on the arm and chest muscles they could keep the unhappy victim alive for days, or they could get it over in a few hours. If a footrest was provided the muscles did not cramp so fast; if the hands and feet were tied to the cross instead of being nailed, the pain from the tearing of the radial nerve was spared, and this reduced the shock that brings on sudden death. Sometimes a sort of peg was provided as a saddle for the victim to sit upon. This also held back tetany.

And they gave Him wine to drink mingled with myrrh This was one of the works of mercy performed by a group of pious women in Jerusalem who had forced the Romans to grant them many concessions both for decency and mercy. The myrrh was a drug which had moderate anesthetic properties. This put the victim into a sort of stupor, and his sufferings were relieved to a degree. Jesus refused even this poor consolation to make a more perfect sacrifice for our sins.

Father forgive them In the process of canonization of saints it is not enough that one be killed for religion. He must forgive his enemies, as Christ did. Forgiveness of enemies is probably the hardest practice in our religion, especially when someone has injured us in a real way.

The amount of suffering that Jesus underwent for us is shown in detail on the Winding Sheet of Turin. While He hung suspended by His hands on the nails, the pulling on His chest muscles would make it virtually impossible to speak. There is on the Winding Sheet a streak of blood from the nail wounds which shows how the blood from the nail wounds coursed down Christ's arms. The scientist who examined the sheet noted there was a change in the angle of the flow of the blood. This led him to conclude that when Christ wanted to speak to us from the Cross He actually raised Himself up on the nail that pierced His feet to relieve the pressure on His arms, and chest while He spoke.

. . . took His garments . . . and also His coat Traditionally personal belongings were the spoils of the executioner, or of the soldiers who performed the crucifixions. Their actions are, as the sacred text notes, a perfect fulfillment of the twenty-first Psalm (twenty-second in Jewish and Protestant versions), verse 19: "They parted my garments amongst them and upon my vesture they cast lots."

Pilate wrote a title Pilate must have had a hateful disposition. Like all cowards he yielded ground when he feared he was about to get into trouble; but when there was no chance of reprisals against him he was brutally overbearing. Here was an opportunity to embarrass the leaders of the Jews by making it appear that they had wanted to have Pilate kill their King. This was exactly what they did want, but they didn't wish to see it flaunted before their faces now. They could not complain of this to Caesar because the more genuine the claims of Christ, the more praiseworthy Pilate's actions would appear to Caesar.

The Jews had made it seem that calling Himself King of the Jews was a crime. Barabbas would have set himself up as a king, and the elders certainly had an interest in him. Jesus was different from the pretenders who rose from time to time. Just the Sunday before, kingly honors had been paid to Him. The thought may have come to Pilate that perhaps Jesus *was* the King of the Jews. It might ease his conscience and increase his "getting even" with the men who had backed him in a corner to put on the placard, "Jesus of Nazareth, King of the Jews."

Then, as befits a king, His title was set up over His cloth of state above His throne—the throne of the Cross. The Jews did not like to see such honors paid, but Pilate for once was firm and definite. "What I have written, I have written." Perhaps Pilate was not being so brave as it appears, since a Roman judge could not reverse a verdict he had once given.

The Sorrowful Mysteries 217

Too bad for his own sake that he could not say: "He is innocent, *therefore I release Him.*"

. . . they that passed by, blasphemed Him, wagging their heads The leaders of the people were so blinded by their lust for power that they missed all the indications that the Messias was in the world in the person of Christ. It should have been very easy for them to see that they were enacting the prophecies about Jesus. Again: "All they that saw me laughed me to scorn; they have spoken with the lips and have wagged the head" (Ps. 21).

Why should these men set up as the test of the mission of Christ this coming down from the Cross? It was the Cross that was to save us, and also the men who persecuted Christ, if they would accept it. God had determined it as the price of our souls, and Christ was willing to pay. Who had any right to determine that there was any importance in His coming down from the Cross?

Some years ago there was a man named Ingersoll who went around making atheistic speeches. One very melodramatic situation which he proposed as a test for God was the supposed fate that God was to be forced to deal out to him if he denied Him. Ingersoll would stand on a platform and hold a watch in his hand. Then he would raise his fist to the heavens and say: "If there is a God I defy Him and I hereby give Him one minute in which to strike me dead as a proof that He exists." Then he would stand there holding the watch and counting off the seconds. At the end of the minute he would turn to the audience, by this time sitting tensely on the edge of the seats, and announce: "See, nothing has happened to me. Therefore there is no God." God was not ready to strike Ingersoll dead, and Christ was not ready to come down from the Cross.

He trusted in God; let Him now deliver Him Again the

blinded leaders bring the twenty-first psalm's prophecy to fruit, with almost the exact words used at the foot of the Cross: "He hoped in the Lord, let Him deliver Him; let Him save Him."

This day thou shalt be with Me in paradise This is the conversion of the Good Thief. In the midst of all the shouting about Christ's helplessness, how did this man ever see through it to conclude that Christ had a kingdom He would ever enter? If God's grace goes to such lengths to save the wretched, who has anything to fear? This is the unfathomable miracle of God's grace. Here were two great offenders against the law; men who would likely be guilty of death in any age of history. Here, between them, is a man who is an utter outcast. His Mother, a few pious women, and only one disciple have seen fit to follow Him in His disgrace. All the power of Jerusalem, both religious and civil, is arrayed against Him. He has just refused to answer a taunt to show His power—if He has any. One of the thieves has even thrown the same challenge to Him: "If Thou be the Christ, save Thyself and us."

Through what kind power of a merciful God did such a man as the Good Thief get the grace to penetrate the blackness he saw all around him, and reach the light he could not see? "Lord, remember me." Any sinner who reads that story and who does not glow with the hope of forgiveness when he turns to Christ on the Cross; any sinner who does not see himself again as a child of God as soon as he turns away from his sins, is in greater danger from despair than he is from his other sins.

It is on the solution of this problem that our unfortunate brother, the late Doctor Luther, went off the pathway. After worrying himself to the point of despair over the problem of the forgiveness of his sins, which probably were not too black, it suddenly occurred to him that he would hurl himself at the feet of the Savior. This, he felt, would be the supreme act of faith which would save him. Of course, this was hope, not faith, and there was nothing new about it. Sinners have always hoped for salvation, relying on the merits of Christ on the Cross. God knows we had no merits of our own when He came to save us, and we have no way of getting any merits apart from Christ, our Savior.

Do the best we can at being sorry and leave the rest to God. He will not merely cover our sins and leave them with us, as Dr. Luther felt—thus clinging to the main point of his despair—but He will wipe out our forgiven sins so completely that they will actually be a consolation to the tortured Christ in His agony in the Garden. Try hard to be sorry and we will never sin again in serious or even in small matters. Just don't turn away from Christ's graces.

Woman, behold thy son . . . behold thy mother At the wedding feast at Cana Christ had said to His Mother that His hour had not yet come, and then He went on to grant her request. Now His hour had come, and to us He gave the dearest treasure He possessed. He did not give her to St. John in a worldly or material sense, because Mary had relatives who would always have taken her into their homes. Many a time He had made it plain that His Mother was not to be honored just because of her natural relationship to Him, but because she had done the will of God. She was the new Eve and she was now being made the "Mother of all the living." She begot on Calvary all the souls of the just who live in Christ. The enmity between THE WOMAN and the Serpent was coming to fruit, and evil was receiving a hurt it will never recover from. This was the will of God that Mary had accepted in assuming the motherhood of the God-man. She had admitted Him into the world and it was for this hour. "For this was I born, and for this came I into the world," Christ had said.

Here in her darkest hour Mary is given the office of searching for souls to bring to Christ. And seeing at what price they were redeemed she will not rest until they are safely home in Christ.

And there was darkness This darkness appears to have been universal. Some pagan and Christian writers refer to the time of the darkness at noon, and the references agree with the time of the Crucifixion. The rationalist writers of the French Encyclopedia of the eighteenth century scoff at this darkness and call it an eclipse, but the Passover is at the full moon, and no such eclipse can take place, since the full moon is opposite the sun. Even a Chinese history, translated into French for the first time during the last century, has references to a midday darkness at about this same date. It may be that God was sending out calls to grace ahead of His apostles so that when the peoples in various parts of the Orient heard the gospel story they would recall from experience or tradition that this darkness had been over the earth at noon.

At least this abnormal darkness should have recalled to the mind of Christ's tormentors that the Prophet Amos had predicted that such would accompany the fall of Israel. In part: "And it shall come to pass in that day, saith the Lord God, that the sun shall go down at midday and I will make the earth dark in the day of light . . . and I will send forth a famine into the land; not a famine of bread, nor a thirst of water, but of hearing the word of God." This was the darkness that had overtaken them.

Eli, Eli, lamma sabacthani To the unwary this may seem to be a cry of despair. In fact, John Calvin, who had accused Christ of cowardice in His agony in the Garden, stated that this was a cry of despair and abandonment by God. Now despair is the sin against the Holy Ghost, and Christ did not commit any sin, let alone such a heinous sin as despair. Neither does God abandon anyone, and Christ could never have said anything such as this. This is a terrible wrong against Jesus Christ, as well as an error in interpretation.

The "Eli, Eli" is a quotation of the opening line of the twenty-first Psalm which the leaders of the people had been enacting during the Crucifixion. Now that the predicted darkness was settling down over the earth, this was the time to call the leaders to repentance. The psalm opens: "My God, My God, look upon me; why hast Thou forsaken me?" Then it continues, and they should have compared it with all that had been done that afternoon. ". . . they cried to Thee, and they were saved; they trusted in Thee and were not confounded . . . all they that saw me have laughed me to scorn; they have spoken with the lips, and wagged the head. . . . He hoped in the Lord, let Him deliver him: let Him save him, seeing He delighted in Him . . . depart not from me for tribulation is very near: for there is none to help me . . . they have opened their mouths against me, as a lion ravening and roaring . . . my strength is dried up like a potsherd, and my tongue hath cleaved to my jaws: and Thou hast brought me down to the dust of death. . . . For many dogs have encompassed me: the council of the malignant hath beseiged me. They have dug my hands and feet: they have numbered all my bones. And they have looked and stared at me. They parted my garments amongst them; and upon my vesture they cast lots."

But they would not heed. All they did was to twist His words into: "This Man calleth Elias . . . let us see whether Elias will come and save Him." Many of us have Christ's message given to us, but choose to distort the language into something far different from what Christ wants from us. Words are very tricky at times, and one needs good will in order not to lead himself astray in his own cleverness in attempting to avoid a call of grace.

I thirst   Jesus was about ready to let natural events take their course and to bring Him to His death. Until He willed it death could not claim Him. There was one more prophecy to fulfill. It was: ". . . they put gall in my food and in my thirst they gave me vinegar to drink" (Ps. 68:22). In His thirst they did give Him vinegar, or the bitter common wine of the soldiers. It was now time for Christ to die, for the Sabbath was coming on and if He were not dead they would break his legs, as they did for the other two. He would have had to intervene with a miracle, else the prophecy, "Neither shall you break a bone thereof" which was commanded for the Paschal lamb and referred to the Messias, would have been unfulfilled.

It is consummated The work of redemption is over and Jesus can return to the Father. The gates of heaven will open again on poor struggling mankind. From this moment it will be a different world from the one of just a moment before.

And Jesus crying with a loud voice said: *Father into Thy hands I commend My spirit* Note that Jesus spoke in a *loud voice*. It would seem that the very last thing that a person could do at the point of expiring from the tortures of crucifixion was to speak at all, let alone in a "loud voice." Anyone who has had a cramping of chest muscles to contend with, or who has had a pleurisy knows that speaking is almost an impossibility. This is ample evidence that Jesus had lived as long as it was His will, and then had freely surrendered His life at the time appointed. He had said: "I lay down My life when I will and I take it up again, and no man can take it from Me." The immolation of Christ for our sins was purely voluntary. No power of evil has any control over Him. Christ could still have come down from the Cross as He had been taunted to do, if He had willed to do so, but He would never will this, for the Father had willed otherwise. Christ had given His enemies a show of His power by speaking in "a loud voice." It was a final call of grace which was refused. They could have opened their eyes now as they could have done the night before when, in the Garden He threw them back like straws by saying: "I am He."

His human soul went to His Father. Around His dead body milled His tormentors, self-blinded by pride at what they thought was a great victory. Jesus was dead and there was now no one to oppose their control of Jewish affairs. They had won; or so they thought. Jesus is dead and we may say with St. John: "Dearly beloved, we are now the sons of God."

The veil of the temple was rent Just the night before, Christ had given Himself to the Church as a sacrifice, to take the place of the sacrifice of animals. "This is the chalice of My blood of the New and Eternal Testament. . . ." Now that His blood had been spilt upon Calvary's hill, the sacrifice of His precious blood in the chalice was as real as it was on Calvary, and this sacrifice is to endure. But the Temple was not to be the place of sacrifice. It passed into oblivion when the guardian angels of the Temple split the veil that separated the Holy of Holies from the Court of the Priests. God had dwelt in that center shrine in an especial way. Now the spot was no more holy than the rest of the Temple and there was no more reason why there had to be a separating veil. The outward appearance of the Temple will continue for a time. The infant Church will even make use of it during a transition period, but the armies of Titus will come in the year 70 and leave it in ruins, not a stone standing on a stone. Nothing remains to show where the Temple stood but a retaining wall that held up the hill on which it stood. This is the celebrated Wailing Wall where Jews come to pray devoutly that Israel may see the end of his exile. Pray God that they may be answered, and that those who were basely sold into spiritual slavery by their leaders by a solemn repudiation, "We have no King but Caesar," may accept the title put up by Pilate, "Jesus of Nazareth, King of the Jews."

Indeed, this was the Son of God The loud cry of Jesus at His death was not lost on the Centurion. He saw all nature in revolt at the sight of a God dead upon a Cross; the darkness, the dead rising, the rocks splitting; and he would have had to be morally obtuse indeed, not to see that something beyond all reckoning was being enacted before his eyes. Let us hope that this is grace and not terror working on him.

Then the Jews . . . besought Pilate that their legs might be broken In the spiritual life there are balances that must be maintained between outward observance and inward devotion. In the fourth joyful mystery we have seen Mary bringing Jesus to the Temple for a religious observance of which they had no internal need. That was good, for there are things of outward observance which we must do whether we think there is much need for them on our part or not. One great fault with the modern world is that many divorce themselves from all manner of outward observance. They do not go to any regular church services; they do not have a stated creed; they do nothing, except what they think or feel at the particular moment is what they want to do. Millions upon millions of our fellow Americans are in this unhappy condition.

Their excuse is that persons who do observe external ceremonies, who do attend church, and who align themselves with regular groups, are no better than they are. That, of course, has truth in it. There are many who give grave scandal in their conduct, yet would not think of leaving out anything external. This was the kind of scandal the Jews gave to the Romans who needed religion. What would they think of a people who felt that it was all right to harry an innocent Man to His death, but that there was something wrong in in leaving His body exposed over a certain day of the week? We all know that God made the Sabbath holy, but He also forbade murder.

The Sorrowful Mysteries

The purpose of breaking the legs was, of course, to hasten death. Whatever little support the legs gave on the cross would be removed, and the added pull on the chest muscles would hasten tetany, and it was also a great shock to one so weakened.

The Sabbath was approaching at sundown, but this day was also a kind of Sabbath itself, being the Festival Day, and no one had objected to breaking it many times. Usually the bodies of the crucified were left on the cross, as we have mentioned above, but the Jews had been able to get some sort of recognition of their beliefs which the Romans respected. The Romans were like the Reds of today in this. In one place they respected local beliefs and customs, and then when it became clear that there was no great danger to them any more they suppressed religions and customs with the utmost ferocity. Thus they treated the Druids in Gaul with brutality and the Jews with tolerance, but when it was no longer politically necessary to humor them they unleashed the horrors of invasion on them.

The soldiers found the two thieves still alive. They administered the brutal leg-breaking to them which killed them at once, or rendered them motionless enough to be dumped into a grave. But they found Jesus already dead. They were surprised at this, but Jesus had already suffered enough to cause death to any ordinary mortal. He had not eaten since the Last Supper the evening before; He had endured the agony in the Garden, and without sleep all night had been scourged and abused before He was crucified. Jesus permitted this treatment to have its natural effect upon Him in time to fulfill the prophecies.

All hell had been turned loose on Him at that hour, and Satan who knows the Scriptures as well as any of us—he showed that at the temptation of Christ—had entered into the hearts of Christ's enemies and torturers to urge them to such excesses of brutality that Jesus would die along the way and so would not be able to fulfill the prophecies. Satan with his bad will could not see the divinity of Christ and so, as must always happen to him, he was brought low by the frustration of his plans by the will of God. Satan did not comprehend that Christ was master of His life and would hold to it until He willed to lay it down.

You who are beset with trials and great troubles—hold fast to God. You can lose wealth, position, honor, and what not. You can be driven from your home and treated as our poor brothers and sisters were treated behind an Iron or Bamboo Curtain; but as long as your will is attached to God's, Satan can make no headway against you. He and all his fallen angels cannot overthrow you.

Christ willed to die before His legs were broken. Thus Providence intervened to see to it that the prophecy was fulfilled and, moreover, furnished the utter incontestible proof that Jesus was truly dead. We may show some surprise that the soldiers did not break His legs anyway, just to be sure. It may have been a little act of mercy.

There was a custom at crucifixions to reduce the amount of suffering to the victims, if they chose to show consideration. They sometimes hit the victim a hard blow over the heart with a blunt instrument to put him into a daze. If it pleased them to make the victim suffer more they delayed this blow until nearer the end. The Centurion may have had this in mind when the thought came to him to use his lance.

One of the soldiers with a spear opened His side St. John knew that he had an important piece of evidence in the fact that blood and water came forth from the side of Christ. This is a complete proof of death as it indicates that the heart muscles were split open; a "broken heart," if you will. It may have been from the pulling up of the chest muscles, or it may have been from the terrible sufferings He had endured, but when the blood poured forth from the broken heart wall into the sac that surrounds the heart, Jesus Christ was dead.

Then the inert blood not being pumped along the arteries, settled down and the red blood corpuscles separated from the colorless serum. St. John did not have a modern scientific name for this blood fraction, so he called it "water."

The Winding Sheet of Turin indicates that a mounted man drove his spear into the right side of Christ's body between the fifth and sixth ribs, into the auricle of the heart. The wound gaped open about a half inch and was a little over an inch and a half long. Such a wound would empty the separated blood from the pericardial sac. The sacred writer would not have known how to outrun medical science and falsify his description, nor would anyone have known how to counterfeit the mingled blood and serum stains on the Winding Sheet of Turin. Truly, they have "looked on Him, whom they have pierced."

Joseph of Arimathea . . . and Nicodemus also came   These men, who were members of the Sanhedrin, now came out into the open in behalf of Jesus and provided for His burial. Carefully they removed the body from the Cross and carried it to the new sepulcher that was the property of Joseph of Arimathea. What with the haste they needed to get Jesus into the tomb before sundown began the Sabbath, they had no chance to wash His body, nor to anoint it for burial, but taking a linen cloth they stretched it out under the body and brought it over the body, and with the aloes they brought for embalming merely strewn over the body and the sheet, they rolled the stone into place and left. The women noted the task was not done completely, so they prepared spices and ointments, waiting only for the first day of the week when the restrictions on their movements would be over, and they could do a more fitting work of laying out the body of Christ in death.

CHAPTER 11

The Glorious Mysteries

THE glorious mysteries are the gathering together of all that has gone before. As Jesus told His disciples on the road to Emmaus: "It was necessary for Christ to die and so enter into His glory." It will be, of course, necessary for us to suffer for Him and fight the good fight so that we, too, may enter into our glory, the glory that was prepared for us from the foundation of the world.

Most of us who have followed Christ have never seen Him, so that there needs to be a way for us to know what He wants from us, and how He expects us to bring what He wishes into our lives. Of those who did see Christ, very few knew the tremendous import of the occurrences that took place before their very eyes. Even the disciples did not know clearly at first what was involved in what Christ suffered for them.

Christ did not make any attempt to prove Himself to His enemies because they would have remained as hardhearted as before. Everything was devoted to bringing home to His friends and followers the truth of His message. They would then pass them on to others, not, however, as dead records of past centuries to be searched out, each one getting further from the source. Christ wished to leave His teachings in the hands of a living teaching agency which would be as new a thousand or even ten thousand years after His death and Ascension as it was when the words came from His own lips.

Christ, therefore, remains with us. He has sent us the Spirit of Truth to keep His teachings from error. He has given us His Mother as an advocate. He has kept His word; He will not leave us orphans.

The First Glorious Mystery: *Christ Returns from The Dead by His Own Power*

Death could have no claim on Christ. He laid down His life when He willed to do so for our sakes. When the work the Father had given Him to do was finished, He could pick up His life again. The Resurrection was necessary by reason of the very nature of Christ. As St. Peter said to the multitude on the day of Pentecost: Death could not hold Him bound.

The manner of the Resurrection was for our benefit, for Christ did not have to be so crushing in His proofs. He had only to rise and then depart for His heavenly home to enjoy His eternal glory; but there is no one thing that Christ could have done for us that He did not do. No man of good will can read or hear of the way that Christ rose from the dead, and the many things He did thereafter to clinch His lesson, without himself being attracted to it. Then, if a man pray for it, Christ will give him the gift of supernatural faith by which he will clearly see that Jesus did rise from the dead in the most literal sense of the terms.

Long before the time of His Passion Christ started to foretell His death and Resurrection, so that the apostles would be strengthened for the shock when He permitted His enemies to have control over Him, and be better able to accept the stunning fact of His return from the dead. For who had ever heard of a man coming back from the dead by his own power? Jesus had raised others to life from death; so had some of the prophets. Once a dead body had come back to life when it touched the relics of the prophet Eliseus. This would be different, Jesus would raise Himself by His own power. That was hard to accept, and now that He lay dead in the tomb, it was impossible to believe.

Jesus always spent much time building up His conclusions, for the truths He taught were so startling that men's minds had to be prepared over a long time to be able to get a basis for belief. Barely was the miracle at Cana performed when Jesus gave a "sign" in Jerusalem. "Destroy this temple and in three days I will build it up again." This will come back to Him at His trial before the Sanhedrin, and it will play a part in His condemnation. His apostles will remember this after the Resurrection and it will help their belief. Then He prepared men's minds for the Resurrection by specifically showing them that He had power, not only over sickness, but over death itself. First, He raised the son of the widow of Naim. This was impressive of course. "And there came a great fear on them all and they glorified God, saying: A great prophet is risen among us and God hath visited His people. And the rumor of Him went forth throughout all Judea and throughout all the country round about."

Then He gave them the sign of Jonas the prophet. "For as Jonas was in the whale's belly three days and three nights so shall the Son of man be in the heart of the earth three days and three nights." Later the Transfiguration with its forebodings of death. "Tell no man until the Son of man be risen from the dead." Next came a new victory over death in the raising of the daughter of Jairus. "And all were astonished with a great astonishment."

By revelation Peter learned that Christ is the "Son of the Living God." Christ told him openly that the "Son of man must suffer many things and be rejected by the ancients and the scribes, and be killed and after three days rise again." When Peter objected that it could never be, Jesus rebuked him and called all the multitude to hear in the presence of all the disciples that, "if any man will come after Me, let him deny himself and take up his cross daily and follow Me."

When Jesus restored the sight of the man born blind His affairs seemed to reach a crisis. For the first time a connection between the miracles of Christ and His office as Messias was brought out by the man born blind. Jesus pressed the issue. "Therefore doth the Father love Me, because I lay down My life that I may take it up again. No man taketh it from Me, but I lay it down of Myself and I have power to lay it down and I have power to take it up again." This was a claim of lordship over life and death which belongs to God alone. Some said: "He hath a devil." Others asked: "Can a devil open the eyes of one born blind?"

We also read of the stupendous miracle of the raising of Lazarus from the dead under circumstances that permit of no denial. The young man of Naim was not long dead; the daughter of Jairus was even called 'asleep' by Jesus, and perhaps men of ill will can, and no doubt do, evade the issue of a power over death by speaking of the girl being aroused from a coma. But with Lazarus the case was different. Christ waited, although His heart was touched with pity for His friends (it was again a case of His Father's business over a natural friendship), because He wished all to know that the decomposition of the tomb had first claimed Lazarus. When He asked that the stone be taken away from the tomb, Martha said: "Lord by this time, he stinketh, for he is now dead four days." This miracle sealed the doom of Christ and His death was decided upon.

The hour of the forces of evil is approaching. Jesus again takes His own and reminds them: "Behold we go up to Jerusalem and the Son of man will be betrayed to the chief priests, and to the scribes and to the ancients, and they shall condemn Him to death, and shall deliver Him to the Gentiles. And they shall mock Him, and spit upon Him, and scourge Him, and kill Him, and the third day He shall rise again."

The last thing Jesus did to foretell His coming death was to institute the Blessed Sacrament, in which He gave His body as delivered and His blood as spilt. His thoughts began to turn to the time after the Resurrection when He must strengthen His friends for His return to His Father. At last He entered His Passion as He had foretold. Now He had been done to death and lay in the cold darkness of the tomb. There remained only His rising again, but how does a man raise himself from the dead by his own power?

The ancients knew about His predictions of rising again. In their zeal to stop Him from having more influence in case He was able to come back, they thought they could prevent Him. All the power of the Temple and all the power of the Roman Empire were employed, apparently to see that there was no fraud done by the followers of Christ, but there was no courage left in any of them that they would try to steal His body and say He had risen again. What would they do after that? They had no power of their own to enforce their frauds. Would they try to form a spiritual kingdom as Christ had planned? No, for they did not understand that Christ had envisaged such a kingdom, because even after the Resurrection the sons of Zebedee, James and John the Beloved, still thought He was going to set up an earthly kingdom in which they wanted to be rulers of the people. Surely, none of them would try to overthrow the Roman Empire. Without Christ they could do nothing, just as we can do nothing without Him. But Christ had not come to establish an earthly paradise. Each of us still has to work out his salvation day by day, but we can have all the graces we need to aid us, and more, if we take the trouble to do serious praying to get them.

Recounting the Gospel story of the Resurrection, it seemed best to go back to Calvary for the setting of the guard and the sealing of the tomb. These things were designed to prevent the Resurrection. All four gospel stories are intertwined.

The Glorious Mysteries

And the next day which followed the Day of Preparation, the chief priests and the Pharisees came together to Pilate, saying: Sir, we have remembered that that seducer said while He was still alive; after three days I will rise again. Command, therefore, the sepulcher to be guarded to the third day: lest, perhaps, His disciples come and steal Him away and say to the people: He is risen from the dead; and the last error shall be worse than the first. Pilate saith to them: You have a guard: go guard it as you know. And they departing made the sepulcher sure, sealing the stone and setting guards.

And behold, there was a great earthquake, for an angel of the Lord descended from Heaven, and coming rolled back the stone, and sat upon it. And his countenance was as lightning, and his raiment as snow. And for fear of him the guards were struck with terror and became as dead men.

When it began to dawn towards the first day of the week, Mary Magdalen, and Mary the mother of James, and Salome brought sweet spices that coming they might anoint Jesus. And very early in the morning, the first day of the week they came to the sepulcher, the sun being now risen. And they said, one to another: Who shall roll us back the stone from the door of the sepulcher? And looking they saw the stone rolled back, for it was very great.

Mary Magdalen, ran therefore and cometh to Simon Peter, and to the other disciple whom Jesus loved, and saith to them: They have taken away the Lord out of the sepulcher and we know not where they have laid Him.

And (Mary the mother of James, and Salome) entering into the sepulcher, they saw a young man sitting on the right side, clothed with a white robe, and they were astonished.

Who said to them: Be not affrighted, you seek Jesus of Nazareth, who was crucified: He is risen; He is not here; behold the place where they laid Him.

But go, tell His disciples and Peter that He goeth before you into Galilee, there you shall see Him as He told you.

But they going out fled from the sepulcher. For a trembling and fear had seized them: and they said nothing to any man; for they were afraid.

(When Mary Magdalen came) Peter, therefore went out and that other disciple, and they came to the sepulcher. And they both ran together, and that other disciple did outrun Peter, and came first to the sepulcher. And when he stooped down, he saw the linen cloths lying, but yet he went not in. Then cometh Simon Peter, following him, and went into the sepulcher, and saw the linen cloths lying and the napkin that had been about His head, not lying with the linen cloths but apart, wrapped up into one place.

Then that other disciple also went in, who came first to the sepulcher, and he saw and believed. For as yet they know not the Scripture, that He must rise again from the dead. The disciples, therefore departed again to their home.

(On Friday, after the crucifixion) the women that were come with Him from Galilee, following after saw the sepulcher, and how His body was laid. And returning, they prepared spices and ointments, and on the Sabbath day they rested, according to the commandment.

And on the first day of the week, very early in the morning they came to the sepulcher, bringing the spices which they had prepared. And they found the stone rolled back from the sepulcher.

And going in, they found not the body of the Lord Jesus. And it came to pass, as they were astonished in their mind at this, behold, two men stood by them, in shining apparel. And as they were afraid and bowed down their countenance towards the ground, they said unto them: Why seek you the living with the dead? He is not here, but is risen. Remember how He spoke unto you, when He was yet in Galilee, saying: The Son of man must be delivered into the hands of sinful men and be crucified, and the third day rise again. And they remembered His words.

And going back from the sepulcher behold Jesus met them,

saying: *All hail.* But they came up and took hold of His feet, and adored Him. Then Jesus said to them: *Fear not. Go tell My brethren that they go into Galilee, there they shall see Me.*

They told all these things to the eleven and to the rest. And these words seemed to them as idle tales, and they did not believe them.

(When Peter and John) departed again to their homes, Mary stood at the sepulcher without, weeping. Now as she was weeping she stooped down, and looked into the sepulcher. And she saw two angels in white, sitting, one at the head, and one at the feet, where the Body of Jesus had been laid.

They said to her: *Woman, why weepest thou?* She saith to them: *Because they have taken away my Lord, and I know not where they have laid Him.*

When she had said that she turned herself back, and saw Jesus standing, and she knew not that it was Jesus. Jesus saith to her: *Woman, why weepest thou? Whom seeketh thou?* She, thinking that it was the gardener, saith to Him: *Sir, if thou hast taken Him hence; tell me where thou hast laid Him, and I will take Him away.*

Jesus saith to her: *Mary.*

She, turning, saith to Him: *Rabboni* (which is to say, Master).

Jesus saith to her: *Do not touch me for I am not as yet ascended to My Father, to My God and to your God.* Mary Magdalen cometh and telleth the disciples. *I have seen the Lord, and these things He said to me.*

When they were departed from the sepulcher, behold some of the guards came into the city, and told the chief priests all things that had been done. And they being assembled together with the ancients taking counsel, gave a great sum of money to the soldiers, saying: *Say you, His disciples came by night, and stole Him away when we were asleep. And if the governor shall hear of this, we will persuade him and se-*

cure you. So they, taking the money, did as they were taught; and this word was spread abroad among the Jews, even unto this day.

And behold, two disciples went, the same day, to a town which was sixty furlongs from Jerusalem, named Emmaus. And they talked together of all these things which had happened. And it came to pass that while they talked and reasoned with themselves, Jesus Himself, drawing near, went with them, but their eyes were held, that they should not know Him.

And He said to them: What are these discourses that you hold with one another as you walk, and are sad? And one of them whose name was Cleophas, answering said to Him: Art Thou only a stranger in Jerusalem, and hast Thou not known the things that have been done there in these days? To whom He said: What things? And they said:

Concerning Jesus of Nazareth, who was a prophet, mighty in work and word before God and all the people; and how our chief priests and princes delivered Him to be condemned to death, and crucified Him.

But we hoped that it was He that should have redeemed Israel, and now besides all this, today is the third day since these things were done.

Yea, and certain women also of our company affrighted us, who before it was light were at the sepulcher, and not finding His body came saying that they had seen a vision of angels, who say that He is alive. And some of our people went to the sepulcher, and found it so as the women had said, but Him they found not.

Then He said to them: O foolish and slow of heart to believe in all things which the prophets have spoken. Ought not Christ to have suffered these things, and so to enter into His glory?

And beginning at Moses and all the prophets, He expounded to them in all the Scriptures, the things that were concerning Him.

And they drew nigh to the town, whither they were go-

ing: and He made as though He would go farther. But they constrained Him, saying: Stay with us, because it is towards evening, and the day is now far spent. And He went in with them.

And it came to pass, whilst He was at table with them, He took bread, and blessed and brake, and gave to them.

And their eyes were opened, and they knew Him; and He vanished out of their sight. And they said one to the other: Was not our heart burning within us, whilst He spoke in the way, and opened to us the Scriptures?

And rising up the same hour, they went back to Jerusalem: and they found the eleven gathered together, and those that were with them, saying: The Lord is risen indeed, and hath appeared to Simon. And they told what things were done in the way; and how they knew Him in the breaking of the bread.

Now when it was late that same day, the first of the week, and the doors were shut where the disciples were gathered together for fear of the Jews, Jesus came and stood in the midst and said to them: Peace be to you. And when He had said this, He showed them His hands and His side, and He upbraided them with their incredulity and hardness of heart, because they did not believe them who had seen Him after He had risen again.

But they being troubled and frightened, supposed that they saw a spirit. And He said to them: Why are you troubled, and why do thoughts arise in your hearts? See My hands and feet, that it is I Myself, handle and see: for a spirit hath not flesh and bones, as you see Me to have. And when He had said this, He showed them His hands and feet.

But while they yet believed not, and wondered for joy, He said: Have you here anything to eat? And they offered Him a piece of broiled fish, and a honey-comb. And when He had eaten before them, taking the remains, He gave to them. The disciples were, therefore, glad when they saw the Lord. He said, therefore, to them again:

Peace be to you. As the Father hath sent Me, I also send

you. When He had said this, He breathed on them; and He said to them: Receive ye the Holy Ghost. Whose sins you shall forgive, they are forgiven them; and whose sins you shall retain, they are retained.

Now Thomas, one of the twelve, who was called the Twin, was not with them when Jesus came. The other disciples therefore said to him: We have seen the Lord.

But he said to them: Except I shall see in His hands the print of the nails, and put my hand into His side, I will not believe.

And after eight days again His disciples were within, and Thomas with them, Jesus cometh, the doors being shut, and stood in the midst and said: Peace be to you.

Then He said to Thomas: Put thy finger hither, and see My hands; and bring hither thy hand and put it into My side; and be not faithless but believing.

Thomas answered and said to Him: My Lord and My God.

Jesus said to him: Because thou hast seen Me, Thomas, thou hast believed: blessed are they that have not seen and have believed (Matt. 27).

And the next day . . . the chief priests and pharisees came together to Pilate The disciples were scattered in complete terror at the arrest of Jesus, and now were huddled together awaiting whatever fate would overtake them after the rest prescribed for the Sabbath. Did the leaders of the people expect for one moment that out of such a group would come enough courage to steal away the body of Christ? If they did that, what would they do next? Jesus alone was the Master; these men had no following either to lead a revolt against Rome or to set up a spiritual kingdom in the face of the Temple.

The scribes and the pharisees well knew what Jesus had taught, and they had seen His power. They had, as they thought, overcome this power by force, and they imagined they could continue to rule by force. It is easier to think that they *did* believe that Jesus was coming back from the dead, than to consider that they imagined that the disciples were bold enough to steal His body away for propaganda purposes. If Jesus did return from the dead they would be there with an armed force to greet Him. If force did it once, force would do it again. They were not going to give up the positions of great influence they held in Jerusalem. This is not farfetched since it seems that one who commits mortal sin implies that he can kill God. They would dress up their motives for Pilate as a fear of fraud. It is well that they acted as they did for they have furnished additional proof for the validity of the Resurrection, which has helped many in Jerusalem to believe in Jesus Christ. An armed guard and the seal of the Empire were enough to cope with whatever zeal remained in the disciples. No one so much as approached the tomb, except the women, and they came only to perform the last sad rites over the dead.

And, behold there was a great earthquake Then took place the greatest event in human history—a man who had been killed by prolonged brutal treatment came back to life by His own power. If it had not been *His own power* He would still be in the tomb, dead. He had said that He would rise again. Everyone knew He had made this statement, time and again. It was precisely on account of the claim of Jesus that He could renew His own life that the guard had been posted over His tomb. Whoever talks as He did is claiming access to the power of God, since only God can make a dead thing live again. "Can a devil open the eyes of one born blind?" Can a devil open the eyes of one who is dead? Jesus did not claim, merely, that God would raise Him as He had raised Lazarus. Jesus claimed that He would raise Himself, which is a claim that He is God. If Christ spoke the truth He was really God, and if He did not speak the truth God could not make Himself a party to a fraud. Thus, Christ has in Himself the power of God. Everything we believe and hold dear depends upon the Resurrection. As St. Paul said: "Unless Christ be truly risen from the dead, your faith is vain and you remain in your sin."

But Christ had risen and as yet no man knew it. How much the guards saw of what really happened we do not know. We do know that they later chose bribery, and like their master, Pilate, turned their backs on truth. The work of salvation had been accomplished. Christ could have returned to His Father and to His glory, but that is not Christ's way. With patience He teaches us and He leads us with example. He goes with us to extremes, demanding of us only good will.

Now Christ was to begin His series of startling proofs to fix the fact of His rising from the dead so firmly in the minds of His followers that they could never again doubt it; and they would then go out into the world, spend themselves, and even give their lives so that man would receive the living teaching of the Resurrection with faith and joy until the end of time.

What a day that first Easter must have been! In spite of all the predictions which Christ made of His death and rising again from the dead; in spite of the fact that many of His miracles were intertwined with predictions of His Resurrection, still His followers were scandalized at His death and were swept from the field. Only the Blessed Virgin kept faith's light burning in her heart. That is why she did not go to the tomb that morning. She alone knew there was no need. From the beginning, as her Son's mission unfolded, "Mary kept all these words in her heart." The Gospel does not tell of Christ's visit to His Mother on Easter morning, as it might cause us to think she had *need* of such a visit to revive her faith. Of course, Christ did visit His Mother. He would certainly go to see her first of all.

The Gospel tells us only of the visits made to those who were in great need of being shocked into realization that

The Glorious Mysteries 241

Christ was truly risen. Non-believers try to make us believe that the apostles and the other followers of Christ were hypnotized into a conviction that Christ would rise. But there never was a lost cause so lost as this one when the large circular stone was rolled into place across the mouth of the tomb, sealed with the seal of Caesar, and guarded by the legionaries of Rome. Christ had told them not long before that "he who will not take up his cross daily and follow Me, is not worthy of Me." Would they follow Him to the cross? Would they hypnotize themselves into being *crucified?* No! They were huddled together in terror, not knowing the great happiness and joy that awaited them. Perhaps we also shrink away from the chastising hand of God, while in that hand awaits the very happiness we thought we had lost.

When it began to dawn The earliest possible moment was chosen by the holy women for their pious work of preparing Jesus for His burial. The first group, headed by Mary Magdalen, moved towards the tomb. Evidently, they knew nothing about the guard; they did not have the men with them to help them, and we shall never know how they expected to have the stone rolled back for them at such an early hour. It is one of those instances where personal charity dictated that they go, and then (as with Mary at the Visitation) God raised their act to a great public revelation. The stones which closed the openings of tombs among the Hebrews were of considerable size in a vault of this kind. This vault was newly cut out and belonged to Joseph of Arimathea. Only one corpse was meant to lie in such a vault, and it was forbidden to disturb the dead once they were laid away. In the case of Jesus, the last rites were prevented by the approaching Sabbath day, and His friends were allowed to come and complete them.

The stone has already been described. Indications from the Scripture in the incident of the raising of Lazarus suggest it needed the help of several men to remove a stone from the door of the tomb. Joseph and Nicodemus had not sealed the tomb, evidently, but this was done by the soldiers. Moving the stone was clearly beyond the strength of three women, and this was on their minds. Imagine their great surprise when the stone was rolled away from the entrance.

Mary Magdalen, ran therefore Mary could think of nothing but running to the apostles with the news that the body of the Lord was missing. She was the sister of Lazarus and had seen the great might of God. We may express some surprise that Mary did not remember what Christ had said about rising from the dead. She could think of nothing except the theft of the body. This shows how far from fraud the thoughts of the followers of Christ were that morning.

. . . entering the sepulcher Mary Magdalen hurried away and the other Mary and Salome entered the tomb where an angel in the guise of a young man gave the first announcement of the Resurrection, and so set in motion a chain of events to establish the fact in the minds of all His disciples. This is the message of Easter which has echoed down the ages: "He is risen, He is not here; behold the place where they laid Him."

Go, tell His disciples and Peter Events began to accelerate from this point. Mary Magdalen was on her way to Peter, and now the two other women rushed back with a different tale. The body was not stolen away: He had risen.

Peter, therefore, went out, and that other disciple This is the touching scene of Peter and John running to the tomb. By reason of his youth and great love, John soon outstripped Peter, who was much older and had no stamina for such violent efforts, even on such a morning as this. John reached the tomb first, but Peter had the primacy and must be per-

The Glorious Mysteries

mitted to enter first. John could not forebear to take a look within, and he saw there the linens that had enfolded Christ lying to one side. There lay a long linen cloth since become known as the Winding Sheet of Turin, and a smaller 'napkin' that customarily covered the face. After they entered the tomb they were convinced that Jesus had risen and the effect on them was immediately apparent. Before this they were penned up with the others in the supper room where they were hiding; now they felt secure enough to return to their homes.

And going in they found not the body of the Lord Jesus This refers to the second group of women; those who had stayed behind to see the hasty preparations Nicodemus and Joseph were making at the tomb. What they saw did not satisfy them, so they went down to the tomb early Sunday morning. A message was given to them, too, at the empty tomb. They remembered the words of the Lord about His rising, and off they went to tell the disciples. Jesus Himself appeared to them so as to strengthen the message they, too, received from the angels. The disciples did not believe them, so it seems that Peter and John went straight home without going back to tell the others what they had experienced. Somewhere along here the Lord appeared to Peter, but when and where we do not know.

Woman, why weepest thou? Mary Magdalen could not be consoled. She had learned nothing of what was going on around her, and in her grief did not even wait for a message from the angels. Jesus then came to her, as He will come to us in our troubles if we seek Him.

Behold, some of the guards Never have men been so upset. These were rough soldiers who knew how to contend with enemies on the battlefield, and how to crush a conquered enemy. Uprisings and plots were all around them, and they were hardened to danger, but never had they seen so much power used before. Like frightened children these tough campaigners fled away. It was not a disgrace to run away from such a demonstration, and it is hard to see why they had allowed themselves to be used to conceal the truth, in a way no soldier should ever have permitted. They confessed that they fell asleep on post. They confessed that they had allowed the seal of the Empire to be broken under their guard. For either of these offenses the death penalty could have been decreed for them. Even today with all the humanitarian advances in the treatment of soldiers, a man can be shot for sleeping on duty. Why did Pilate not punish them? By this time he was so badly driven from control that he swallowed even this flagrant insult to his rank of Commander—that his men would openly admit to sleeping on post and permitting the Emperor's seal to be broken. The soldiers received much gold for their parts, but what did Pilate get? In another run-in with the Jews Pilate was recalled to Rome in disgrace some time after this, and it is believed that he ended up a suicide. The soldiers' story was spread all over Jerusalem as the leaders wanted the story that Christ's body was stolen away to be believed. The sacred writer says that the story has persisted "even to this day," meaning the first century, and it keeps cropping up even in the twentieth century.

And behold, two disciples went . . . to Emmaus Even after the evidence of the Resurrection got to the disciples, they were still not too convinced. Two men were leaving the city of Jerusalem as others will soon be doing. Sabbath restrictions on travel were over and it was time to get away from the wrath of the Sanhedrin. The beautiful possibility of redemption for Israel was over for them. They saw this, not with bitterness but with sad regrets. Men such as they do not steal bodies and lead revolts in the name of falsified resurrections.

The Glorious Mysteries

Why could not the leaders have read the Scriptures and recognized in Jesus the Messias? Had His disciples been learned men they would have seen what these two men were to see now for the first time. It was only when Jesus took bread, blessed it and said: "Take ye and eat for this is My body," that they knew clearly who it was that was with them. When we are in travail and in trouble we can have our eyes opened at the Holy Sacrifice of the Mass by these same words.

Poor men! So great was their joy that they could not wait to get back to Jerusalem to bring the good news to the others. It was well on to evening, but they went back over the seven miles or more to the Holy City; through the small night gate and then across the city to the Cenacle, where the others were gathered. Jesus was kind enough to let them get there first.

. . . late that same day . . . Jesus came Then the supreme proof was given them. Jesus came through locked doors, barred solid, to stand in the same room with all of the disciples. They might well be troubled because this was an event that had never happened before in this world. The disciples were slow in believing, and even with Christ standing among them they were still slow to accept the testimony of their own senses. Even the sight of His wounds did not convince them. But at last when Christ ate with them they did accept the tremendous truth, that Christ was alive in the flesh.

Whose sins you shall forgive, they are forgiven them This was the first fruit of the Resurrection, and it is most fitting that Christ conveyed this power on the very day He rose. When Christ rose from the dead the grip of sin was broken and already the power to bring forgiveness was being given to the apostles to be passed on to their successors, and so to continue till the end of time.

Now Thomas . . . was not with them Thomas has to take a lot of undeserved blame for being a skeptic, but the others were hard to convince even while Jesus stood before them. When Christ showed Thomas His wounds, he believed, whereas the others held off until Christ ate with them as a final proof He was there in the flesh. Thomas represents us. Jesus was soon to leave this world and return to the Father, but men still would need to receive the message of Christ with faith, although they will not get an opportunity of seeing Him visibly amongst them. We are the ones whom Christ calls blessed because we have received Him with joy in faith. We shall see Him when we are called home to the Father. Our first glimpse of Him will be when He says to us: "Come ye blessed of My Father."

In vain the enemies of Christ tried to scoff at the evidence of the Resurrection, but there is no event in all history so fully documented as this. Monuments, documents, the evidence of the Catacombs, ancient texts of Scripture, so well preserved throughout the centuries. We have the writings of the Fathers of the Church which evidence their succession from the apostles. For example, there is the testimony of the martyr bishop, St. Irenaeus, who said to prove the truth of his teachings: "I have this from Polycarp, who had it from John, who had it from Christ." There is the unbroken succession of the popes and the councils down to the present living teaching of the Church; all of which is overwhelming to an honest searcher. But Christ through His herald angels promised peace only to men of good will. If we let the implications of the Resurrection sink deep into our souls we shall never swerve from the Faith.

The Second Glorious Mystery:
Our Lord Ascends into Heaven

The sacred humanity of Jesus Christ was united to the second Person of the Blessed Trinity from the first moment of His conception, so that everything He did had infinite efficacy for our redemption from the effects of sin. This was the divine aspect of His nature.

Christ was man also—a truth we are prone to overlook because we keep the stress on the fact that Christ is God. We do well to keep insisting on His divinity since the modern tendency is to forget or even to deny this. But Christ was man, and as man He had an eternal reward due to Him just as we shall have an eternal reward for working out the will of the Father.

Christ, then, ascended into heaven to enter upon His reward. Hence the necessity of returning to the bosom of His Father. Christ also returned to heaven for our sakes. If He had, in some way, stayed with us He would have had to be the visible head of the Church. This was not His plan. He willed to remain with us in the Blessed Sacrament, and to make us His members—the very members of His body—in the mystical body of Christ, which is the Catholic Church.

The details of the Ascension are found in the first chapter of the Acts.

The former treatise I made, O Theophilus, of all things which Jesus began to do and to teach, until the day on which, giving commandment by the Holy Ghost to the apostles whom He had chosen, He was taken up.

To whom also, He showed Himself alive after His Passion, by many proofs for forty days appearing to them and speaking of the kingdom of God. And eating together with them he commanded them that they should not depart from Jerusalem, but should wait for the promise of the Father, which you have heard (said He) by My mouth. For John indeed baptized with water, but you shall baptize with the Holy Spirit not many days hence.

They, therefore, who were come together, asked Him saying: Lord wilt Thou at this time restore the Kingdom to Israel? But He said to them: It is not for you to know the times or moments which the Father hath put in His own power, but you shall receive the power of the Holy Spirit coming upon you, and shall be witnesses unto me in Jerusalem and in all Judea and Samaria, and even to the uttermost parts of the earth.

And When He had said these things, while they looked on, He was raised up; and a cloud received Him out of their sight.

And while they were beholding Him going up to heaven, behold two men stood by in white garments, who also said: Ye men of Galilee why stand you looking up to heaven? This Jesus who is taken up from you into heaven, shall so come, as you have seen Him going into heaven.

And they returned to Jerusalem from the mount which is Olivet, which is nigh Jerusalem, within a Sabbath day's journey. And when they were come in, they went up into an upper room where abode Peter and John, James and Andrew, Philip and Thomas, Bartholomew and Matthew, James of Alpheus and Simon Zelotes, and Jude the brother of James.

All these were persevering with one mind in prayer with the women and Mary, the mother of Jesus, and with His brethren.

He showed Himself alive . . . for forty days Jesus would not return to His glory until He had done everything to strengthen His chosen followers to a point where they could launch His work. He had promised at the Last Discourse that He would not leave them orphans. We know that grace works through nature, and Jesus was not going to leave the disciples at loose ends waiting for the coming of the Holy Spirit. Finding them fishing, He duplicated the miracle of the draft of fishes, loading their nets after a fruitless night, as He had done when He first called Peter, and James, and John. Then from this simple background which must have recalled to them all the events of the past three years, He

The Glorious Mysteries

began His final work. He had not removed Peter from the primacy because of his denial, but no one could be sure. Peter had sinned through panic, and now, through love, he was given an opportunity to work out expiation. Here it was settled for all to know that Peter would feed, not only the lambs, but the sheep.

Christ had already provided through the sacrament of penance the means of destroying actual sin, and He next instituted baptism, about which He had told Nicodemus long ago. This is the gateway to salvation. Only through baptism does a soul reach the supernatural life; else it cannot hope ever to see God face to face.

In our remarks above on faith we decried the harshness of zealots who make this mean an outward formal membership in the Catholic Church. God looks upon the good will of the soul first of all, and grants baptism of desire to all who seek after Him according to their lights. We must avoid being zealots but neither should we follow the laxists who declare that it does not make any difference what a person believes. Earnestness is not indifference, and we must be careful not to close the gates of heaven on anyone for whom God has left them open.

The apostles were unlettered men, for the most part, and there are instances where they did not understand the simple parables Christ used. Surely, most of them, if not all, did not understand the Scriptures about Christ. Accordingly, Jesus opened their understanding that they might see clearly the prophetic teachings about Himself.

Not content with the official witnesses He had for His Resurrection in the apostles and the holy women closest to Him, Jesus appeared to more than five hundred persons at one time in Galilee, so that His work could get off to a start. Nothing was left undone that would prepare the chosen band for the time when He had to leave them for "a little while."

. . . speaking of the Kingdom of God   This was a time of

retreat, a preparation for labors that were to come. "My Kingdom is not of this world," Christ had told Pilate, and one of the hardest things to do was to get this thought into the minds of those who had been with Him for three years. All that was required of them Jesus told them, commanding them to wait in Jerusalem, in the center of opposition until the Holy Spirit, the Helper, should come. There would be a change from symbols to reality—as from the baptism of John, which was a sign of internal cleansing, to the coming of the Spirit which would burn all else away as fire does.

Lord, wilt Thou at this time restore the kingdom of Israel?
It was known to all the Apostles that Jesus was the Messias who was to come to save Israel, and we must not be too hard on them if they expected the temporal kingdom to be restored as well. For about fifteen hundred years, since the time of Moses, there had been a blending of the spiritual and the temporal in Israel. Now a foreign invader occupied their country that God had blessed and promised to make a mighty nation. It was difficult for simple minds to take in. How could there be a spiritual kingdom without a temporal protector? In the beginning Israel had been a theocracy until the people demanded of God that they should have a king as other nations. God granted their request, but it had not gone well with them and in time the kingdom split and was overrun by enemies. The kingly line was now extinct; the only king was Caesar. There would be no restoration of the political kingdom, but all boundaries of race and place were to be ignored and this new kingdom was to be preached in Judea to friends, and in Samaria to enemies, and then in all the world to strangers. This was the last kingdom of Daniel which in time will overcome the opposition of the Roman Empire and become a universal kingdom to endure forever. "I am with you all days even to the consummation of the world."

And when He had said those things . . . He was raised up
Long ago, after the multiplication of the loaves and fishes, when Christ walked upon the waters to prove His control over nature He followed with the stupendous promise of His body and blood as food for their souls. He had given a sign: If you shall see the Son of man ascend up where He was before. . . ." Now He was being taken up into heaven where He shall live and reign with His Father forever, but He has left for us His body and blood in the Blessed Sacrament.

The apostles under Peter were now the rulers of the Kingdom of God. It was theirs to organize as they saw fit, to preserve and to develop the teachings of Christ without corrupting them. Jesus was gone from their sight but not from their hearts. To them and to us was given the work of becoming more and more like Christ.

Christ, the promise of our future glory, has gone back to the Father to prepare a place for us. Do we see how our daily tasks and sufferings are only the prelude to what is coming? Are we running away from the risen Christ as the two disciples on the road to Emmaus, thinking He was not to be found? If we are, Christ will overtake us on the road and teach us that we ought to have suffered and so entered into our glory.

St. Augustine says: "Let us follow Christ to heaven by faith and love here below, so that we may follow Him thither on the day designated by eternal promise. If the Ascension of the Lord is to be celebrated fittingly, faithfully, and holily and piously by us, we shall ascend with Him, and have our hearts joined with Him in our celestial homeland."

This Jesus . . . shall so come as you have seen Him going into Heaven This is not the end of things. Jesus has not gone away from us. He abides with us to be our strength, for, as He has told us: "Without Me, you can do nothing." But at the end of time this same Jesus will return with all

His power and majesty to be the judge of the living and the dead. In the living He will see His own life reflected, because these living are those who live in Christ. These He will take to Himself. The dead will have no part with Him since they have cut themselves off from the divine life, the only life that will avail at this awful judgment seat. Was this the terrible vision before Christ in His agony; the thought that many would not avail themselves of His saving grace, and that he would as judge have to condemn them forever? The judgment seat will stand where Christ ascended near to the place of His agony.

Then they returned to Jerusalem The apostles were to receive the direct visitation of the Holy Spirit to preserve them from error in their mission. The holy women were to be filled with the Spirit as Sanctifier. The Blessed Mother was to be given further work to do, nurturing the early Church until it was time for her to go back to her Son and to her eternal reward.

All these were persevering with one mind in prayer with the women and Mary, the mother of Jesus, and with His brethren The number of the apostles instituted by Christ was twelve, but "all these" designates only eleven, since Judas had hanged himself. Peter, as leader, rose up and decided upon the election of a successor to Judas. A choice was made of Matthias, and so was performed the first administrative act of the Catholic Church through her bishops and the pope in council. Matthias was an apostle just as much as he would have been if Christ had picked him in person. "Whatsoever thou shalt bind upon earth it shall be bound also in heaven."

Mary was with them during the first stirrings of the Church to be born on Pentecost, and that Church, the mystical body of Christ, has always striven to see that she is with us. It is in Mary, and through Mary, and by Mary that Christ sends His graces down upon us. He came to us through her and wills that we shall go back to Him through her.

*The Third Glorious Mystery:
The Descent of The Holy Spirit upon The
Apostles and The Blessed Virgin*

The Holy Spirit is the Helper, the Paraclete that Jesus had promised His apostles; the Spirit of Truth who would remain with them and guide them until the end of time. At the Last Supper He had told them: "I will not leave you orphans." Therefore He left them and us Himself in the Blessed Eucharist—in the Mass and as Holy Communion. He left us all the other sacraments as means whereby we could avail ourselves of the infinite merits He had won for us on the Cross.

When Christ ascended to His Father the apostles and the holy women made a novena of preparation for the great coming of the Sanctifier. When the Holy Spirit came there came with Him the final act of change from the personal rule of Jesus Christ to rule through His Vicar, St. Peter and his successors. The Catholic Church came into being at the moment of the descent to preserve intact until the end of time all the teachings of Jesus Christ. This is the public mission of the Holy Spirit. He guides priests in the confessional, He preserves infallibly through the bishops the ordinary teachings of the Lord through the Catholic Church; He keeps the pope from error when he speaks in matters of faith and morals to the whole world.

To each man personally He is the Sanctifier, coming into the soul at baptism and remaining there until driven forth by mortal sin. He guides us, admonishes us, and encourages us in the struggle against evil. He helps us to regain the virtues which we lost as gifts of our human nature through the Fall of our first parents. Somewhere in the human heart there is a longing for the lost terrestrial Paradise. All false teachers say they will restore this, and man listens to his sorrow.

The world is now going through one of those periods of mass delusion in which chemistry and mechanics, technics and electronics promise to bring "happiness" to all. Besides this false belief which has penetrated almost all ranks, the excesses of Communism are trifles. There is no other way to explain the way the Reds took over entire nations without firing a shot unless we understand a frame of mind that took the heart out of possible defenders. Communism must have been speaking to the inner aspirations of many who would be horrified at the thought that they are like the Reds.

There are so many people looking for the kind of world in which all evil will be destroyed so that they can all be good in the way they want to be "good," without effort or struggle; or they seek to throw off all restraints so that what men call "good" and "evil" will be exactly what attracts them or repels them at a given time. These men deny that there is a good or an evil outside their own thinking. That is not the sort of world we live in. There is evil in the world and it will remain—the cockle in the wheat—until the end of time. The Holy Spirit came down to dwell with us, to give us strength to overcome evil in ourselves through regeneration. God will not destroy evil at this time. He will give us all the graces we need to fight the evil around us, and so to root it up from our own lives. These helps are supernatural, given to help man to overcome the downward pull in his nature from original sin. The Holy Spirit came to help us in a struggle; not to take us out of it.

The story of the coming of the Holy Spirit is in Acts, the second chapter.

And when the days of the Pentecost were accomplished, they were all together in one place: and suddenly there came a sound from heaven as of a mighty wind coming, and it filled the whole house where they were sitting.

And there appeared to them parted tongues, as it were, of fire, and it sat upon every one of them. And they were filled

The Glorious Mysteries

with the Holy Ghost, and they began to speak according as the Holy Spirit gave them to speak. Now there were dwelling at Jerusalem, Jews, devout men out of every nation under heaven. And when it was noised abroad, the multitude came together and were confounded in mind because that every man heard them speak in his own tongue. And they were all amazed, and wondered saying: Behold, are not all these that speak Galileans? And how have we heard, every man our own tongue wherein we were born? Parthians, and Medes, and Elamites, and inhabitants of Mesapotamia, Judea, and Cappadocia, Pontus and Asia, Phrygia, and Pamphilia, Egypt, and parts of Lybia about Cyrene, and strangers of Rome, Jews, also, and proselytes, Cretes and Arabians: we have heard them speak in our own tongues the wonderful works of God.

And they were astonished and wondered, saying one to another: What meaneth this? But others, mocking, said: These men are full of new wine.

But Peter standing up with the eleven, lifted up his voice and spoke to them: Ye men of Judea, all that dwell in Jerusalem, be this known to you, and with your ears receive my words. For these are not drunk, as you suppose, seeing it is but the third hour of the day. But this is that which was spoken of by the prophet Joel:

And it shall come to pass in the last days (saith the Lord) I will pour out my spirit upon all flesh: and your sons and daughters shall prophesy, and your young men shall see visions, and your old men shall dream dreams. And upon my servants, indeed, and upon my handmaids will I pour out in those days of my spirit, and they shall prophesy. And I will shew wonders in the heaven above, and signs on the earth beneath: blood and fire and vapor of smoke. The sun shall be turned into darkness, and the moon into blood, before the great and manifest day of the Lord come. And it shall come to pass, that whosoever shall call upon the name of the Lord shall be saved.

Ye men of Israel, hear these words: Jesus of Nazareth, a man approved of God among you, by miracles and wonders, and signs, which God did by Him. In the midst of you as you also know:

This same being delivered up by the determinate counsel and foreknowledge of God, you by the hands of wicked men have crucified and slain. Whom God hath raised up, having loosed the sorrows of hell, as it was impossible that He should be holden by it, for David said concerning Him:

I foresaw the Lord before my face: Because He is at my right hand that I may not be moved. For this my heart hath been glad, and my tongue hath rejoiced; moreover my flesh also shall rest in hope, because Thou wilt not leave my soul in hell, nor suffer thy Holy One to see corruption.

Thou hast made known to me the ways of my life: Thou shalt make me full of joy with thy countenance.

Ye men, brethren, let me speak freely to you of the patriarch David; that he died and was buried; and his sepulcher is with us to this present day, whereas therefore he was a prophet, and knew that God hath sworn to him with an oath that of the fruit of his loins one should sit upon his throne.

Foreseeing this, he spoke of the resurrection of Christ, for neither was He left in hell, neither did His flesh see corruption.

This Jesus hath God raised again, whereof we are all witnesses. Being exalted, therefore, by the right hand of God, and having received of the Father the promise of the Holy Ghost, He hath poured forth this which you see and hear.

For David ascended not into heaven; but he himself said: The Lord said to my Lord: Sit Thou on My right hand until I make Thy enemies Thy footstool.

Therefore let all the house of Israel know most certainly that God hath made both Lord and Christ this same Jesus, whom you crucified.

Now when they had heard these things they had compunction in their heart and said to Peter, and the rest of the

The Glorious Mysteries

apostles: What shall we do, men and brothers? But Peter said to them:

Do penance, and be baptized every one of you in the name of Jesus Christ for the remission of your sins; and you shall receive the gift of the Holy Spirit. For the promise is to you and your children and to all that are far off, whomsoever the Lord our God shall call. And with very many other words did he testify and exhort them saying: Save yourselves from this perverse generation.

They, therefore, that received his word were baptized: and there were added in that day about three thousand souls. And they were persevering in the doctrine of the apostles, and in the communication of the breaking of bread, and in prayers.

And when the days of the Pentecost were accomplished The Pentecost amongst the Jews was the harvest feast which occurred fifty days after the Sabbath of the Pasch. This Sabbath was the day after Christ was crucified. The Roman Empire saw to it that crucifixion took place during the Paschal season when Jerusalem was jammed with visitors numbering in the millions. The next day when the city was again filled with visitors was the Pentecost, when as many as three millions were said to have passed through the city gates. God saw to it that He was to manifest Himself and begin the work of His Church when the maximum of Jews from scattered provinces all over the eastern world were in Jerusalem.

. . . and suddenly there came a sound from heaven . . . and there appeared to them parted tongues of fire When God was ready to begin His work He used the noise of the winds to bring the crowd, and perhaps the fire coming down from heaven was visible generally, as well. At the dedication of Solomon's Temple fire came down from heaven to sanctify it; this the Jews would recall. To the apostles, the Blessed

Mother, and the holy women this meant the coming of the Holy Spirit, the Spirit of Truth, and the Catholic Church was brought into being.

. . . every man heard them speak in his own tongue This was a gift which was bestowed for the sake of the impact it would make on the crowds that came running from everywhere to see what was taking place at the Cenacle; and it also had the very practical effect of making the message understood by all simultaneously. These gifts were common in the early Church, but were withdrawn from men when the stupendous miracle of the founding of Christianity was accomplished. God in His wisdom saw fit to touch hearts by external signs, although He could have quietly moved them by invisible grace. But God uses nature to support grace, since He leaves the will free to follow or reject His grace. If we were not free to turn away from God there would be small virtue in following Him. Men, hearing on that day from Galileans who knew only their own tongue, and perhaps a little Greek, were deeply moved.

But note that there were none there surprised to hear Greek spoken. In those days Greek was the universal language of the people in the peculiar form known as "Koine." This is the language of the New Testament, and not so long ago rationalists used this form of Greek as a reproach to the Church, saying that God should have spoken better Greek, and drawing odious comparisons between the language of St. John and that of Homer, for example. However, discoveries that began at Oxyrhynchus in Egypt have finally proved that this Greek was universal, even in Rome at the dawn of the Christian Era, and formed a basis on which the word of God could spread far and wide, even without the gift of tongues. But the other tongues aroused the attention of all the bystanders who were ready for Peter's message.

The Glorious Mysteries

These men are full of new wine No matter what takes place in this world there are always those who are so shallow that a sneering comment is their best weapon. They pose as the liberal, the advanced, the emancipated; everything but what they are—shallow. We must guard against such as these who do more damage to the weak and struggling than argument and brutality ever can do. The sneers at the apostles must have come from men who had just witnessed wonders they had never before experienced. Ignorant men were speaking, according to the testimony of hundreds, and perhaps thousands of witnesses, in fifteen or more strange tongues. They were speaking these diverse tongues in such a way that whereas one man understood the speech in Arabic, another took it for his native Egyptian. This was the one great fact to be accounted for. What did wine have to do with it in any way?

When Communism was expanding twenty some years ago men were planted to ridicule everything that others held sacred. Patriotism was scoffed at. Heroes were given the so-called "de-bunking" treatment to show that they, after all, were only human as the rest of us. Of course, the Reds tried to make religion into something to be ashamed of in one who pretended to any good sense. The poison pen is the weapon of all men who wish to overthrow any established order.

Peter standing up . . . these are not drunk . . . seeing it is but the third hour of the day I can remember when Peter's simplicity would have brought a smile to my lips. It seemed to me that he should have used more of an argument based upon the logic of the situation. It looked as if he was giving in to the scoffers, by seeming to agree that the only reason these men were not to be considered drunk was the early hour of the day. The third hour was nine o'clock in the morning. But on the harvest feast or Pentecost, because of a very human tendency for men to partake too freely of all the food and the new wine—brought out customarily at this festival—all were required to fast until the sixth hour, or about noon. St. Peter is, then, asking the scoffers if they are accusing the apostles of breaking the solemn religious fast. It is one thing to make a loose charge that one has been drinking too much to reject something that cannot be explained, but it is another thing to have to back up an accusation of breaking the religious ceremonial law of Moses. One who made such a charge might have to substantiate it. Which, of course, he could not do.

Thus we see that making false charges against religion and those in religion is the oldest trick of unbelievers and so-called rationalists, who seek to offset the effects of religious teaching. History is full of such attempts. Nero did it; Henry VIII did it; Hitler did it, too. The glorious work of Chesterton and Belloc in rehabilitating historical persons who had been blackened by interested schemers, was a good beginning but there is still much to be done.

This is that spoken of by the Prophet Joel When the scoffers were silenced Peter could plead the cause of Christ to those who would listen. His was the outpouring of the Holy Spirit, according to the prophecy which was recognized as Messianic.

. . . Jesus of Nazareth, a man approved of God among you Peter was no longer scared and cringing in the shadows for fear of his life. His denial was behind him; no longer did he have to stay hidden. Thus started his career which would end in his crucifixion, head down, and his burial under what is now St. Peter's in Rome. The Jews were ready for the coming of the Redeemer and would have received Him if the leaders of the people had not hardened their hearts against Him. His hearers are now ready to accept the Resurrection, although in this very crowd were many who had cried: "Crucify Him." It only goes to show us that God in His

patience in waiting for us is good beyond measure. He could have killed these men in their sin, but here they are only a few short weeks later, ready to turn over their whole lives to Christ. Of these who stood before Peter there were, no doubt, many who later died for Christ.

Now when they heard these things they had compunction God has told us so many times that if we turn away from our sins, even though they are as scarlet, He will wash them away and make us as white as snow. "What shall we do?" The answer given to the throng was the same as the one repeated many times since: "Do penance," that is, "Be sorry in such a way that you can undo the evil that was in the sin." It is one thing simply to be sorry; it is another thing to be sorry in a manner that effects repudiation of the sins committed, and makes up for the damage they have caused.

And there were added in that day about three thousand souls The small company that awaited the coming of the Holy Spirit numbered about 120. This vast gain was the result of one talk. Such was the small beginning of the chain of events that was to bring into the fold almost one third of the Jews. At first there was not a complete repudiation of Jewish services. In fact during the time of waiting for the Holy Ghost the apostles went every day to the Temple to pray. Moreover, the first part of the Mass as we know it today in the Roman rite, resembles the Jewish synagogue service. The Last Supper is added, giving the full ceremony. When the Protestants left the Church they kept the first part, or the synagogue services, in the reading of the Scriptures and the singing of hymns.

Those outside the Church try to make it appear that she has got away from the customs of the apostles. The purpose of this is to make it seem that the Church has turned her back on Christ, and that the self-styled reform was a restoration of apostolic teaching. An example is the **ceremonies** surrounding baptism. Some of the Protestants say that baptism among the ancients was by immersion. It is true that the ancients used to submerge those being baptized, but this was merely a symbol of Christ's burial and not an essential part of baptism itself. Here we behold a gathering of over three thousand people being baptized in a small area without previous preparations, and with an inadequate water supply for baptism by immersion. It is likely that there was not even an opportunity to pour on the waters of regeneration; the only feasible way of baptizing so many at a time was by sprinkling.

And they were persevering in the doctrine of the apostles, and in the communication of the breaking of bread and in prayers Such is the test of the true Church even today. Hold to the teachings of the apostles; show the death of the Lord in Holy Mass, and pray. Christ left the earth to go back to the Father, and it was fitting that He do so. Men are to be saved by working out their salvation according to the truth left us, with the guidance of the Holy Spirit. Christ taught the truth, but without a living guide to keep His teachings pure and unadulterated it is a foregone conclusion that man would have fallen into error by this time. No records can replace the living guide. After two thousand years who could know which records to trust?

As for prayer, we do not make enough of its force; we tend to rely too much on our own efforts, as though there were something degrading about going to God with our troubles. The apostles prayed; the Blessed Mother prayed; and Christ Himself prayed most of all.

Jesus laid upon His followers the most difficult task ever given to humankind; the establishment of His Church in the face of the entrenched position of the Jewish priests, leaders, scribes, and pharisees. These had so violent a desire to remain in power that they did not hesitate to hand Jesus over to the invading enemy of their country to have Him killed. If they killed the Christ of whom the prophets had spoken, they would not hesitate to kill His followers.

Jesus Himself never assailed the religious institutions of the Jews. In fact He had told the people always to obey the leaders whose power was from God, but not to imitate their lives. Even after His death the apostles continued to go to the Temple, although the veil of the Temple had been rent at the death of Christ and the scepter has passed to the Gentiles. Those who accepted the teachings of Christ felt no great wrench as they passed from Judaism to Christianity. Christ had not come to destroy but to fulfill.

However, there was a New Testament, and the leaders looked upon this as the setting up of a rival camp. Recall how Annas and Caiphas resisted. The break between observances will widen after the first general council at Jerusalem, in which it was decreed that the Judaic observances were no longer to be required. The persecution flared up and thousands of Christians were killed, but the scales were tipped to the Christian side when so many Jews were slain at the fall of Jerusalem, while the Christians saved themselves by fleeing across the Jordan to seek refuge in the caves at Pella. The Roman Empire which had undertaken the destruction of the Jews would have drawn no distinction between Jew and Christian. If distinction had been made it would still have been death to the Christians, since the persecutions had broken out under Nero. Caesar-worship was then beginning, and if Caesar was to be a god there was no room for Jesus Christ. The idea of a God-man who had died the shameful death of the Cross and now expected, through His followers, to be exalted above Caesar, was revolting to them. But God's work was begun and it will continue till time shall be no more.

The Fourth Glorious Mystery:
The Assumption of The Blessed Virgin into Heaven

Our Lady must have had few unalloyed joys while her

Son was on earth, since the shadow of the Cross always hung over Him. At last the sword of sorrow did pierce her soul, only to give way to the joys of the Resurrection.

The time after the Ascension of Christ into heaven must have been a kind of exile for Mary, but she still had work to do for Her Son in heaven and for all the rest of her sons still on earth. It was her task to pray for the infant Church, and to obtain graces for its spread in the face of the terrible odds that were against it. Twelve men and a few disciples stood on one side, and on the other was the entire hostile world. Mary prayed for the Church because a work destined under divine promise to spread over the entire earth still had to be supported by prayer. Perhaps the Catholic Church would sustain fewer hurts if more of us thought about our duty of praying for her welfare.

The time came when Mary could return to her divine Son to receive her reward. It has been asked: "Why did Our Lady have to die when her work was finished on earth? She was sinless. Why did she have to pay the penalty of sin, which is death?" Mary had a human nature exactly the same as ours but she was preserved from all taint of sin through the redeeming merits of Jesus Christ. Mary *was* redeemed as we were but since she was to be the Mother of Jesus it was not fitting that Satan have her under his dominion for even the shortest fleeting instant.

If Our Lady did not *have* to die, why did she die? Would not this give death the victory? No, death would not have dominion over her any more than it had a victory over Christ, her Son. Christ died for sin, it is true enough, but He died for our sins, and by His death the rest of us who are to be saved will have a final victory over death. Now, since Our Lady was associated with Christ in the victory over death she could offer herself up for us so as to be like her divine Son. Again, in a world steeped in paganism it might have been dangerous to the Faith if she were not subjected

The Glorious Mysteries

to the separation of body and soul in death. Some heretics would have picked this up to exalt her above her Son; a thing she would never permit to happen.

But the corruption of the tomb could never claim her, as it could not claim her Son. Corruption of the tomb would surely have been a victory for sin. Therefore, the Church teaches us that Mary was taken up into heaven body and soul. In the same way we shall be taken up but not until the end of time. In Mary we can look forward to the time we shall rise at the end of the world. In Mary we can see the promise fulfilled to each of us.

It has been objected to our belief in the Assumption of Mary that the Scriptures are silent about this event. It is true that there is no account such as that of the Resurrection of Christ, or of His Ascension into heaven, but this does not affect our belief. In Scripture there is a clear statement by Christ: "This is My Body." But willful men who do not wish to follow the evident sense of Scripture have invented over two hundred explanations that attack each of these four simple words, all trying to refute the words of the Lord that this indeed is His body.

St. Paul taught that we must follow all teachings given by the apostles whether written down in Scripture or taught by tradition and handed down by word of mouth. We must not forget that we have the Scriptures because the Catholic Church preserved them, so that the Scriptures are themselves a part of Catholic tradition.

We believe what the Catholic Church teaches because it is in direct, unbroken contact with the apostles and remembers what they taught. This is what we mean by the word "tradition," but in general speech with an eye to the Reformation, it has come to mean some sort of tale or legend passed on from father to son over a long period of time, with the added idea that the sources are hazy, uncritical, and usually incorrect. To the Church tradition means the living teachings of Jesus Christ as He gave them to the apostles, to be taught to their successors, either in writing, as in the Scriptures, or by individual instruction.

The teachings of the apostles concerning Mary's Assumption were thus handed down, although no report of this teaching made its way into the Scriptures and little of it appears in the writings of the Fathers until after the close of the Canon of the Bible. In the beginning the teachings about our Blessed Mother had to remain in the background, while the claims of Christ were advanced and developed for the pagan world. There would have been too much temptation to raise her to the status of a goddess, as the Collyridians did. But Mary was certainly not neglected. In the Catacombs there are frescoes that depict the Blessed Virgin as our advocate in the modern sense, praying for us with Christ. This painting is almost as old as St. John's Gospel itself. Other representations show her not merely seated, *but seated on a throne* with the Infant Jesus on her knee. In 340 the Council of Ephesus met to protect her honor as "Mother of God," defining her motherhood as Catholic teaching handed down from the apostles, just as Pius XII did in the matter of the Assumption in 1950.

When our Holy Father defined this doctrine no one felt that something new was being declared. In Rosaries said ages before the definition this mystery was presented for meditation. Every Catholic in the world from pope to the humblest layman was in peaceful possession of this teaching and continues so, thankful that the time has come for the proclamation of this great privilege of Our Lady—the sure sign of the beginning of the Marian Age.

The Assumption is the great mystery of hope. When Christ cancelled the handwriting that was against us, nailing it to the Cross, the curse of Adam was broken, and "dust thou art and into dust thou shalt return" was not to be the eternal lot of man. Christ had broken it in Himself, but since He was divine in His Person He was above the curse. However, Mary was redeemed as the rest of us and her victory is the promise of our victory. We shall have to wait for our rising, as is fitting since we were under the sway of Satan at some time, at least in original sin; but it was never fitting that Mary should be under this penalty, and hence she rose body and soul into heaven as we all hope to do at the end of the world.

Another great hope for us lies in the fact that there is a world where what is "fitting" is true. It is likewise true that the Assumption is of faith because it was the fitting reward, and hence had to be given to her that earned it.

We live in two worlds: one natural and the other supernatural. In the world of nature things go wrong; justice is not always given to him that deserves it; persons who try to do what is right are opposed and misunderstood even by those who are trying to do the same things themselves. Even saints are at odds with saints. Fraud and force can put the unworthy into high places. We see this too often to have it surprise us any longer. Under the sway of all the mishaps in the natural order the weak give up hope and become cynics, thinking there is no other order of things.

There is, however, a supernatural order where order from God prevails. All the good we do is noted, but we err if we expect to receive our supernatural reward from the natural world. That was the deformed doctrine of Calvin who taught that the good can be known by their temporal prosperity; that we may know the predestinated by seeing who has the largest share of this world's goods. Earnest souls who are deceived by this are led to despair when they find that their practice of the supernatural life has not given them what they want in temporal riches, and often not even what they desperately need. How many of our brothers have been torn away from their homes to be sent like beasts to slave camps while their families are scattered to a fate they know not what? Most of us will never have to suffer in this way, but we all have suffering to endure in times like these, and it is only through the exericse of great patience that we can restore the balance. In normal times most persons find a niche where they no longer have to put up a losing struggle, and life raises no tremendous questions for them, unless there is a depression or a mass displacement of populations. A few like St. Benedict Joseph Labre can turn their backs on the whole economic order, although this procedure is not open to most of us. Even this attitude will not banish the urge for possessions, which followed St. Benedict all his life.

The Church teaches it was fitting that Christ should raise His Mother from the grave before the corruption of the tomb could claim her, and that since it was fitting, He did just that. We were all thrilled at the news that the body of St. Peter was certainly located under the foundations of the Basilica of St. Peter, but should we ever come upon a spot that was supposed to contain the lifeless relics of the Blessed Mother we should feel we were in the presence of a great injustice. The angel greeted her: "Blessed art thou amongst women," but where would her blessing be in the punishment of the tomb?

The Fifth Glorious Mystery:
The Coronation of The Blessed Virgin As Queen of Heaven

We have come to the closing of the cycle of the Rosary, a series of mysteries begun by the consent of Our Blessed Lady to be the Mother of the Redeemer. In this consent she cooperated with the divine will in bringing the work of redemption to a suffering human race. It is idle, perhaps, to speculate on what would have been the fate of human kind if Mary had refused to be the way by which the Savior could come to us. Adam refused; Eve refused; in heaven itself, Lucifer refused. We may well suppose it would have been indeed a rugged pathway that we should have had to tread to get back to God. As we noted above, God in His foreknowledge knew that she would not refuse, but her choice was as free as any human act ever was.

The Glorious Mysteries

Mary remained on earth for years to help the infant Church, and then was transferred to the larger scene of activity as the channel of graces for us all. Her crowning is the symbol of her place in bringing Christ to us and of bringing us back to Christ.

Non-Catholics often say that we make too much of the Virgin Mary, but the saints have said: "Of the Blessed Mother there can never be too much." We do not wish to make her divine with our great devotion to her, but we do seek to exalt her above every creature. If we can speed the Age of Mary we shall speed the Age of Peace. Until she comes into her own the Church can never come into full flower.

There is in the Apocalypse of St. John (c. 12) a vision of the Catholic Church, but the passages are also applied to the Blessed Virgin as Queen of Heaven, because of all women they are true of her alone.

And a great sign appeared in heaven: a woman clothed with the sun and the moon under her feet, and on her head a crown of twelve stars: and being with child, she cried travailing in birth, and was in pain to be delivered.

And there was another sign in heaven: and behold a great red dragon, having seven heads and ten horns: and on his heads seven diadems. And his tail drew a third part of the stars of heaven, and cast them to the earth: and the dragon stood before the woman who was ready to be delivered; that when she should be delivered, he might devour her Son.

And she brought forth a man child who was to rule all nations with an iron rod; and her Son was taken up to God and to His throne."

And a great sign appeared St. John was writing a revelation of the last things, when time should be no more, and when God would wipe away the tears of the martyrs who had suffered for Him in patience, so that He might convert sinners and not destroy them.

This marks the fulfillment of the first promise made to man since He began to carry the burden of sin. "Behold I will place an enmity between thee and THE WOMAN between thy seed, and her seed, and she shall crush thy head." It makes little difference that it is the woman in one version or the woman through her seed that will overcome Satan. Mary is THE WOMAN both of the prophecy in Genesis and its fulfillment in the Apocalypse.

. . . she cried travailing in birth Mary was without sin, of course, and she was not subject to the pain of childbirth as other women because these are a part of the original curse laid upon Mother Eve. At the foot of the Cross Mary brought forth in pain and sorrow all the souls for whom Christ was suffering on the Cross. It was at the foot of the Cross that she was proclaimed our mother.

Behold a great red dragon The dragon is not only Satan himself but all the forces of evil that were to battle against THE WOMAN and her Son. They would sweep some of the stars from heaven; not all men would allow themselves to be saved, but THE WOMAN would triumph, both as the sign of the Church and as the Blessed Virgin, and Jesus Christ would reign over all, above the highest heavens.

Here in heaven, also, is brought about the close of the cycle begun by the angel's message: "Blessed art thou amongst women." There is also fulfilled Elizabeth's voicing the prophecy: "Blessed art thou amongst women and blessed is the fruit of thy womb (Jesus)." Our Lady through the inspiration of the Holy Spirit completed the prophecy: "Behold from henceforth all generations shall call me blessed."

When Our Lady foretold that she was to be called "blessed" she meant something more than will be our common lot: all of us are to be called blessed in heaven. How can we restrict the crown of glory that Mary received since all are to receive a crown? "Be ye faithful to me even unto

The Glorious Mysteries

death and I will give you a crown of glory." If we are to have a crown for being faithful, the Virgin Most Faithful shall be crowned above all of us. Can we deny Mary the crown of Queen of Angels, if we recall the words of St. Paul: "Of which of the angels has He said, This is My Son?" Shall the Son who is above all the angels place His Mother beneath any of them?

We believe that man will take over the places vacated by the fallen angels: places vacated even by Seraphim: and even the place vacated by Lucifer, once the brightest of the angels, now fallen to be Satan, the serpent whom THE WOMAN has overcome. Will she defeat him on earth and then take a lower place than once was his in heaven? Someone such as St. Francis of Assisi is now in glory on the throne vacated by Satan, but it is more fitting that the Blessed Mother have a place over all the angels and saints—a place closest to her Son. In this world what is apt and fitting does not always carry away the victory; in the world of the supernatural the fitting is always true.

Mary, translated into heaven has ever turned her eyes to her children who are still struggling towards final perseverance. That struggle goes on, and when the foe presses too closely upon us Our Blessed Mother comes down with a message, or a warning; with a new devotion or holy practice to bring us back to Christ. She has come time and again to the founders of religious orders to inspire them to their good work; she has filled the earth with the shrines of her apparitions and visitations.

If you have enjoyed this book, consider making your next selection from among the following . . .

The Facts About Luther. *Msgr. P. O'Hare*	13.50
Eucharistic Miracles. *Joan Carroll Cruz*	13.00
The Incorruptibles. *Joan Carroll Cruz*	12.00
Little Catechism of the Curé of Ars. *St. John Vianney*	5.50
The Curé of Ars—Patron St. of Parish Priests. *O'Brien*	4.50
The Four Last Things: Death, Judgment, Hell, Heaven	5.00
Pope St. Pius X. *F. A. Forbes*	6.00
St. Alphonsus Liguori. *Frs. Miller & Aubin*	15.00
Confession of a Roman Catholic. *Paul Whitcomb*	1.25
The Catholic Church Has the Answer. *Paul Whitcomb*	1.25
The Sinner's Guide. *Ven. Louis of Granada*	12.00
True Devotion to Mary. *St. Louis De Montfort*	7.00
Life of St. Anthony Mary Claret. *Fanchón Royer*	12.50
Autobiography of St. Anthony Mary Claret	12.00
I Wait for You. *Sr. Josefa Menendez*	.75
Words of Love. *Menendez, Betrone, Mary of the Trinity*	5.00
Little Lives of the Great Saints. *John O'Kane Murray*	16.50
Prayer—The Key to Salvation. *Fr. Michael Müller*	7.00
The Victories of the Martyrs. *St. Alphonsus Liguori*	8.50
Canons and Decrees of the Council of Trent. *Schroeder*	12.50
Sermons of St. Alphonsus Liguori for Every Sunday	16.50
A Catechism of Modernism. *Fr. J. B. Lemius*	4.00
Alexandrina—The Agony and the Glory. *Johnston*	4.00
Life of Blessed Margaret of Castello. *Fr. Bonniwell*	6.00
The Ways of Mental Prayer. *Dom Vitalis Lehodey*	11.00
Fr. Paul of Moll. *van Speybrouck*	9.00
Communion Under Both Kinds. *Michael Davies*	1.50
Abortion: Yes or No? *Dr. John L. Grady, M.D.*	1.50
The Story of the Church. *Johnson, Hannan, Dominica*	16.50
Hell Quizzes. Radio Replies Press	1.00
Indulgence Quizzes. Radio Replies Press	1.00
Purgatory Quizzes. Radio Replies Press	1.00
Virgin and Statue Worship Quizzes. Radio Replies Press	1.00
The Holy Eucharist. *St. Alphonsus*	8.50
Meditation Prayer on Mary Immaculate. *Padre Pio*	1.25
Little Book of the Work of Infinite Love. *de la Touche*	2.00
Textual Concordance of/Holy Scriptures. *Williams*. H.B.	35.00
Douay-Rheims Bible. Leatherbound	35.00
The Way of Divine Love. *Sister Josefa Menendez*	17.50
The Way of Divine Love. (pocket, unabr.). *Menendez*	8.50
Mystical City of God—Abridged. *Ven. Mary of Agreda*	18.50

Prices guaranteed through December 31, 1995.

Title	Price
Ven. Jacinta Marto of Fatima. *Cirrincione*	1.50
Reign of Christ the King. *Davies*	1.25
St. Teresa of Ávila. *William Thomas Walsh*	18.00
Isabella of Spain—The Last Crusader. *Wm. T. Walsh*	20.00
Characters of the Inquisition. *Wm. T. Walsh*	12.50
Philip II. *William Thomas Walsh.* H.B.	37.50
Blood-Drenched Altars—Cath. Comment. Hist. Mexico	18.00
Self-Abandonment to Divine Providence. *de Caussade*	16.50
Way of the Cross. *Liguorian*	.75
Way of the Cross. *Franciscan*	.75
Modern Saints—Their Lives & Faces, Bk. 1. *Ann Ball*	18.00
Modern Saints—Their Lives & Faces, Bk. 2. *Ann Ball*	20.00
Saint Michael and the Angels. *Approved Sources*	5.50
Dolorous Passion of Our Lord. *Anne C. Emmerich*	15.00
Our Lady of Fatima's Peace Plan from Heaven. Booklet	.75
Divine Favors Granted to St. Joseph. *Pere Binet*	4.00
St. Joseph Cafasso—Priest of the Gallows. *St. J. Bosco*	3.00
Catechism of the Council of Trent. *McHugh/Callan*	20.00
Padre Pio—The Stigmatist. *Fr. Charles Carty*	13.50
Why Squander Illness? *Frs. Rumble & Carty*	2.00
Fatima—The Great Sign. *Francis Johnston*	7.00
Heliotropium—Conformity of Human Will to Divine	11.00
Charity for the Suffering Souls. *Fr. John Nageleisen*	15.00
Devotion to the Sacred Heart of Jesus. *Verheylezoon*	13.00
Sermons on Prayer. *St. Francis de Sales*	3.50
Sermons on Our Lady. *St. Francis de Sales*	9.00
Sermons for Lent. *St. Francis de Sales*	10.00
Fundamentals of Catholic Dogma. *Ott*	20.00
Litany of the Blessed Virgin Mary. (100 cards)	5.00
Who Is Padre Pio? Radio Replies Press	1.50
Child's Bible History. *Knecht*	4.00
The Life of Christ. 4 Vols. H.B. *Anne C. Emmerich*	55.00
St. Anthony—The Wonder Worker of Padua. *Stoddard*	4.00
The Precious Blood. *Fr. Faber*	11.00
The Holy Shroud & Four Visions. *Fr. O'Connell*	2.00
Clean Love in Courtship. *Fr. Lawrence Lovasik*	2.50
The Secret of the Rosary. *St. Louis De Montfort*	3.00
The History of Antichrist. *Rev. P. Huchede*	3.00
Where We Got the Bible. *Fr. Henry Graham*	5.00
Hidden Treasure—Holy Mass. *St. Leonard*	4.00
Imitation of the Sacred Heart of Jesus. *Fr. Arnoudt*	13.50
The Life & Glories of St. Joseph. *Edward Thompson*	13.50

At your bookdealer or direct from the publisher.

Prices guaranteed through December 31, 1995.

NOTES

NOTES

NOTES